AVIATION & MARITIME SECURITY INTELLIGENCE

Hassan M. Eltaher, B.A. Pol. Sc., MBA Aviation

E&W Communications

Ottawa, Ontario - Canada

2012

Library and Archives Canada Cataloguing in Publication

Eltaher, Hassan M.
  Aviation & maritime security intelligence / Hassan M. Eltaher.

Includes bibliographical references.
ISBN 978-0-9784760-1-4

1. Merchant marine--Security measures. 2. Aeronautics, Commercial--Security measures. 3. Intelligence service--Management. 4. National security. 5. Terrorism--Prevention.
  I. Title. II. Title: Aviation and maritime security intelligence.

VK203.E48 2011   363.12'3   C2011-906999-7

Printed in Canada by:
MISSION STREAM
14 Concourse Gate, Suite 400
Ottawa, Ontario K2E 7S6

Published by:

E&W Communications
eandwcommunications@gmail.com
www.eandwcommunications.com
407 - 1440 Heron Road
Ottawa, Ontario K1V 0X2
Canada

All warfare is based on deception.
Hence, when able to attack we must seem unable.
When using our forces, we must seem inactive.
When we are near, we must make the enemy believe we are away
When far away, we must make him believe we are near.

THE ART OF WAR
According to Sun Tzu

CONTENTS

Inside photo credits:
- Somalia and a comparison to the Eastern Coast of the United States - Government Accountability Office (GAO) "Counter Piracy Report", Washington, D.C., p. 103
- Successful and attempted pirate attacks of the Coast of Somalia, January 2007 to February 2 Government Accountability Office (GAO) "Counter Piracy Report", Washington, D.C., p. 104
- Dramatic increase in total hostages captured by Somali pirates, 2007 to 2010 - Government Accountability Office (GAO) "Counter Piracy Report", Washington, D.C., p. 106
- Somali pirates surrendering - European Naval Force Somalia (Operation Atalanta) - By permission, p. 114
- Map of the Iran, Pakistan, Afghanistan border, p. 226
- The China Gwadar proposed pipeline and highway route - www.truthwinds.com, p. 227
- The m/v Sirius Star - US Navy photo - By permission, p. 231

Cover photo credits:
- A320 Simulator - By permission from Captain Ralf Rohner, Switzerland
- Washington National Airport terminal - By permission from the AirNikon Collection - Pima Air and Space Museum, Tucson, Arizona.
- Satellite intercepts - By permission from Bild, RDB, Switzerland
- The m/v Sirius Star - US Navy photo - By permission

FOREWORD

This book is not about adding more barriers and multiplying obstacles and security layers that turn the life of travelers, those employed in transportation, and those in charge of administering security into a daily unpleasant obstacle course. The book is not meant to be an academic "publish or perish" exercise. Now that we have established what the book is not about, it may be useful to state what purpose it is meant to serve. It is meant to help render aviation and maritime security more efficient, more effective, less cumbersome, less expensive, and certainly more logical by looking at it from the vantage point of intelligence as opposed to simply from that of physical security.

The idea of a book came as an afterthought. Originally it was intended to be a training program. But because of the relatively large amount of material involved and the desire to make it accessible to a much larger and diversified professional audience, the idea of a book imposed itself, took a life of its own, and eventually took root. However, due to the obviously sensitive nature of the subject matter discussed, a sizeable bloc of operational information that should have normally formed an integral part of the book to render it more useful cannot be published for obvious security reasons. That's the nature of the beast.

People within the security and intelligence community, as well as those in the fields of transportation security, and in particular those on the operational side of the industry, will find this book of particular interest and usefulness. The academic community as well as students and teachers of transportation management will equally find much interest in the academic-cum-applied approach to the subject matter.

Not everybody may agree with some of the approaches recommended in the book, or with the proposed solutions to some of the major international security-related problems. Suffice it to say that it provides a different approach to thinking outside the box that must be taken into consideration. After all, intelligence is a kaleidoscope of infinite possibilities, and herein lays the challenge to both the intelligence community and to the transportation security professionals.

Why does a book need to be published about this topic?

The fields of intelligence, security and transportation are the subject of hundreds of books. None has all three of them addressed in one treatise, while also offering solutions and not just analysis and discussion. They hardly touch on the intelligence side of security, other than just mention the word 'intelligence' perhaps not more than a couple of times. Books reflect the particular experiences of their authors, and in a sense, each book is good and unique in its own way.

Since this book is essentially about the intelligence function within the overall theme of transportation security, it will concentrate on security intelligence and not on physical security such as port or airport perimeter fencing, passenger frisking and patting and cargo searches, or the assignment of air marshals aboard aircraft, etc. Security Intelligence within the context of transportation security, which is the main theme in this book, considers threats that have a rather political agenda to be no different from threats with a criminal intent.

Since the best protection starts with prevention, the book will discuss practical means for pre-empting threats to the aviation and maritime sectors by addressing the following nine major topics:

- Defining the important role, workings and limitations of intelligence
- Synthesizing intelligence analysis, assessment and interpretation
- Confronting cultural bias and narrowing the security intelligence gap
- Highlighting the defining role of leadership in intelligence
- Putting the threat of terrorism in its proper context
- Assessing the aviation and maritime threat environments
- Building the structure and management of the transportation security - intelligence function
- Managing the threat and risk assessment process
- Managing the ongoing interaction between intelligence and the stakeholders

ACKNOWLEDGMENTS

This book is dedicated to those who contributed to making a better world for everybody to live in without fear. Some of these people are respected public figures, and some were truly unknown soldiers. The vast majority of those who work in intelligence in one capacity or another fall within the latter category.

The book is also dedicated to those who espoused their nation's struggle for freedom, dignity, and the place it deserves among nations. In the history of nations some may have had recourse to the sword as an ultimate recourse, though, in the end, the pen is always mightier than the sword.

It would be ungrateful not to recognise those who made it possible for the author to become part of the professional fields which offered him the hands-on experience without which he would not have been able to handle the subject matter of the book authoritatively. It is also a nod to those who did their best to trivialise his capacities purposely, or simply out of sheer ignorance.

There are always those who contributed to the book knowingly or unknowingly such as the authors who were quoted in the book and the publishers who gave their formal authorization to use the selected quotations. A special "Thank you" equally goes to all those who believed in the book without seeing it and provided permission to quote from their work or artwork at no charge. Some of those have passed away before the author got the chance to acknowledge their contribution adequately. So the book is also a tribute to their memory.

My children, Shirine, Ramsay and Wally took successful control of their lives at a relatively young age, and thus provided me the time and peace of mind to continue my intellectual pursuits. Wally and Shirine dived into the post-editing stage with hawk-eyes, while Ramsay provided the invaluable IT support when needed. Not only that; but the three of them contributed immensely in keeping me in step with the changing perspectives of the younger people of this generation, and keep up with the constantly evolving technologies that only young people can contribute. My former spouse of many years continued to believe in my capabilities even years after our divorce. To her I owe much too.

My best reward will be to see today's adversaries stop, think, and ask themselves: "*Quo Vadis?*" Where are we going? To come to realise that this is possible and that there is indeed room for accommodation and possibly peace even among former enemies, they must have the will to sail or fly in that direction.

TRANSPORTATION SECURITY
AN INTRODUCTION

A multi-modal (Aviation – Maritime – Surface) security directorate, division or branch is a must for any transportation department or ministry. Without such a directorate which possesses a wide-angle view of transportation security as an integrated system, the security of the overall national transportation system will always be at risk of falling not just victim to occasional terrorist acts, but also to permanent criminal exploitation.

Managing security and intelligence efficiently calls for ongoing, constant cooperation, coordination, centralized command and control, but especially the candid exchange of security and intelligence related information among all players involved.

In the area of transportation security, particularly aviation and maritime security, the players include the extended network comprised of the Department of Transport's geographic regional security managers and inspectors, private sector stakeholders'[1] security managers, and law enforcement agencies at the national, provincial/state and local levels. While most of the transportation security intelligence requirements are the same, it remains that the aviation, maritime and surface transportation modes each has its own specifics.

By necessity, governments everywhere create branches, units and sections within departments. Unfortunately, and mostly for intangible reasons, these organizational units often not only do not talk or listen to each other, but occasionally compete with each other, hide information from each other, or sometimes obstruct each others' work. In this fashion, they collectively help defeat the purpose for which they were created. It may be possible to manage the operational aspects of their functions separately from the policy side, though at great cost to operational inefficiency. But; when it comes to security and its intelligence component, it is simply counterproductive and ultimately seriously harming to national security to manage the security of each mode of transport in isolation of the other modes.

Therefore, for transportation security to be handled properly from all its aspects, it must all be integrated into one centralised multi-modal unit, managed by a small group of individuals, in order for the right hand to know what the left hand is doing, and not divided among the various transportation sectors as is the case in some countries.

---

[1] The term "stakeholders" as used hereafter refers to all those who have an active role to play in matters related to transportation security such as governmental departments, law enforcement, security and intelligence agencies, airlines, airports, shipping lines, port authorities, freight forwarders, etc.

When a threat to aviation for example is detected, all the other modes; i.e. maritime, surface and rail must be informed about it immediately and vice versa. Why? Because the would-be perpetrators, whether groups or individuals, could have also been involved in threats against other modes of transport whether in their own country or in other countries, or that they should be flagged as potential future threats to those modes. It is also possible that if terrorists were originally targeting aviation for instance, and failed to reach their target, that their fall-back plan could be an attack against one of the other modes of transport. Furthermore, the terrorists could also be planning a terrorist act against either a multi-modal target such as a seaport or against more than just one mode of transport simultaneously.

In a nutshell, working in aviation and maritime intelligence in the context of an integrated inter-departmental setting should be no different than being on a football/soccer or hockey team: working together and making passes to each other, with the aim of scoring against the other team while protecting their own goal.

PART I

DEFINING THE IMPORTANT ROLE, WORKINGS AND LIMITATIONS OF INTELLIGENCE

"An intelligence service is a permanent corps of professionals working for politicians who are part time rulers."
Anonymous

"One of the most important lessons the FBI learned from the September 11th attacks was the need for better intelligence - better collection, better analysis, and better dissemination."
Robert S. Mueller, III
Director, FBI

CHAPTER 1

"Ask and it shall be given you; seek, and ye shall find it; knock, and the door shall be opened unto you. For every one that asketh receiveth."
(Matthew VII: 7)

UNDERSTANDING THE ROLE OF INTELLIGENCE

Every time a terrorist attack is successful such as 9/11, or very close to succeed such as the "underwear bomber" arrested at Detroit Airport in 2009, it means essentially, or at least partially, that there was a failure of timely counter-intelligence or counter-terrorism to prevent the occurrence from happening. This may not necessarily mean that intelligence was asleep at the wheel, but it could be an indication that intelligence may have been looking in the wrong direction. It could have also simply fallen short of tying the dots together, or has not analyzed the intelligence available quickly enough, or the terrorists proved to be ahead at their game.

Countries self-described as democratic pride themselves for their judicious use of intelligence according to the rule of law, while countries described as non-democratic rely almost exclusively on unbridled intelligence to run their affairs. Warts and all, the inside workings of the intelligence organizations of both systems are practically the same, though the dose of extra-legal actions by the latter that is not subject to controls, review and audit is generally much more pervasive and often simply considered as "tools of the trade."

THE FOUR PILLARS OF INTELLIGENCE

The first pillar of intelligence is the fact that in the first place it is a **cause**, then; after that, a public service career. To be in intelligence with the main objective being simply to establish a long career in the Public Service does a disservice to intelligence. Hence intelligence itself must be the main objective, which is rewarded by promotions and adequate financial rewards. To achieve this level of dedication to the profession calls for outstanding leadership and deep knowledge of the issues at hand, rather than just administrative skills on part of senior intelligence bureaucrats. A good intelligence service is directed and run by highly professional intelligence officers, not by administrators, former human resources clerks and accountants in search for something less boring in their lives.

The second pillar of intelligence is to **know,** not only the bad about the adversary or the enemy, but also the good. Since conflict and violence shape and influence the views of each party involved, there is a tendency to attribute all negative epithets to the other side. This is dangerously blinding because the 'enemy' also possesses strengths and not just weaknesses. Besides, like in every society, there is the good, the bad and the ugly on either side. If politicians and the media often thrive on these generalisations, intelligence should not fall in that trap.

Knowing both the good and the bad about the adversary allows intelligence officers and analysts to properly assess and 'size' that adversary, then draw an accurate multidimensional and comprehensive picture of his capabilities in terms of strengths and weaknesses. It will also allow us to learn from the enemy, and, why not, also be ready to deal with him amiably when the situation changes in the future. When we look back at history, as close as to the fall of the Berlin Wall in 1991 and the end of apartheid in South Africa in 1994, we all know that with time situations do change, and many of the historic "nevers" have taught us to never say never!

The third pillar of intelligence is to **communicate** what you know. In English the term 'intelligence' is rather subjective. Its equivalent in French is *'renseignements'*, i.e. information. Intelligence in Arabic is referred to either as *'moukhabarat'*, i.e. communications, or as *'istikhbarat'*, i.e. information gathering, which is a more comprehensive definition. Communication or dissemination of intelligence by the producers to the consumers is done in a variety of formats, some through personal interaction, some as messages, and others in the form of briefing notes or reports, at various levels of classification depending on their content and the end-users who will receive them. Intelligence agencies also disseminate unclassified reports that serve as a means of keeping the industry at large as well as the general public aware of the fact that "we are not asleep", but also to help keep them informed about the major issues of interest that could affect them. After all the industry and the public are the ultimate beneficiaries since the final objective of the work undertaken by the intelligence service is the nation's safety and security.

The fourth pillar of intelligence is to **act** on the intelligence. There is a ton of raw intelligence being collected every minute by intelligence agencies, but not all intelligence can be acted upon. That is why today the buzz word is "actionable intelligence."[2] Acting on intelligence, namely preventing the would be terrorists from reaching their objective as early as possible before they go into action, could be a long process, and may not always succeed. The involvement of the industry during some of the intelligence gathering phases, whether it is aviation or maritime, could provide the necessary heads-up details related to their operating environment that could speed the intelligence collection, analysis and assessment process, or help put it on the right track.

---

[2] "Actionable Intelligence" is defined as intelligence information that could be acted on. A good deal of intelligence consists of raw information that is not corroborated, and no evidence is available to ensure its plausibility, hence cannot be acted upon.

WORKINGS OF AN INTELLIGENCE SERVICE

Unless they worked with or in intelligence, most people either make wild assumptions as to how intelligence works, or simply have no clue. Therefore, a reasonable understanding of the workings of an intelligence service is of great help to transportation security professionals. Why? Because they will be able to know how to <u>obtain the information</u> they need, as well as <u>how to identify</u> and share information of interest with the intelligence agencies.

It is equally important that intelligence services <u>understand the workings</u> of the transportation industry. This will allow them <u>to be familiar</u> with the environment in which the industry works, and which intelligence <u>to collect</u> that the transportation industry requires, to be able to protect itself from threats to its operations <u>as early in the process as possible</u>. It is a two-way street.

Intelligence services do not exist just to collect intelligence, then lock it up. If the intelligence they collect is not used in a timely manner for the purpose of protecting national interests, then the whole exercise defeats its purpose. To understand where intelligence successes and failures happen, and how to remedy to certain shortcomings and failures, let us look at how intelligence services work.

Intelligence agencies are organized along either geographic or functional divisions. Which is better? Each concept has it strong points and its adherents, yet experience tells that the root-base of the organization must be geographic, with the functional requirements called upon as the case may arise. Depending on the investigation to be carried, certain cases may call for a full time functional organization as opposed to a purely geographic organization. Flexibility, versatility and adaptability are the name of the game here as opposed to the traditionally rigid bureaucratic structure.

Main components of an intelligence service

Anywhere one looks, intelligence services are to a great extent similar to each other. Some may have more means, additional refinements, more money, ambitious objectives, or better capabilities. But roughly speaking, the key operational foundations of an intelligence service rest mainly on:

1. Intelligence and counter-intelligence operations
2. Counter terrorism functions and operations
3. Training, technical, scientific and logistical support
4. Analysis and assessment.

The main role of an intelligence service is to protect the country from threats to its security as a result of:

(a) Espionage or sabotage, or activities directed toward or in support of such espionage or sabotage,

(b) Foreign influenced activities within or relating to the country that are detrimental to its interests and are clandestine or deceptive or involve a threat to individuals or institutions,

(c) Activities within or relating to the country that are directed toward or in support of the threat or use of acts of serious violence against persons or property for political, religious or ideological objectives, and

(d) Activities directed toward undermining by covert unlawful acts, or directed toward or intended ultimately to lead to the destruction or overthrow by violence of the constitutionally established system of government in that country.

To perform its duties, the intelligence service uses covert and overt means to collect, investigate, analyse and retain information and intelligence respecting activities that may be suspected of constituting threats to national security. Such information is then reported to government along with assessments and advice.

A - INTELLIGENCE OPERATIONS

Intelligence operations include aggressive intelligence and defensive intelligence. Even though intelligence is intelligence; both aggressive and defensive intelligence include elements of each other. One of the modern refinements of intelligence is what is called "Security Intelligence" which may have a more defensive than aggressive role to play; and this is where transportation security mainly falls as will be discussed later in the book.

It is essential to underline the fact that "intelligence" could mean different things to different people. The impact of culture, geography, the environment and history upon a country's intelligence service and the people who work in intelligence is phenomenal. Yet, this aspect is often not taken seriously or simply ignored. This important point is further elaborated in Chapter 3.

Under the umbrella of Operations, one will certainly find an intelligence branch, a counter-intelligence branch, and a counter-terrorism branch. The terrorist events that spanned a good part of the past two to three decades have called for the dedication of a Counter Terrorism branch as an independent operational branch in its own right.

1 - Intelligence (espionage) and counter-intelligence (counter espionage)

This is the traditional 'old fashioned' spying, which never goes out of style. It has always existed and will always be there. When individuals spy for personal reasons, it is called 'snooping around'. When governments do it for 'national security purposes', it is called intelligence. Those who are being spied on call it 'espionage'.

Intelligence activities cover a number of fields such as:

- Political intelligence
- Economic intelligence
- Industrial intelligence
- Military intelligence
- Security intelligence

2 - Intelligence and counter-intelligence functions

Whether it is intelligence or counter-intelligence, the functions involved are relatively similar and could include the following desks:

- Country-specific geographic/regional desks
- Functional specialty desks (Political, military, economic, industrial, leadership, scientific, technical, and weapons intelligence)
- Intelligence and counter-intelligence joint task-forces are also created when needed across organizational lines to manage a particular intelligence or counter-intelligence operation.

Clandestine operations, also known as covert action, or special operations are conducted by intelligence services that have a mandate to carry out espionage or special operations overseas. These types of operations are mainly conducted by major or regional powers, and even by certain small and middle-sized countries with aggressive foreign policies. Keeping in mind though that some smaller countries have been known to conduct first class intelligence operations, though rather pretty quietly. Some countries think they are important and run spies too, though mostly against their own citizens at home or among their immigrant communities overseas. These are the countries that confuse between spying for national security purposes, and spying on their own citizens for the purpose of harassing their political opponents.

B - COUNTER-TERRORISM

Counter-terrorism functions & operations

Fighting terrorism could be more complicated than countering espionage, and while the latter can be countered by resorting to traditional counter-intelligence crafts that most of the time do not involve armed intervention, terrorists may need to be handled with traditional criminal police-like investigative methods, which may occasionally call for, or result in full-fledged armed intervention at one point or another as happened in Afghanistan.

While states, or at least some of them, engage in espionage, they normally do not engage in terrorism. That is except in the case of a small number of countries who have a tendency to sponsor undercover terrorist actions, which are referred to by the euphemism "disruptive operations", i.e. state-sponsored terrorism in plain English. Whatever the terminology and the semantics, the purpose is the same. It all depends on which side of the fence one happens to be.

A generic counter-terrorism branch may be comprised of the following sections:

- Geographic, regional, country-specific, issue-specific, and even individual-specific desks
- An interdepartmental and intra-departmental counter-terrorism task-force ('Cellule anti-terroriste' in French)
- A disruptive or instigative counter-terrorism action group or commando

With time, espionage and counter-espionage have been defined and the actors involved identified. Historically-speaking, espionage was the domain of politics and military necessities. In modern times economic and industrial espionage made their entry, and are equally harmful to both the state and to private entreprise.

In relative terms, combating terrorism has not always been as successful as counter-intelligence, particularly because of the time element involved. Terrorism is event-controlled and has to happen as soon as possible. As if they were members of the historic British pre-World War I Fabian Society whose motto was: "For the right moment you must wait…but when the time comes you must strike hard." Intelligence is a long term process that certainly does not want to be eventful and strives to remain undetected as long as possible. Because this book is essentially about threats to civil aviation and to maritime targets, it will therefore dwell more on terrorism, why it happens, the reasons of failing to understand it or combat it, and ensuring that it is at least successfully contained, if not eradicated.

C – TRAINING, TECHNICAL, SCIENTIFIC & LOGISTICAL SUPPORT

To carry out intelligence, counter-intelligence and counter-terrorism operations, calls for a major sophisticated logistical support infrastructure that is constantly technologically upgraded. Without the logistical support and without close cooperation with other players and allies nationally and internationally, operations will come to a standstill. Hence, most, if not all intelligence services will roughly have the following logistics and support branches:

1. Training
2. Technical support
3. Intelligence collection and signals intercept
4. Field, or special operations
5. Multilingual translation
6. Security screening
7. Open and classified info library
8. International cooperation and joint operations
9. Surveillance
10. Human sources recruitment, development, retention, protection and management
11. Internal security
12. Review, audit and operational quality assurance

Because of the large number of employees working in the aviation and maritime security sector who require a security clearance, the department of transport, which coordinates this function with intelligence and law enforcement agencies, is usually one of the largest applicants for such clearances, which are delivered by the Security Screening Branch.

The international cooperation function is also of particular interest in the area of aviation, maritime or surface security. Such cooperation is normally conducted through bilateral intelligence arrangements between a given country's intelligence service and its counterpart in other countries.

Intelligence cooperation, not just with countries that do not uphold the same human rights standards, but also among some G8 countries are a cause of concern, especially when false information is manipulated and purposely exchanged by design, by ignorance or erroneous analysis that leads individuals being tortured if not assassinated. Occasionally, the same states that legislate laws to protect human rights, issue regulations and implement procedures to circumvent those same laws. Sometimes information shared with foreign countries could be wrong, inaccurate, or fabricated, or it could be sent to a country whose human rights record is known universally to be abysmal. Indeed, there have been several cases where this has led to serious injustice against the person concerned, as well as his family.[3]

Bilateral liaison arrangements between intelligence agencies are usually set up formally, with the signing of a Memorandum of Understanding, or informally (on the basis of an unwritten, gentlemanly agreement). They usually cover a wide range of issues, such as sharing of assessments, raw data, or training facilities and the conduct of joint operations.

"Arrangements or exchanges are subject to the third-party rule, which means that intelligence supplied by a party to another cannot be shared with a third one without the originator's consent. Without such a rule, intelligence shared with an ally could end up in the hands of a third party friendly to the original recipient but an adversary of the originator."[4] This rule is designed to protect confidential sources of information and keep a liaison relationship secure. It is necessary to protect the identity of sources and to respect the conditions imposed on the sharing of information from foreign agencies to ensure the continued flow of such information.

"Intelligence agencies cooperate for many reasons. No one agency can do and know everything. But, they act primarily in support of their nation's foreign policy objectives and in their self-interest. The United States, France, Germany, and the United Kingdom are particularly attractive partners for less fortunate services that can trade human intelligence for the more sophisticated and expensive technical products to which they would not otherwise have access."[5]

"Filling identified gaps, reducing operational costs, and replacing nonexistent diplomatic relations are among the major benefits of intelligence cooperation. Others may include some ability to influence where applicable the policies of other countries, or "affect the course of a military conflict," as happened in 1984 after Iraq received U.S. intelligence useful in its war against Iran (during the reign of Saddam Hussein)."[6]

---

[3] For more in-depth analysis consult Helga Hernes' article in Hans Born, Ian Leigh and Aidan Willis, "International Intelligence Cooperation and Accountability", Routledge Studies in Intelligence, UK, p. ix (2011).

[4] Jeffrey T. Richelson, "The Calculus of Intelligence Cooperation," International Journal of Intelligence and CounterIntelligence, v.4, number 3, fall 1990, pp.315-316. Cited in Stéphane Lefebvre, "The Difficulties and Dilemmas of International Intelligence Cooperation."

[5] Stéphane Lefebvre, "The Difficulties and Dilemmas of International Intelligence Cooperation", International Journal of Intelligence and CounterIntelligence, v.16 number 4, pp.527-542 (2003).

[6] Jeffrey T. Richelson, "The Calculus of Intelligence Cooperation", pp.307-323 p.314. Cited in Stéphane Lefebvre, "The Difficulties and Dilemmas of International Intelligence Cooperation".

D - ANALYSIS AND ASSESSMENT

The work being done by the previous three branches essentially consists of collecting and processing information about foreign states, suspect groups and individuals. Some intelligence agencies follow a specialized path, others follow the vacuum-cleaner approach, i.e. they collect everything and anything, then sort it out later. An essential part of the work consists of testing the raw intelligence that has been collected for quality, and try to fact it and corroborate the evidence thus gathered. The next phase they must proceed with would be to evaluate, corroborate, analyze and assess the filtered product. Sometimes the analysis is discussed with allied intelligence agencies to see if they concur, or hold differing views.

Some of the major intelligence failures in history were not failures in collection, evaluation or analysis, but failure in the proper assessment and interpretation of analysis, or the wilful misinterpretation of the analytical facts by the political echelons. This has happened regarding the imminent threat of Iraq's 'nuclear weapons', the association of Iraq with Al-Qaeda[7], and finally including the attribution of a role to Saddam Hussein in the 9/11 attacks. Everybody else on the planet knew for fact that these were untenable fabrications.

Analysis of intelligence must be seen as a combination of two elements, operational analysis, and analytical interpretation. Furthermore, intelligence analysts must go beyond simply reporting facts like a laundry list and be able to synthesize the facts within the analysis. To be able to do that adequately and effectively, "the intelligence analyst must possess the requisite knowledge and abilities; be able to perform the specific tasks associated with the job; and finally exhibit personality traits compatible with intelligence analysis work."[8]

Chapter 2 hereafter is dedicated entirely to a discussion of the role of intelligence analysis and assessment, which are of major importance to transportation security.

To ensure that the above mentioned tasks work properly, there must be a management mechanism that defines the direction taken by the intelligence service and plans its moves in sync with the internal and external policies of the government. This also calls for the presence of formal and independent auditing and oversight mechanisms in place to monitor the ongoing quality and relevance of the work being done; to ensure that the principle of accountability is adhered to; and to prevent excesses, fabrications and third-party manipulation, which are quite likely to take place even in countries priding themselves of respecting the rule of law.

---

[7] Depending on the context, the name "Al-Qaeda" in Arabic could have different meanings, such as "a rule". In a military context such as in Afghanistan, it means "base", like a military base.

[8] Lisa Krizan, "Intelligence Essentials for everyone", Occasional Paper Number six - Joint Military Intelligence College, Washington, DC, p.55, June 1999.

CHAPTER 2

"While you can teach someone to paint, it is not possible
to teach someone how to paint a masterpiece or become a great
painter."[9]
Professor Stephen Marrin

INTELLIGENCE
ANALYSIS, ASSESSMENT AND
INTERPRETATION

Throughout history intelligence has always been the cornerstone of defence and protection. The important question is: What type of intelligence? Without timely, precise and reliable actionable intelligence that is at least partially corroborated, properly interpreted and analysed, accurately assessed, and adequately shared, it is quite difficult to do an efficient job in order to keep the threat away from territories, ports, airports, ships and airplanes.

The fact that an increasing number of terrorist acts are carried out by lone terrorists makes the task of intelligence even more difficult. In a conspiracy where a number of players are involved, there are better chances that their action could be intercepted by intelligence.

Every country has, and will continue to have, an ongoing intelligence gap that it is constantly striving to reduce. In some cases the gap is simply the result of good operational secrecy practices by the enemy, but it could also be caused by intelligence shortcomings. In other cases, the problem lies with either wrong analysis or assessment of the intelligence, or both.

CHALLENGES IN ANALYSIS AND ASSESSMENT

American vs. British intelligence culture

In his analysis "At Arm's Length or At the Elbow?"[10], Stephen Marrin, an academic and former intelligence analyst with the CIA, who knows what he is talking about, points to the different cultures characterizing the American and British attitudes towards intelligence.

---

[9] Stephen Marrin, "Improving Intelligence Analysis: Bridging the gap between Scholarship and practice", Routledge, Studies in Intelligence Series, UK (2011) p.94. By permission from Professor Marrin.

[10] Stephen Marrin, "At Arm's Length or At the Elbow? Explaining the Distance between Analysts and Decision makers", International Journal of Intelligence and CounterIntelligence, v.20 number 3, (2007) pp.401-414

Marrin points out that "…the United States national security decision-making culture is both hierarchical and adversarial, and tends to keep all-source intelligence analysts at arm's length from national decision makers, with the heads of the various departments providing conflicting advice to the President regarding what to do and how to do it."

According to Marrin, "this adversarial approach to decision-making leads to greater distance between intelligence agencies and decision makers because of how information is used in the decision-making process." Marrin quotes Columbia University Professor Robert Jervis saying in 1991, that information is "often used, not to shed light on issues, but as tools of persuasion, if not as weapons with which to beat adversaries within the government over the head."[11]

"In the American system", Jervis continues, "decision makers do not always appreciate all-source analysis, whether it comes from independent analytic organizations such as the CIA's Directorate of Intelligence or departmentally-affiliated organizations such as State Department's Bureau of Intelligence and Research. This is because the interpretation of information - otherwise known as analysis or assessments - can be a critical component of the interagency disputes over policy, with departmental advocates for each policy putting forth their best case for the President to decide. Intelligence agencies can be perceived as intervening in the policy process by providing alternative interpretations of the intelligence that appears to support the position of one of the sides in the policy debate.

By way of contrast, Jervis points out that "the United Kingdom's national security decision-making is decentralized rather than hierarchical, and frequently collegial rather than adversarial, and these combine to push intelligence analysis and decision-making closer together."

According to Martin J. Smith, Professor of Politics and Faculty Director of Research and Innovation (Social Sciences) at the University of Sheffield, "intelligence, because of its particular nature, creates a series of power asymmetries that favour those with the most direct access to intelligence. Intelligence therefore is shaped by the power relations that exist within the core executive because the Prime Minister is at the centre of the network of government and not only has access to intelligence but is able to shape the interpretation of that intelligence and so is in a strong position.[12]

"Where intelligence analysis takes place separately from decision-making, as is the case with both the (U.K.) Defence Intelligence Staff and the Joint Intelligence

---

[11] Robert Jervis, Strategic Intelligence and Effective Policy. Security and Intelligence in a Changing World: New Perspectives for the 1990s, 1991, p.179. Quoted in Stephen Marrin, "At Arm's Length."

[12] Martin J. Smith, Professor of Politics and Faculty Director of Research and Innovation (Social Sciences) at the University of Sheffield. "Intelligence and the Core Executive Public Policy and Administration" (January 2010), v.25 number 1, pp.11-28, p.21.

Committee (JIC), the integration of the analysis into decision-making is facilitated by the collegial and collaborative aspects of British national security decision-making."

"In British practice, raw intelligence moves straight into policymaking circles without passing through a separate intervening analytical stage...the British Joint Intelligence Committee (JIC) assessments are almost completely integrated into decision-making" says Philip H. J. Davies.[13] "This is because the JIC is an interdepartmental Cabinet Office staff made up of officials from both intelligence and policy organizations, that integrates intelligence into decision-making at the national strategic level primarily through weekly meetings and other forms of personal interaction..."[14] The JIC and its [Current Intelligence Groups] says Michael Herman, are partly meetings of intelligence professionals, but partly also a means of 'gathering the voices' within government as a whole."[15]

In a very recent article published by Philip Davies in the International Journal of intelligence and CounterIntelligence, Davies updates the intelligence community as to the diminishing role of the JIC at the present time saying that "for three-quarters of a century, the JIC and the Joint Intelligence Organization (JIO) set the global gold standard for national intelligence coordination."

Davies explains that "the conventional understanding of the British system is that, since the dark days of the Blitz, the Joint Intelligence Committee (JIC) has provided a continuously operating, tried and true apparatus for coordinating and managing Britain's national intelligence effort... But for some time, this has not, in fact, been an accurate description of how British intelligence is actually run. Since the summer of 2009, in particular, the JIO's functions have been steadily divided and redistributed within the Cabinet Office, and the JIC has itself been increasingly marginalized and ineffectual. For seven decades, the JIC has been seen as an enviably successful example to the rest of the intelligence world, with even American observers often looking to its collegiality and atmosphere of trust and mutual support as desirable, albeit not necessarily easy to emulate. That the UK has effectively abandoned such a tried and true formula is, therefore, somewhat surprising, still more so that such significant changes should have been undertaken with so little real debate and deliberation both within government and without."[16]

---

[13] Philip H. J. Davies, "Ideas of Intelligence: Divergent National Concepts and Institutions." Harvard International Review, v.24 number 3, fall 2002, pp.62-66. Quoted in Stephen Marrin "At Arm's Length."

[14] For additional information on the JIC, see Percy Cradock, Know Your Enemy: How the Joint Intelligence Committee Saw the World (London: John Murray, 2002). For a history of the JIC process, see Philip H. J. Davies, "Organizational Politics and the Development of Britain's Intelligence Producer-Consumer Interface", Intelligence and National Security, v.10 number 4 (October 1995), pp.113-132. Quoted in Stephen Marrin "At Arm's Length."

[15] Michael Herman, "National Intelligence Machinery - Assessment Machinery: British and American Models," Intelligence and National Security, v.10 number 4, October 1995, p.28. Quoted in Stephen Marrin "At Arm's Length."

[16] Philip H. J. Davies, "Twilight of Britain's Joint Intelligence Committee?" International Journal of Intelligence and CounterIntelligence, v.24 pp.427-446, 2011.

Governments do that quite often and go against the popular saying "if it is working, don't fix it!" They thus ruin something that is working, albeit when it occasionally does not operate efficiently. Instead of trying to pin-point the problem, they circumvent it and rush to create yet another "joint something" or several of them. By doing so, they defeat the whole purpose behind a centralized intelligence coordination body. So instead of fixing the problems that could have arisen within that organization, including shuffling staff and removing a possible incompetent chief, they just leave the organization spinning its wheels, duplicating what others are doing, or finding itself deliberately starved from intelligence. The terrorists on the other hand do not face these kinds of problems at least during the initial phases of their birth. All the government could simply do is to look at major banks, financial institutions and corporations and learn from their example when one of their subsidiaries or branches faces a problem or becomes less productive.

Myths reinforcing distance

In many countries, government officials at the management level tend to hold expertise and experience rather in low esteem, perhaps even contempt. "Beyond technical subjects like ballistic missiles, or nuclear power, specialization in a single issue, say, Latin America, Islam or South Asia for example, classifies officers as narrow-minded with no management potential. Expertise then becomes a career killer, especially in the intelligence community. Most prized is the "generalist", the officer who changes jobs every two years, flitting from Europe to East Asia to arms control, to narcotics. Conversant in many topics, expert in none, these usually male - but also female - officers are fast-tracked for senior management. In command are the glib but clueless appointees building an impermeable, self-perpetuating wall between officers, who in the generalist's eyes, "waste" their careers developing expertise. Thus, if and when elected leaders call for intelligence advice, they get access to articulate and politically manipulative dilettante careerists, and hear nothing from reality-prone experts who are carefully hidden away and only brought out when the going gets tough, and usually when it is too late."[17]

"In the United States, the distance between intelligence and decision-making has been legitimized and reinforced by a myth that is embedded in intelligence culture. This is again a reflection where the non-specialists and the mediocre cover their ignorance by relegating the specialists to a secondary support role and belittle their knowledge, with the pretext that generalists have a clearer image of the overall picture than the specialists."[18]

---

[17] Adapted from "Imperial Hubris" by Michael Scheuer - Brassey's Inc. Publishers; Dulles, Virginia 2004, p.245. www.potomacbooksinc.com

[18] For general comparisons of the British and the U.S. intelligences systems, see John Ranelagh, "Through the Looking Glass: A comparison of United States and United Kingdom Intelligence Cultures." Also see Michael Herman, "Assessment Machinery." Quoted in Stephen Marrin "At Arm's Length."

"According to the late intelligence scholar, Professor Michael Handel of the Naval War College, "it has often ... been assumed that intelligence work can be pursued by professional, detached experts working within an objective environment, and that they will be able to present the truth, as best they can determine it, to the policymakers. The policymakers in this scenario will of course recognize the quality and relevance of the data provided them, and will use this information in the best interest of their country (as they identify it)."[19]

"Intelligence analysis is both an art and a science. It is not and cannot be objective in an absolute sense, and even if it could be objective, practical reasons determine why that may not be such a good thing. Analytic objectivity in an absolute sense is not achievable because biases consisting of cognitive frameworks are necessary in order to infer meaning from incomplete data. Some degree of bias is inevitable ...Good analysts will question their own biases and revise them in the face of contrary evidence, but they cannot get along without some set of working assumptions.

"Many intelligence analysts and managers continue to believe in the myth that intelligence should remain distant from decision-making, due likely to their possession of a normative belief that intelligence should be a precursor to and foundation for decision-making. This myth may be all the stronger because it also exaggerates the importance of intelligence analysis in national security decision-making, thus creating a self-reinforcing mechanism."[20]

In her article entitled "Defending Adaptive Realism", Jennifer Sims proposes that "an intelligence service must have the ability to collect against targets, without decision-makers approval."[21]

"According to the myth, then, the distance between intelligence analysts and decision makers is in fact a protective mechanism to prevent decision makers from politicizing finished intelligence. Yet many intelligence analysts and managers continue to believe in the myth that intelligence should remain distant from decision-making.

"In the end, the collegial approach to decision-making leads to greater proximity between Britain's intelligence agencies and decision makers than in the U.S.

[19] Michael I. Handel, "Intelligence and the Problem of Strategic Surprise," Journal of Strategic Studies, v.7 number 3, September 1984, p.235. Quoted in Stephen Marrin "At Arm's Length."

[20] Richard K. Betts, "Intelligence for Policymaking," Washington Quarterly, summer 1980, pp.118-129. For additional information on the existence, effects, and inevitability of cognitive biases in intelligence analysis, see Kevin Russell, "The Subjectivity of Intelligence Analysis and Implications for the U.S. National Security Strategy," SAIS Review, v. XXIV, number 1, winter-spring 2004, pp.147-163; and Richards J. Heuer, Psychology of Intelligence Analysis (Centre for the Study of Intelligence: Central Intelligence Agency; 1999, p. 111.) Quoted in Stephen Marrin "At Arm's Length."

[21] Jennifer Sims, "Defending adaptive realism: Intelligence theory comes of age", appeared in "Intelligence Theory: Key Questions and debates", Edited by Peter Gill, Stephen Marrin and Mark Phythian; Routledge, London, UK p.157 (2009).

because of how information is used in the decision-making process. Therefore, "an ... equivalent to the JIC might be useful as a way to close the distance between intelligence analysts and decision makers without necessarily compromising analytic independence along the way."[22]

An institution such as the JIC requires a combination of highly experienced subject-matter analysts, who are skilled at integrating the various reaches of intelligence, history, diplomacy, strategic, economic and security, which renders analysis and policy recommendations multi-dimensional and realistic. The leaderships of such an institution must be of the highest calibre. When all these essential factors are absent, the institution could turn into a stagnant cemetery. There are examples of similar institutions today that produce no more than occasional toothless term papers collated from different domestic and foreign intelligence and law enforcement agencies. Their product is not taken seriously by anybody, because much of the raw data and/or analysis would have already been communicated to these client organizations by the original agency that produced the intelligence in the first place.

According to Michael Herman, "what the JIC produces is arguably not really 'intelligence assessment,' but just 'assessment.'[23] Philip Davies proposes that "The decentralization of power in the British cabinet system is undoubtedly a factor in the decentralization of all-source analysis, much as executive centralization under the US presidency influences the centralization of analysis."[24] He has also observed that in the UK "individual [policy] departments [are] highly autonomous in their formulation of policy, and their power [is] highly centralized in the Cabinet." As a result, "ministers and civil servants have traditionally held a proprietary attitude towards analysis and decision-making enhanced by the very small size of the UK central government." Accordingly, "Centralized analysis is anathema to the twin doctrines of ministerial responsibility and the constitutional role of the civil service under British parliamentary democracy."[25] This explains, according to Marrin, "why most intelligence analysis and assessment is conducted by Britain's decision makers rather than by its intelligence analysts."[26]

More recently, "Richard K. Betts noted that decentralization has always persisted in the overlapping division of labor among numerous agencies. Some theorists of bureaucracy see such duplication as beneficial because competition exposes disagreement and presents policymakers with a wider range of views.

[22] Stephen Marrin, "At Arm's Length or At the Elbow? Explaining the Distance between Analysts and Decision makers", International Journal of Intelligence and CounterIntelligence, v.20 number 3, (2007) 401-414.

[23] "National Intelligence Machinery" Michael Herman, "Assessment Machinery: British and American Models," Intelligence and National Security, v.10 number 4, October 1995, p.28. Quoted in Stephen Marrin "At Arm's Length.

[24] Philip H. J. Davies, "Ideas of Intelligence: Divergent National Concepts and Institutions." Harvard International Review, v. 24, number 3, fall 2002, p.63. Quoted in Stephen Marrin "At Arm's Length."

[25] Philip H.J. Davies, "Organizational Politics and the Development of Britain's Intelligence Producer -Consumer Interface", Intelligence and National Security, v.10, number 4 (October 1995), pp.114-115. Quoted in Stephen Marrin "At Arm's Length."

[26] Stephen Marrin, "At Arm's Length or At the Elbow?" p.407.

Redundancy inhibits consensus and impedes the herd instinct in the decision process, thus reducing the likelihood of failure due to unchallenged premises or cognitive errors. To ensure that redundancy works in this way, critics oppose a process that yields coordinated [intelligence] estimates that are negotiated to the least common denominator and cleared by all agencies before they are passed to the principals."[27]

Interaction between intelligence officers, collectors and analysts

Some intelligence agencies separate their analysis branch from the operational branch. Their reasoning is that analysis must be neutral and not 'tainted' by operational details or personal value-added by the intelligence officers or the analysts. This means that they deny themselves the most important ingredient of intelligence: experience and ability to detect trends. In actual fact, for analysis to be meaningful, realistic and useful as actionable intelligence, it must be done cooperatively between the two branches.

Keeping the analysts and the operational intelligence officers at arms length could distance them from the ongoing trends within a given group of potential terrorists they each observe from their own vantage point. Sometimes intelligence officers may be absorbed by operational matters and specific targets, which could lead them to miss the forest from the trees. On the other hand, intelligence analysts may find themselves drifting away from the investigation underway and lose sight of the overall case. Working in tandem will help minimize such occurrences to a great degree and give meaning to the expression "actionable intelligence."

From the point of view of intelligence analysis, "the Intelligence Community is far more diversified in its tasks than is generally realized. Where analysis is done and for whom makes a large difference in its effectiveness. Moreover, changing technology is altering how it is done, where, and by whom. The border between what is 'strategic' or 'national' intelligence and 'tactical' intelligence is much diminished. That requires understanding the proper role and responsibility of intelligence analysis, especially at the national level."[28]

But it also requires putting intelligence analysis – that is, intelligence products used by policy-makers and military commanders – in its proper context within overall intelligence operations. An enlightening study of the problem for intelligence chiefs during World War II is found in Harold Deutsch's article on 'Commanding Generals and Uses of Intelligence'. "The overpowering status and

---

[27] Richard K. Betts, "Enemies of Intelligence: Knowledge and Power" in American National Security (New York: Columbia University Press, 2007, p.39. Quoted in Thomas H. Hammond, "Intelligence Organizations and the Organization of Intelligence", International Journal of Intelligence and CounterIntelligence, v.23 number 4, pp. 680-724, 2010.

[28] William E Odom. "Intelligence Analysis", Intelligence and National Security, (2008) v.23 number3, 316-332 p.316.

authority of the commander, Deutsch argued, inevitably causes the intelligence officer to make analytical judgments more or less in line with what the commander will accept, and what he believes is reasonable and prudent." [29]

"Where intelligence analysis is done has huge implications too often ignored or misunderstood. Analysis at the national level differs in one respect from analysis within departments and military commands. Deutsch, for instance, was studying intelligence officers on military staffs." According to him "they are an organic component inside the organization that uses the analysis."[30]

"The analytic component of the CIA, the Directorate of Intelligence (DI), does not belong to any intelligence user's organizational staff. It is, therefore, separated from the planning and operational processes at the White House and elsewhere in departments and agencies.[31]

"The CIA/DI's organizational autonomy has another effect that is important to notice, not least because it tends to justify the assumption that the CIA should provide intelligence that forces a president to make effective decisions. As mentioned above, this unrealistic assumption is reinforced by the CIA's ethic of wholly 'objective' and 'apolitical', or purely 'professional judgment' in analysis and intelligence production. With their organizational autonomy, they insist that they are positioned to discern and report the unvarnished truth while those working under policy-makers and commanders are subject to their superiors' political biases. Indeed they are, as Deutsch cogently demonstrates. But that raises another question: do or can intelligence analysts know the full and unbiased truth about adversaries? The answer is clearly 'no'. They can only make best guesses.[32]

"For anyone who doubts this, simply observe the academic world where social sciences and historians, presumably working with all the facts, arrive at radically different answers to the questions they address. True, a strong effort is made to maintain scholarly objectivity, and that is as it should be, but it does not remove the normative biases humans inherently bring to their research."[33]

In the intelligence environment on cannot overstate the value of the small diversified group of younger analysts led by a specialist in producing not just high quality intelligence analysis, but analysis rooted in realities on the ground. Besides, it mixes the younger and more adaptive and inquisitive mindset with that of the established and experienced leader. This structure has the potential of producing more realistic analysis and estimates. This is similar to ensuring that

[29] Harold C. Deutsch, "Commanding Generals and the Uses of Intelligence", Intelligence and National Security v3 May 1988, pp.194-260. Quoted in Odom "Intelligence Analysis p.318.
[30] Odom, p.320
[31] Ibid., p.320
[32] Ibid., p.321
[33] Ibid., p.321

such groups be composed of both men and women, due to their different outlook on things. A good example in a different field would be the team of diverse physicians performing surgery in an operating room working as a team under the baton of a chief surgeon.

"In most federal agencies that use intelligence, intelligence analysts are grouped into a single intelligence unit. Unlike the DI of CIA, they have an executive official or policy-making agency head directly above them, and they are part of the user organization. Their integration into the planning and policy-making elements of each agency, however, varies considerably. In most, it is limited. Two reasons explain this. First, it must work in a fully secure set of offices with secure communications and storage space for its (electronic and paper) files and documents. Second, most of the information needed for planning and operational decisions in the civilian agencies is unclassified. The need for classified intelligence analysis is not great most of the time.

"Moreover, interactions with the media and with foreigners – diplomats and others – create a serious problem for securing intelligence documents. In the State Department, a large user of intelligence, where much of it is very sensitive, this is an especially difficult problem. It can also be a problem in Treasury, Energy, Transportation, Commerce, and Justice, the other departments that use intelligence more or less extensively. Homeland Security, a relatively new department, is still evolving in its use and the location of intelligence analysts, but it should have more in common with the Defense Department than any others, and therefore fewer problems of integration."[34]

Countering the threat by detecting and identifying trends and patterns

The role of intelligence is to think in terms of the future, and not in terms of what has already happened yesterday; i.e. intelligence must be at least one step ahead of the enemy. But this cannot be achieved if the collected intelligence is not analyzed and assessed in good time, or if it is not intelligently shared within the security and intelligence community to start with. These cardinal rules of detecting and identifying trends and patterns by the various players within the community was subject to an extensive analysis by Dr. Thomas H. Hammond, Professor of Political Science at Michigan State University and other universities, who specialized in the scientific study of bureaucratic hierarchies.

In an extensive article published in the International Journal of Intelligence and CounterIntelligence, under the title "Intelligence Organizations and the Organization of Intelligence", Dr. Hammond notes that "a puzzling aspect of many successful surprise attacks in modern warfare is that, after the attack, the defender discovered that it had already possessed, before the attack, substantial information suggesting that an attack was on the way. Among such "intelligence

---

[34] Ibid., p.321

failures" are the German invasions of France and Norway in 1940 and the Soviet Union in 1941, the Japanese attack on the American fleet at Pearl Harbor in 1941, the German attack on British and American forces in the Ardennes in 1944 in the Battle of the Bulge, the Tet Offensive by the North Vietnamese and Viet Cong against American and South Vietnamese forces in 1968, and the Egyptian attack on Israeli forces in the Sinai in 1973. In each case, later assessment revealed that essential information had already been collected by the defenders' intelligence agencies but that the data had been ignored, overlooked, or interpreted in ways that limited, or even completely negated, an effective response."[35]

"… had this information been properly analyzed, the defender should have been able to anticipate, disrupt, or perhaps even prevent these attacks. Similar observations have also been made about the al-Qaeda attacks on the Pentagon and the World Trade Centre on 11 September 2001 (9/11): intelligence agencies in the U.S. had already had in their possession information that, had it been properly disseminated and assessed, might have allowed them to anticipate, disrupt, or perhaps even prevent these disasters."[36]

As mentioned above, one of the pillars of forward-looking intelligence is following trends and patterns over a long period of time. During the summer of 2001 i.e. prior to 9/11 a senior intelligence analyst working for the intelligence service of a G8 country had observed while monitoring several targets in a completely different investigation that a specific city in a European country had become a hub for several plotters from a variety of countries, but all belonging to, or affiliated with Al-Qaeda. The post facto investigation of the 9/11 bombings confirmed that at least some of the terrorists involved in the attack on the World Trade Centre in New York were members of those networks operating out of that European city.

This trend, which was apparent a good two to three months before the attacks, was shared with another major allied agency. It is not known though if the intelligence services of the two countries involved acted on the information, or checked it with the European country involved. Had the information based on trend analysis been quickly actioned, chances are that the 9/11 attacks could have been prevented.

---

[35] Thomas H. Hammond, "Intelligence Organizations and the Organization of Intelligence", International Journal of Intelligence and CounterIntelligence, v.23 number 4, pp.680-724, 2010. Also see Richard K. Betts, "Surprise Attack: Lessons for Defense Planning" (Washington, DC: The Brookings Institution, 1982).

[36] See National Commission on Terrorist Attacks upon the United States, The 9/11 Commission Report (New York: W. W. Norton, 2004) and Amy B. Zegart, Flying Blind: The CIA, the FBI, and the Origins of 9/11 Princeton, NJ: Princeton University Press, 2007) for thorough reviews. Cited in Thomas H. Hammond, "Intelligence Organizations and the Organization of Intelligence."

Improving intelligence analysis,
Optimizing its interpretation, and increasing its impact

"At the centre of the intelligence machine lies the analyst, and he, or she, is the fellow to whom all the information goes so that he can review it and think about it and determine what it means."[37]

"Analysts must learn how to 'task' collectors. Collectors cannot perform effectively unless they know what analysts and users want to know and need to know. 'Need' and 'want' to know are not always the same. Most operations staffs, commanders, and policy-makers have little or no idea of what intelligence or another part of the Intelligence Community can provide. Thus they do not know whom to ask for what.[38]

"To become more specific about how 'analysis' is done, it should be noted that there is no set of 'rules' or principles that, if followed, guarantee effective results. Even the best analysts must work within organizations locked in preconceptions and strong normative biases. Inevitably they will absorb many of those biases, just as historians inexorably interpret the past through the prisms of contemporary problems, ideologies, political and social beliefs, and personal preferences about how the world 'ought to be'. All that either the analyst or the historian can do is to strive for detachment, to criticize one's own analysis to the extent possible, to be skeptical. Yet excessive skepticism can induce indecision, and at some point that is no longer an option."[39]

In a "letter to the editor" of the Washington Times published on February 22, 2004 under the title "Improving the CIA's Analysis", Stephen Marrin highlights the fact that "Intelligence analysis should include not only what analysts know, but also what they don't know." In view of the importance of Marrin's arguments and their applicability, we are reproducing the article almost integrally hereunder.

"Uncertainty is part of the intelligence production process. Intelligence collected rarely provides analysts with a complete picture of what is occurring in a foreign country. When an intelligence analyst taps into all the various data available to him [or her[40]] through intelligence collection or open info material, the first sense is of an overwhelming amount of information about all kinds of topics. When precise information is desired, the analyst puts together bits and pieces of

---

[37]William Colby, "Retooling the Intelligence Industry", Foreign Service Journal v.69, number1. (January 1992). Quoted from Stephen Marrin, "Improving CIA Analysis by Overcoming Institutional Obstacles." "Bringing Intelligence About: Practitioners Reflect on Best Practices." Russell G. Swenson, Editor Joint Military Intelligence College. May 2003. p.2.

[38] William E. Odom. "Intelligence Analysis", Intelligence and National Security, (2008) v.23 number 3, 316-332 p.325.

[39] Ibid., p.326-327

[40] Women are extremely good analysts because of their natural attention to detail as well as their perspective that often sees things from yet another angle. Besides, women have the additional innate gut feel about people, that not all men can claim and that is so important in intelligence.

information to form a picture or story and frequently discovers many gaps in the data. As a result, an intelligence analyst's judgment rests on a rickety foundation of assumptions, inferences and educated guesses.

"Caveats are necessary in finished intelligence as a way to communicate analytic uncertainty. Intelligence agencies would be performing a disservice to policy-makers if their judgments communicated greater certainty than the analysts possessed. In the case of Iraqi weapons of mass destruction, if the CIA's analytic caveats effectively captured their uncertainty and relayed this uncertainty to the policy level, there was no intelligence failure at the analytic level. Accurately reflecting uncertainties when they exist is crucial.

"Unfortunately, caveats also complicate assessments of intelligence accuracy. Words such as "probably," "likely" and "may" are scattered throughout intelligence publications and prevent easy assessment of accuracy. For example, if CIA analysts had said Iraq probably had weapons of mass destruction, would that analysis be considered accurate or inaccurate? There is no way to tell, given the use of the word "probably," which communicated the analyst's uncertainty.

"Removing caveats for the sake of simplicity in assessing intelligence accuracy also unfairly removes the record of analytic uncertainty and, in the end, assesses something with which the analyst never would have agreed. Therefore, all assessments of intelligence reporting must be very careful in their use of accuracy as a measuring stick, and it is for this reason that former-CIA Director George J. Tenet said, "In the intelligence business, you are almost never completely wrong or completely right."

"If intelligence does not provide policy-makers with answers, what does it provide for them? Intelligence agencies provide policy-makers with intelligence reports that help them make decisions in two ways: by informing them of what is going on in foreign countries, and by warning them of possible developments that could harm U.S. interests." Crucial foreign policy matters are made in so many countries without being assessed by intelligence before implementation for possible effects and repercussions of one type or another.

"Validation of intelligence requires two levels of fact-checking. The first is to ensure that the finished intelligence accurately captures the information contained in the raw intelligence reports; the second level is to ensure that the raw intelligence reports themselves are accurate.

"Analysts in general link their analysis to source reports, but only do a cursory examination of the accuracy of the source reporting raw intelligence." This is especially the case of second-tier G8 countries that rely partially on first-tier countries to provide them with raw intelligence.

"Intelligence agencies must be able to warn policy-makers about issues that might negatively affect the national interest by emphasizing alternative possibilities rather than just provide a single assessment of the future. Analysts usually provide their assessment of the most likely outcome, but many times that single assessment turns out to be wrong because of factors the analysts did not incorporate into their analysis.

"The usual way other professions that deal with complex subjects such as meteorology or epidemiology forecast the future is by providing a range of possible outcomes and highlighting the factors that could change the outcomes. The adoption by intelligence agencies of a scenario-based warning system highlighting multiple possible outcomes would more effectively capture analytic uncertainty than the popular practice of providing a single assessment of the most likely outcome...Relaying this information in a way that highlights uncertainty through formats that emphasize multiple possible outcomes would provide policy-makers with a better sense for what the intelligence agency does not know."[41]

We would like to argue that while this is a reasonable approach, it is still important that the lead intelligence analyst put his or her expertise on the line and put his/her weight behind the most likely estimate in his/her assessment and why. After all, the accuracy of intelligence analysis depends in part upon an individual analyst's expertise. And we must always remember that this person must be at all times a permanent partner of the government policy-making pool comprised of the Intelligence Service, the Cabinet, the Department of Defence, and the President's team depending on the political system of the country.

"After all, these are not academic exercises but action-orientated briefs", says former chief of the Israeli Intelligence Service Efraim Halevy. "When there is no agreement, the time comes for an intelligence chief to step in and determine what the official estimate shall be. He could and should indicate if there are major reservations, and what these might be, but the ultimate responsibility lies with the chief. He must state his view and he, and he alone, must bear official responsibility for the estimate. Nobody else shoulders real and accountable responsibility, either for the estimate, or for the ultimate mistake, if it emerges that there has been one."[42]

While almost everything published about intelligence analysis zooms on intelligence analysts and intelligence agencies, scant attention is given to policy makers. In the vast majority of cases professional intelligence analysts do know what they are talking about, and the assumption that policy makers, or policy pushers, possess the same level of knowledge is not totally accurate; at least not in all cases.

[41] Stephen Marrin, "Improving the CIA's analysis" - The Washington Times, February 22, 2004. Letters to the Editor - www.washingtontimes.com - Article ID: 200402230933260007.

[42] Efraim Halevy – "In defence of the intelligence services" - The Economist print edition, July 29, 2004.

Furthermore, there are cases where the agenda of certain elected officials does not necessarily correspond to national interest. Their agenda may be biased towards the interests of certain influential groups within a vocal, ideological or financial minority which does not take into consideration the generally silent majority. At the end of the day the analysis produced by the intelligence community may be used, or misused, by these elected politicians to advance the interests of a few among those they represent to the detriment of the long term national interest. For some reason, many politicians in various countries continue to do that, thinking that the general public is either blind or stupid. Then they are surprised when they are uncovered.

The danger of politicization or partisanship, i.e. the potential for higher echelons in the intelligence community to distort information or judgment in order to please political authorities especially at the very senior levels is real. The challenge is to develop reasonable safeguards against such situations by protecting intelligence analysis and analysts from predatory politicians and special interest groups.

In his book "Intelligence and Strategic Surprises" Ariel Levite provides the following analysis: "Intelligence information may be "compartmented" to protect the collecting agencies' sources and methods of collection, but this may limit dissemination of relevant information to analysts and policymakers if the defender's intelligence analysts are too closely linked to policymakers, the analysts may provide "intelligence to please",[43] whereas if the analysts are too isolated from policymakers, the analysts' information may address the wrong questions or concerns; in either case, the policymakers will be less than adequately informed. Finally, Levite cites Roberta Wohlstetter's argument that intelligence analysis almost always involves the difficult process of extracting a small amount of meaningful information from a large mass of meaningless noise; as a result, the inferences that are made are almost inevitably uncertain and error-prone."[44]

Enhancing analytic expertise by enlisting expert support

High-quality analysis starts by bringing in high quality analysts from the outset into the process. Intelligence analysts must be given the same basic training as intelligence officers, and occasionally involved in operations to maintain them on the same wavelength with the operational intelligence officers.

Quality analysis also requires reducing the isolation of the intelligence community. A greater flow of talented people into the agency not just from

---

[43] Ariel Levite, "Intelligence and Strategic Surprises", New York: Columbia University Press, 1987, pp.9-12. Quoted in Thomas H. Hammond, "Intelligence Organizations and the Organization of Intelligence", International Journal of Intelligence and CounterIntelligence, v.23 number 4, pp.680-724, 2010.

[44] Roberta Wohlstetter, "Pearl Harbor: Warning and Decision", (Stanford, CA: Stanford University Press, 1962). Quoted by Ariel Levite, "Intelligence and Strategic Surprises" (New York: Columbia University Press, 1987), pp. 9-12, in Thomas H. Hammond, "Intelligence Organizations and the Organization of Intelligence", International Journal of Intelligence and CounterIntelligence, v.23 number 4, pp. 680-724, 2010.

academia, but particularly among businesses and individuals with hands-on experience or expertise in a variety of trades, professions and industries such as the aviation and maritime industries for instance is essential.

In his very appropriate article 'Soldiers, Scholars and Spies'[45] Bowman H. Miller touches on a particularly important topic, namely the relationships between specialized academia and intelligence. In our estimate the importance of this topic cannot be overemphasized especially when dealing with threat sources in foreign countries or in specific industry sectors such as aviation and maritime to cite one example among many.

"Those in the U.S. intelligence community, and there are some, who conclude that "outsiders" have nothing to offer them since only "insiders" holding security clearances have access to the nation's collected intelligence are guilty of the utmost in short-sightedness - if not intellectual hubris.

"By the same token, there are some in academia who claim that the involvement of scholars with "the national security state [sic]" constitutes an infringement on, or threat to, their intellectual integrity, morality, or professional or ethical obligations to their given discipline. Both perspectives are off the mark. Government needs some expertise it does not have and cannot retain in its ranks. But there are better and worse ways of obtaining that expertise. Engaging the expertise of qualified outsiders becomes a "force multiplier" for the intelligence community and the military, one that they can ill afford to shun or alienate since the mandate for intelligence (and for military operators) is to exploit the best minds and most relevant knowledge, wherever they are or it is to be found. By the same token, those in the defense and intelligence enterprises need to recognize and sensitively manage the concerns of scholars and other outside subject matter experts, who may be wary of involving themselves and their disciplines in issues of secrecy, lethal operations, covert actions, aggressive interrogations, and the prosecution of acts of war, lest their future ability to do research and their standing in the scholarly or medical community be imperilled.

"Preceding the present constellation of intelligence, military, and outside experts, there is a rich history of involvement by scholars in national intelligence in the United States for much of the twentieth century. "Old-timers" will recall that in the fateful, founding era of the Office of Strategic Services (OSS) during and after World War II, some of the titans of American academia were summoned to Washington to lead strategic and other analysis on the part of the nascent intelligence community. In mid-1941 William Donovan recommended to President Roosevelt that, in organizing the foreign intelligence service with which he had been tasked, the effort should "draw on the universities for experts, with long foreign experience and specialized knowledge of the history, languages, and

---

[45] Reminds one of John Le Carré's 1974 spy novel "Tinker, Taylor, Sailor, Spy!"

general conditions of various countries."[46] That core focus resulted in the essential composition of the OSS. Its staff members were, in many respects, the intellectual elite of the country; they represented the cream of the Ivy League and other top-flight American institutions of higher learning."[47]

"It was this special generation that broke adversaries' codes in the war, provided the judgments that guided postwar policy formation and led the process of National Intelligence Summary and National Estimate production, as well as efforts to produce net assessments. Indeed, it had been anthropological expertise on Japan that played a pivotal role in convincing President Roosevelt to exempt the emperor from the terms of surrender, lest Japanese culture suffer an irreparable wound. When the Board of National Estimates was created, it replicated the OSS approach in culling out the brightest minds in American academe to draft the estimates. There is, indeed, a pantheon of these path breakers recorded in U.S. political and intelligence history, and most of them emanated from, and often later returned to, the halls of academe. The relationships between those still "inside" the intelligence world and those on its margins were sustained - and they fed off each other's expertise and insights.

"Jumping ahead into the 1950s, 1960s, and early 1970s - in the era of Vietnam, the Bay of Pigs debacle, and abuses of U.S. intelligence capabilities in Latin America, elsewhere in the "Third World," and at home - the intelligence relationship with the academic world became strained, nearly to the breaking point. The Church - Pike congressional inquiry into domestic spying, the fatal overreaction of Ohio National Guardsmen at Kent State, FBI illegal monitoring of the civil rights movement, and other developments prompted many academicians publicly and stridently to distance themselves from any cooperation with U.S. intelligence, particularly the CIA. Agency (and military) recruiters were banned from or spurned on campuses, professors were excoriated for contracting or consulting with intelligence agencies, and "intelligence" seemed to have become a four-letter word.

"Even though various levels of policy makers in Washington saw (and, at times, were responsible for) the ebb and flow of the intelligence - academic relationship (to include think tanks and technology development entities), at a more discreet level it was being sustained and expanded all along. This clearly featured close cooperation and huge amounts of funding for pivotal advances in technologies with specific, sensitive intelligence aims and applications. In analytic collaboration, this prominently featured Soviet studies and analysis. The intelligence agencies also gave strong backing to the study of foreign languages and cultures, even as

---

[46] Quoted by then-Deputy Director of Central Intelligence for Intelligence Robert M. Gates, "CIA and the University," speech at Harvard University, February 13, 1986, in Bowman H. Miller, Soldiers, Scholars and Spies.

[47] For a fuller, if often critical, account of these formative years and leaders, see Tim Weiner, "Legacy of Ashes: The History of the CIA" (New York: Doubleday, 2007), 3-70.

U.S. intelligence furnished many graduates - holding degrees in these areas - with postgraduate employment where their knowledge and expertise could be utilized well and commensurately be rewarded."[48]

When it comes to seeking academic views on events happening or originating overseas, most intelligence agencies tend to call on professors from universities established in their own countries or in countries belonging to the same culture. What they get is mostly the same occasionally inaccurate, or slanted, analysis present in the media or that parrots the official government line. The end product will not be much different from what's being published in local newspapers or academic journals. They almost never try to go out of the box they put themselves in, and indirectly seek the opinions and perspectives of academics from universities in other countries to get their perspective too, including from those countries where the trouble is coming from or generated as a result of foreign interference.

Miller underlines the fact that "two heads are better than one" and trusting in the "wisdom of crowds." At the same time that the government's human intelligence collectors are seeking to spot, assess, and recruit clandestine agents to report on foreign capabilities and intentions, many U.S. (and foreign) scholars have an impressive cadre of their own informative contacts, counterparts, and "sources" in virtually every society on earth.

"On the other hand, for their part, government intelligence analysts (leaving aside clandestine collectors) in a number of countries may be lucky to visit their overseas "portfolios" for two weeks every two or three years and are, in many agencies, banned from communicating with or attending conferences involving foreigners. They often lack the depth of experience, language skills, and cultural *Fingerspitzengefühl* (fingertips knowledge) of their academic counterparts. Indeed, it is the smart analyst who keeps open a channel to his or her former university instructors from whom he or she may acquire unique insights, even if second-hand.

"Some of these in academia compose a cadre of "reserve experts" or "associates" who draw a small retainer and can be called on to review analyses, render their own assessments, present views and moderate panels at symposia, and monitor foreign developments and trends.

"Thus, it is not simply an added convenience that the government can call on outside experts who do track what are otherwise too often neglected corners of the globe; it often has proven to be essential, if the (country) is to see problems looming on the horizon or is to quickly react to an unexpected event, be it a riot, a coup d'état, a disease outbreak, a civil war, or a tsunami. For those and other

---

[48] Bowman H. Miller, "Soldiers, Scholars, and Spies: Combining Smarts and Secrets", Armed Forces & Society, (2010) v.36 number 4, 695-715

reasons, the most capable government analysts have an electronic (data base) of outside experts on whom they can call for information, to cross-check data, and to share analytic views.

"It is they, as resident scholars or ad hoc consultants, who also can often spot the frailties and potholes in the community's analytic culture and processes from the standpoint of an objective, observant outsider. If "groupthink" tends to mark the analytic approach to a key issue, the outsider is more likely to spot this phenomenon and call it to the attention of those who can repair the damage and ward off its recurrence.

"So-called outsiders are not immune from some of their own frailties, however. For their part, many academic experts bring with them their own foibles and misguided preconceptions. Hubris is not unique to bureaucrats. More than occasionally one encounters the university scholar whose egotistical intellect cannot imagine that anyone in government has a fresh, informed, or even useful idea - or any observation worth hearing.

"Getting academics to write tersely, to focus more on their findings and less on the contextual background, and to venture future outlooks in their *written* assessments has often proven difficult. Thus, the tendency in an organization such as the Department of State's Bureau of Intelligence and Research is not to ask academics or think tank specialists to *write* analyses but rather to have them participate in symposia where the academic participants can be enjoined to focus on core questions, are bound by short speaking time limits, and, most importantly, can make their comments and appraisals with the added assurance that they are speaking in an off-the-record, not-for-attribution setting. This condition is crucial if one is to expect conference participants (and all outside experts) to speak candidly and to "think out loud" without fear of being quoted, if one is to reap the full value and richness of the insights of "outsiders."[49]

This is exactly what the British Foreign Office does through an executive agency operating under the name "Wilton Park", which offers conference programs for discussion and debate on world political, security and economic topics to which British as well as foreign speakers from all political and non-political fields are invited to address issues of importance to the British Government.[50]

Provision ought to be made also for appointing specialists and not just academics through lateral and mid-career entry as well as for short-term entry (measured in weeks, months, or years) or even for just a single, short-duration project. In this way the intelligence community could attract and exploit some of the best minds

---

[49] Ibid., pp.695-715

[50] See Wilton Park's website www.wiltonpark.org.uk

from various walks of life that would otherwise not be available to them within the ranks of the intelligence agency itself. The resulting two-way enrichment and "knowledge transfer" will be tremendous.

While some intelligence services bring in outside experts for short tours as scholars-in-residence, others keep them for good. A third type unfortunately gets rid of them and relies on permanent in-house term-paper writers with no hands-on operational or in-country residence experience. A fourth type makes the subject matter experts report to novices who have no clue as to what's going on out there.

As the reader will remark in this book, we are encouraging the move towards both specialisation and decentralisation of sectorial intelligence, but also for centralisation in those areas that call for such an approach. i.e. versatility. The Department of Transport for example understands its environment better than any other department, the same goes for the Department of Industry, the Department of Defence, the Department of Foreign Affairs, etc. Each department should have its own intelligence analysis team who concentrate their work on the various major areas under the department's mandate. In the case of the Department of Transport for example, this team will analyse intelligence pertaining to the aviation, maritime, surface transportation and mass transit sectors. Each of the other departments will have the same type of specialisation in its own domains. Ultimately all these analytical teams will be working jointly with the intelligence service(s) in relation to aviation and maritime security, with each contributing to the other's input, as discussed later in more detail.

Arthur S. Hulnick made a comparable observation when he wrote saying that "there are good reasons to have duplication in some areas [of the intelligence community], especially in both collection and analysis. Collecting data from a variety of sources, even if there is overlap, is just what analysts need to solve the mysteries. From the analyst's perspective, there is never too much raw material. Analysts are comforted when several analytic units go through the data and reach similar conclusions. When they disagree on the interpretation, then there is a good reason to confer and sort things out. Competitive analysis is a good way to avoid intelligence failure. One could conclude from this that redundancy in the substantive areas of intelligence is generally a good thing and should not be cut back."[51]

For intelligence professionals and analysts to better understand the needs of policymakers and vice versa, career intelligence professionals must undergo regular rotations into positions in the policymaking departments or ministries (Foreign Affairs, Defence, Treasury, Industry, Transport, Immigration, the private sector, etc.). Such rotations should be required for promotion to junior and senior

---

[51] Arthur S. Hulnick, "Fixing the Spy Machine: Preparing American Intelligence for the Twenty-First Century" (Westport, CT: Praeger Publishers, 1999), p.206. Quoted in Thomas H. Hammond, "Intelligence Organizations and the Organization of Intelligence", International Journal of Intelligence and CounterIntelligence, v.23 number 4, pp.680-724, 2010.

levels. The same logic argues for assigning career public servants normally in the governmental security policymaking divisions to periodic tours within the intelligence community.

Not every analyst needs or chooses to pursue a career with a management component. Given an adequate incremental pay scale will encourage many analysts who are just as happy to do what they like most, namely analysis, to do just that. A special career path for this category needs to be created. While there is a universal trend to consider university professors as the most eminent in a given subject matter, this is not universally true. Some professors hold the position only because they have a PhD. But not every PhD holder is necessarily a knowledgeable person. Besides, the diversity of expertise required by the intelligence community calls on people with long professional experience, and perhaps with a bachelor's or a master's degree only. Having said that, intelligence management level staff must be knowledgeable in either a functional or a geographic area. They also require formal management and leadership training as well as demonstrated competence as a prerequisite for promotion. The tendency in some intelligence services of appointing accountants and administrators who have no clue about the outside world as managers in operational or analysis areas is a grave mistake that will seriously harm the service.

Capturing institutional memory

As noted earlier by Miller "some small-minded intelligence officials still harbor the misguided view that only those with a security clearance and access to sensitive intelligence can possibly know and analyze the world as, and as well as, they do."[52]

"One added element for consideration in examining the ties between insiders and outsiders in the world of analysis, in particular", he points out to, "is the vast diaspora of retirees from the worlds of both analysis and academe. [I would also add "ex's" who left the service practically by choice or by electing to go on early retirement and wish to return on part-time or contractual duty]. Many of them carry decades of institutional memory, analytic tradecraft practice, and the wisdom of earlier policy and intelligence successes and failures. Taking advantage of such experience is a boon to analytic accuracy and output. Moreover, some of these same seasoned analysts particularly those hailing from other cultures serve as vital mentors and educators for a generation of successors. They bring different backgrounds, technology orientations, and challenges than those of the departing generation. It is a wise use of an available talent pool whose insights and bureaucratic experience can be usefully deployed to the benefit of a younger, energetic, and highly educated group of up-and-coming analysts."[53]

---

[52] Bowman H. Miller, "Soldiers, Scholars, and Spies: Combining Smarts and Secrets", Armed Forces & Society, (2010) v.36 number 4, 695-715.

[53] Ibid., p.710

Intelligence analysis rarely impresses itself upon politicians and policymakers, who in certain cases are full of themselves, and who are understandably busy and inundated with more demands on their time to ensure they get re-elected, keep their jobs and retire comfortably. Unlike in business, the intelligence customer is not always king. The leadership of the intelligence community should reinforce the ethic that speaking the truth without adverse effect on their careers from those in power is a must.

Another serious problem to be avoided is mindset. Any intelligence agency can fall into the trap of not questioning basic assumptions that affect much subsequent analysis. It is essential that competitive or redundant analysis be encouraged when required. Not all duplication is wasteful. Intelligence analysts must draw attention to their product and market their ideas. This is especially true in the case of any early warning or intelligence-related development that has potentially significant political, economic or security consequences. This calls for their supervisors, who are expected to be competent and knowledgeable people, to create the required atmosphere that encourages intelligence officers and analysts to speak up.

In his book 'Psychology of Intelligence Analysis, Richards Heuer talks about how the then CIA Deputy Director of Intelligence (DDI) Robert Gates reviewed intelligence analysis. Heuer said that "Gates' main impact ... came from practice--from his direct involvement in implementing his ideas. Using his authority as DDI, he reviewed critically almost all in-depth assessments and current intelligence articles prior to publication. With help from his deputy and two rotating assistants from the ranks of rising junior managers, Gates raised the standards for DDI review dramatically--in essence, from "looks good to me" to "show me your evidence. As the many drafts Gates rejected were sent back to managers who had approved them--accompanied by the DDI's comments about inconsistency, lack of clarity, substantive bias, and poorly supported judgments--the whole chain of review became much more rigorous. Analysts and their managers raised their standards to avoid the pain of DDI rejection. Both career advancement and ego were at stake."[54]

"There has to be a clear understanding among the clients of (intelligence) that, in the final analysis, any institutional evaluation is a "group-think" effort. Officers can sit around a table and hotly debate an issue but, at the end of the day, someone has to be assigned to draw up a draft that is designed to reflect the mainstream consensus. If there is consensus, is this "group think"? If there is no agreement whatsoever, what benefit can a political master derive from receiving a paper with five or six conflicting opinions on a given issue?[55]

---

[54] Richards J. Heuer Jr., "Psychology of Intelligence Analysis", Centre for the Study of Intelligence, CIA (1999). Introduction by Jack Davis, p. xvii - www.cia.gov/csi/books/19104
https://www.cia.gov/library/centre-for-the-study-of-intelligence/csi-publications/books-and-monographs/psychology-of-intelligence-analysis/index.html

[55] Efraim Halevy, "In defence of the intelligence services", The Economist print edition July 29, 2004.

CHAPTER 3

CULTURAL BIAS AND
THE SECURITY INTELLIGENCE GAP

When the Shiite community in Iraq rose against Saddam Hussein in 2003, the U.S. Administration viewed them as natural allies of Iran, which is a predominantly Shiite country. Even though the Iranians are Persians and the Iraqis are Arabs, i.e. two radically different ethnic groups, the misjudged assessment in Washington was that sectarian ties among the Shiites were stronger than cultural ties among the Arabs. This overlooked the fact that Iraqi Shiites had fought Iran for eight years during the Iran-Iraq War of 1980-1988. It also showed serious ignorance as far as the divide between Arabs and Persians. It is pretty unlikely that such an assessment would have been made by specialized intelligence analysts within the U.S. intelligence community. So, either they were not asked for their opinion, or their analysis was disregarded for political expediency.

Cultural hazards associated with intelligence

Even though the tasks performed by intelligence agencies across countries are similar, Philip Davies has observed that intelligence practices can vary by country."[56] Similarly, intelligence scholar Kevin O'Connell has observed that nations may have different intelligence "styles"- or cultures - resulting from "their societal, political, and historical context" which affects how they collect and analyze intelligence.[57]

To better evaluate, analyse and assess the value of the raw or finished information they have access to, it is extremely important for intelligence analysts to possess a close understanding of the people and nations involved, be they friends or foes. One way of ensuring that, is talking and listening to people who know what cannot be gleaned from books, through classified reporting or open sources. As elementary as this may sound, it is not always the case that certain intelligence agencies would encourage their analysts to talk to such people. It is still much better to have the analysts spend a couple of years in the country and region they will be covering, as well as getting at least a basic knowledge of the local language.

In Chapter 4 of his book, 'Psychology of Intelligence Analysis', Richards Heuer observes that "to see the options faced by foreign leaders as these leaders see them, one must understand their values and assumptions and even their misperceptions

---

[56] Philip H. J. Davies, "Intelligence Culture and Intelligence Failure in Britain and the United States," Cambridge Review of International Affairs, v.17, number 3, October 2004, pp.495-520, 496. Quoted in Stephen Marrin "At Arm's Length."

[57] Kevin M. O'Connell, "Thinking About Intelligence Comparatively", The Brown Journal of World Affairs, v. XI, number 1, Summer - Fall 2004, pp.189-199. Quoted in Stephen Marrin "At Arm's Length."

and misunderstandings. Without such insight, interpreting foreign leaders' decisions or forecasting future decisions is often nothing more than partially informed speculation. Too frequently, foreign behavior appears "irrational" or "not in their own best interest." Such conclusions often indicate analysts have projected American values and conceptual frameworks onto the foreign leaders and societies, rather than understanding the logic of the situation as it appears to them." [58]

Certain Western cultures are rather conservative, or hesitant, when it comes to interacting with other people in general, and establishing networks in particular, especially among people from other cultures[59]. This natural trait does them a disservice when it comes to intelligence. In certain countries this is exacerbated by the formal requirement some intelligence agencies impose on their officers and analysts prohibiting them from mixing or socializing with anybody outside their circle of work colleagues. They cannot talk to their neighbours for instance! We are not referring to under-cover agents of course, but just regular nine-to-five desk officers, who would normally have a plausible and well-rehearsed cover story as to their profession

This is unhealthy and detaches the analysts and intelligence officers from the reality surrounding them in their own country. On the other hand, the uneasiness regarding establishing specific networks for the purpose of collecting intelligence or recruiting quality human sources, leads them to over-rely on technical intercepts and the printed or electronic media, or rely on intelligence shared by other intelligence agencies to remedy this deficiency. That is aside from finding themselves having to glean their required cultural profile through paid human sources.

The other important mistake they make is not to seek a second opinion, particularly in the areas of intelligence, foreign affairs and national security, which should be a very wise thing to do. This should be the case, not only if the in-house subject-matter expertise is not available to provide expert counsel; but also for the benefit of such in-house expertise if it is available, to corroborate its own analysis and assessment. This approach will go a long way in helping avoid costly mistakes based on misunderstandings, pre-conceived notions, judgmental errors, or simply ignorance.

One should not underestimate the excitement generated by operational activities. Once excitement enters into play, caution and sobriety go out the window, and excesses, or shortcomings, may prove fatal. Very much like driving under the

---

[58] Richards J. Heuer Jr., "Psychology of intelligence analysis", Centre for the Study of Intelligence, CIA (1999) Introduction by Jack Davis, p. xxii - www.cia.gov/csi/books/19104.

[59] For further reading on intelligence networking see Barak, Oren and Sheffer, Gabriel, "Israel's Security Network" and its Impact, International Journal of Middle East Studies, v. 38 (2006) pp.235-261.

influence. Hence, as discussed earlier, calling on trusted, knowledgeable and balanced subject-matter specialists, or even better, former and retired qualified intelligence analysts and officers possessing these attributes, beside having the insider 'feel', should narrow the margin of error appreciably, especially prior to operational action.

The blind fighting the blind and the rest of humanity pays a hefty price

Intelligence, foreign affairs, national defence, diplomatic reporting, open info, signals and technical intercepts are certainly key sources of information. However, members of the security and intelligence community require training programs, or at least in-depth briefings, in intercultural particularities and sensitivities of both individuals and foreign societies. They also need to understand the thinking process and the communications patterns of these national groups to better gauge their targets. While this sounds like pretty elementary, it does not always happen. This gap is not just apparent in Western countries, but also in many other countries, where most of what they know about the West is based on assumptions, Hollywood movies, and half-truths, if not outright ignorance.

Such training programs would be most useful to intelligence collectors, analysts and operational intelligence officers, particularly those who are deployed overseas. While training programs of that kind may be offered occasionally to new intelligence officers, they are not offered to senior management who make the final decisions on intelligence matters. Having contributed to the training of hundreds of military, intelligence and law enforcement officers deployed overseas for many years, a now retired senior intelligence analyst specialised in the Middle East, its cultures, languages and religions in a G8 country, confided that he was always puzzled by the fact that among the hundreds of people he had given pre-deployment briefings to, almost all of them were young recruits, lower ranks personnel and non-commissioned officers. Only a very small number of commissioned officers attended these programs, but never any officer above the rank of Captain or Major. As if the senior ranks from Colonel up who draw the war plans and make the major decisions which will result in many of their own men getting killed, and not just enemy personnel, know everything about the enemy.

When it comes to knowing about "the other", the frightening part is that their political masters also know practically nothing about these foreign cultures either, and what they profess to know is usual pretty sketchy and mostly based on preconceived ideas, or even more dangerously, religious beliefs pertaining to mythologies such as Armageddon and the end of times. Believe it or not, these are concepts which the three major monotheistic religions preach, and which are considered by some politicians today as a factual template for their political platform.

Interestingly enough this is exactly the same situation among the "bad guys", who also judge Western culture based on preconceived ideas, movies and outlandish interpretations. Aside from those who lived in America, almost nobody in other countries knows of the amount of good, fairness, justice and openness that exist in the West in general, and in the US in particular, whether within society or within the system as such.

After retiring from the public service, the same analyst mentioned above had communicated with the Chief of Staff of the Prime Minister of his country's newly elected government, as well as with the chiefs of staff of various key ministers and offered to give their bosses short intercultural briefings above and beyond the usual security and foreign affairs briefings they receive prior to meeting with their foreign counterparts in that part of the world. The idea was to make their first contact with these foreign heads of state have better chances of success, and possibly also avoid stupid misunderstandings and embarrassment.

Some of the Chiefs of Staff did not respond at all, while some of those who responded encouragingly and saw the benefit of the proposal suggested that the retired analyst contact this or that person within the department concerned. The Chiefs of Staff of two key ministers responsible for national security replied and explained to the analyst how to apply for a job with the Public Service. They probably never read his original correspondence carefully as he had made it very clear to them that he had already retired from the Public Service two years earlier! None of them asked for more details as to what it is he was proposing. This situation is pretty unfortunate, especially that the Prime Minister, was known to be completely and intentionally ignorant about other parts of the world, and what he was committed to ideologically as an individual is centuries removed from the twenty-first century. Following some of the public declarations of his ministers showed clearly that they did not know much more than him either. These people were democratically elected by the majority of the population of their country. This is what the people wanted.

In general, Western countries know the people of a country through the types of individuals they frequent, some could be graduates of Ivy League universities, others could be wheelers and dealers. Taking the case of Iran under the Shah for example, many Western intelligence agencies as well as the diplomatic and political establishment could not conceive that the population of Iran included people who still lived intellectually in the eleventh century. The Iranians with whom the Westerners normally associated on the cocktails circuit lived in Tehran. They had no contact with the average people in the bazaar and the die-hard Shiite clergy and population in the vast country-side. When the revolution against the Shah exploded, all these Westerners were taken by surprise. So was the Shah and his entourage.

It will be unfair to only castigate the West for that. Today many Arab governments do not have real understanding of the vast majority of their own population and what goes on within the narrow alleys of society. They actually do not want to know. Then they are surprised when the kettle starts to boil and overflow. Two years after these lines were initially written, the kettle did indeed boil over in Algeria, Egypt, Jordan, Syria, Tunisia, Bahrain, Libya and Yemen; and it is not over yet. Riots forced some rulers like the president of Tunisia, Zein El-Abdine Ben Ali, and the Egyptian president Hosni Mubarak to abandon ship along with their families carrying with them billions of dollars of the "foreign aid" money, or better expressed "bribe money" they were showered with by their Western allies. Others like the "Leader of the Great Arab Jamahiriya", namely Libya, were killed ignominiously.

Intelligence means different things in different cultures

Wilhelm Dietl, a former agent with the German intelligence service, the Bundesnachrichtendienst (BND) in the Middle East, reflects what everybody knows in the region that "most of the Arab intelligence services are completely different from what people in the West are familiar with when they think about intelligence services."

The definition of intelligence among countries is not the same. In some countries, when people talk about intelligence, they think in terms of the intellectual and operational dimensions required to acquire and understand the raw information collected. In these countries intelligence is considered to be one of the means of protecting the country from foreign interference.

In a book titled "Schattenarmeen: Die Geheimdienste der islamischen Welt" (Shadow Armies: the Secret Services of the Islamic World) about the history of intelligence agencies in Islamic and Arab countries, Dietl points out that "Most of the work of the BND, for example, is to collect information of strategic, political or military value, and to understand, evaluate and analyze trends; not killing people and not torturing them. Arab agencies see their primary task as preserving the regime or the political leader and therefore, they are cruel and without limits. They are above the law; they are the law itself. They see themselves as a divine entity. They torture suspects relentlessly, so it is not surprising that many suspects are willing to confess to every crime. He adds that members of the Arab intelligence services are more worried about making mistakes that may cost them their jobs if not their lives, than they are about doing their jobs in a professional manner."[60]

Like in all dictatorial regimes that were not chosen by the people through transparent democratic elections, Arab countries, whether monarchies, republics,

---

[60] Quoted in Yossi Melman, "Arab intelligence agencies too busy protecting regimes to be effective", Haaretz, July 29, 2010.

or under Islamic clergy rule, maintain a whole panoply of intelligence services. Their main role is to spy on their populations; but especially on anybody who thinks or expresses himself or herself.

The intelligence services exist then to maintain the ruler and the immediate circles surrounding him in power. Another important function for them to fill is to spy on other Arab and Muslim countries and their embassies. When it comes to serious stuff like resorting to intelligence to protect the country and the nation from foreign threats such as those emanating from foreign countries including their main adversary Israel, they remain woefully unprepared.

In some Western countries intelligence agencies advertise vacancies in the media. Some particularly qualified people may also be approached directly by their nation's intelligence service for recruitment, while in the majority, interested individuals simply apply for a job with their country's intelligence service, and their application is considered, approved, or rejected.

Applying to work at an intelligence service in many Arab countries is something that does not exist. Intelligence services do not advertise vacancies, and prospective interested candidates cannot simply call or visit the intelligence service's office and ask for an application for employment. To start with, the prospective candidates will never be able to even reach the building where the intelligence service is located. The way it works is that those already working for the intelligence service or those who occupy a relatively high position in government, the armed forces or the police will intercede with counterparts, friends, relatives and colleagues among the intelligence service management on behalf of family members, friends and acquaintances. It is only then that the service may proceed with an interview with the individual to envisage his/her potential recruitment.

Qualified or not, the main factor that will ultimately tilt the balance towards recruiting the individual or not, is the degree of seniority, friendship, or family-relationship that exists between the intelligence manager and the person who intercedes with him. This means that the nepotistic relationship between the service and those who rotate around the clique in power will be the decisive argument. This eventually leads to an unhealthy partnership between the service and the political leadership, with the end result being an intelligence service that is totally manipulated by the ruler, and without which the ruler can fear his demise. So, to expect these services to really do intelligence for the sake of national security as opposed to displaying gang-like behaviour at the highest levels is pretty slim.

When we deal with these types of services and establish bilateral relationships and cooperation agreements with them, we are playing in the hands of organized crime-like agencies with chiefs holding impressive titles or military ranks at the highest level[61]. We do that when we do not want to dirty our hands, and subcontract the task to them, such as under the rendition program. It does not matter whether it is Syrian, Egyptian, or Saudi intelligence or other, as long as they do the job. This is not much different from the type of cooperation that existed between the Soviet Union and the Warsaw Pact countries which we decried during the Cold War era.

Avoiding Cultural Bias

> "We Judeo-Christian Westerners, when we want to be polite, we wear our shoes andtake off our hats. The Muslims wear their hats and take-off their shoes. Who is right?[62]
> **Comte Alexandre de Marenches**
> **Former Director General of the French S.D.S.C.E. (now DGSE)**

The epitome of successful intelligence and even successful warfare is to remove the element of hate from adversity. Nations and armies continue to be injected with ongoing hate propaganda vis-à-vis their enemy to the extent that the enemy is either totally discredited or represented as being much stronger than he is. The result is invariably either discounting the enemy or fearing him more than he is really worth.

By concentrating only on the negative characteristics of the enemy you could be in for a surprise. Prior to the 1904 Russo-Japanese War the Russians always stated that the Japanese could not fight because of physical limitations, but also didn't have the will to fight one of the great powers. The Japanese surprised everybody and easily defeated Russia. Some four decades later the United States and Great Britain said practically the same thing about Japan, to be served a devastating blow by the supposedly inferior Japanese at Pearl Harbor, the Philippines, Singapore, and Hong Kong.

In 1991 former DCI Stansfield Turner noted that "another reason for many of the analytic shortcomings is that (US) analytical agencies do not have an adequate grasp of the cultures of many countries with which we must deal."[63]

---

[61] Some time in the 1960s, Syrian Prime Minister Maarouf El-Dawalibi was received in Paris by French President General De Gaulle. The visit took place a few days following a state visit by then President of Iraq Marshal Abdel-Salam Aref. The Syrian Prime Minister asked General De Gaulle about his opinion of Marshal Aref. According to Dawalibi, who told the story to a person close to the author, the De Gaulle responded in one of his typical fashions, saying: "I met a policeman with the rank of Marshal!" ("J'ai rencontré un gendarme au grade de maréchal!").

[62] French original: "Nous dans l'Occident judéo-chrétien, quand nous voulons être polis, nous mettons nos souliers et enlevons notre chapeau. Les Musulmans mettent leur chapeau et enlèvent leurs souliers. Qui a raison?" Christine Ockrent et Comte Alexandre de Marenches, "Dans le secret des princes", Éditions Stock, Paris 1986 (Comte Alexandre de Marenches was Director General of the French Service de Documentation extérieure et de Contre espionnage (S.D.E.C.E) from 1970 to 1981 which preceded the current Direction générale de la Sécurité extérieure (D.G.S.E.). p.184.

[63] Stansfield Turner, "Intelligence for a New World Order," Reprinted by permission of Foreign Affairs, v.70, number 4, (Fall 1991): p.163. By the Council on Foreign Relations, Inc. - www.ForeignAffairs.com.

"A better acquaintance with the Arab Security Sector ... may lead to more informed decision-making processes, especially at critical policy junctures", says Oren Barak in an article about the 'Arab Security Sector'. A good example he gives "is the United States' decision to disband the Iraqi Army following the United States - led invasion of Iraq in 2003. "A better appreciation of the role of the Iraqi Army in the process of state formation could have resulted in a decision to reform this institution, which at the time, had about 350,000 troops. In addition, greater awareness of Iraq's complex political - military relationship could have led to the imposition of effective - and not merely formal - civilian control over the newly established Iraqi Security Forces.

"Finally, a deeper understanding of the relationship between the Iraqi Army and the pattern of intersectorial relations in the state could have suggested that replacing a military institution dominated by Sunni Arabs with one dominated by Kurds and Shiites would be liable to impinge not only on the legitimacy of the new security sector but also on that of the United States-sponsored "nation-building" project as a whole.[64]

We all see the world and make decisions using values and standards we have been taught since childhood. When assessing the capabilities or situation of those of a foreign land, we employ our own values and cultural biases in determining the situation. This hinders us from thinking the way the enemy, or even an ally, may think. It also affects the quality of the advice we give to policymakers regarding the reaction of foreign governments to our policy.

"In 1991 Turner suggested that analysts should be provided with "a better opportunity to attend academic institutions, participate in professional conferences, travel and live abroad, acquire language skills and thus become true experts in their areas."[65] The average analyst in many intelligence services has 2 to 5 years experience. Most of them have not been to the countries they are analyzing. They don't have the country's language skills, the historical knowledge, the in-country residence time, or the respect of their private-sector peers.

Prior to the 1973 Yom Kippur War, the Egyptian armed forces undertook a series of military exercises similar to those that led to the October 1973 attack; each time Israel mobilized in response, and nothing happened[66]. Just prior to the 1973 Yom Kippur War, Egyptian President Sadat, while hosting a meeting with Palestinian guerrillas, made the following statement: "Prepare yourselves, we are going to war." At the same time his Prime Minister Aziz Sedki presented a war budget to Parliament because, "Egypt is going to war." Both these statements were very

---

[64] Oren Barak and Assaf David, "The Arab Security Sector: A New Research Agenda for a Neglected Topic", Armed Forces and Society, (2010) v.36, number 5, pp.804-824.

[65] Stansfield Turner, p.164.

[66] For detailed analysis see Avi Shlaim, "Failures in National Intelligence Estimates: The Case of the Yom Kippur War", World Politics, v.27 (April 1976).

strong indicators as to the disposition of Egypt towards Israel. A few weeks later Egypt announced that it had to postpone one of these often publicized planned attacks on Israeli lines on the eastern bank of the Suez Canal because of "heavy fog" in the region.

All these statements were either largely ignored or misinterpreted by Israeli intelligence analysts. President Sadat spoke of war with Israel so often that little credibility was given to those statements. In his book "The Art of War", Sun Tzu said that "all warfare is based on deception", Sadat actually used this tactic to deceive his enemy. He eventually attacked the Israeli defences at a time of his choice and breached the Bar Lev Line along the Suez Canal successfully at least during the initial phases of the war.

In this context it is quite educating to see what the Israelis themselves said about this war as described by Efraim Halevy, who was head of the Israeli Intelligence Service from 1998 to 2002. Halevy said that: "It seems only logical that the more you know, the safer you are and the greater the chance that you will get things right. "Yet Israel's most costly failure was its mistaken estimate of Egyptian and Syrian intentions on the eve of the Yom Kippur war in 1973, when the two armies unexpectedly attacked Israel in a bid to regain the territories lost in the 1967 war. At the time, Israel had it all:

a) Superior intelligence coverage,
b) Excellent human resources with good access,
c) High-level and discreet dialogue with more than one Arab or Muslim leader, and
d) An intelligence-evaluation arm that had provided an early warning several months before the war.

"But despite all of the above, the Israelis got it all wrong according to Halevy. The abundance of information, he said, led the Israeli intelligence community to what he called "intelligence hubris": We trusted our superior analytical prowess rather than ominous indicators on the ground.[67] "Intelligence is not a natural science. It is an art or a craft, and as such it cannot be governed by the basic tenets of logic…Intelligence officers must be gifted with imagination and creativity, enabling them to peer behind the curtain of apparent reality."[68] Like the Russians, the Americans and the Brits before them, the Israelis underestimated Sadat, as they usually consider the Arabs to be some kind of a lower species.

---

[67] Prior to both the 1956 Suez War and the 1967 Six Day War, President Gamal Abdel-Nasser of Egypt, based on cultural bias, made the same judgmental error by contradicting the situation analysis on the ground of his own intelligence services. He simply discounted the political and military ability of the Israelis to launch a war. They did, and they won. For more information please consult Owen L. Sirrs' book "A History of the Egyptian Intelligence Service: A History of the Mukhabarat, 1910-2009", Routledge, New York (2010).

[68] Efraim Halevy, "In defence of the intelligence services", The Economist print edition 29 July, 2004. Since 2003 he has been head of the Centre for Strategic and Policy Studies at the Hebrew University of Jerusalem.

LEADERSHIP IN INTELLIGENCE

There are two types of people who work in intelligence. For some it is simply a job, a career like any career in the Public Service, for others it is a commitment, almost a call.

The way some governments and their intelligence services are set up places paper pushers, accountants, former clerks, former police constables and cronies at the top levels of the organization. They are given managerial positions because they are considered to be "untainted" by any particular specialty, and thus viewed as better capable of managing. In the meanwhile the professional specialists are relegated to lower levels in the hierarchy and prevented from rising above those levels. Because they are specialists, they are considered unqualified for managing according to the definition of those who are fast-tracked to the upper echelons. There are times where total incompetents, or cowboy types, are put in charge of sensitive and complicated areas such as the Middle East, or Asia about which they have no clue whatsoever.

To put it in different words, those who are the least qualified to run intelligence, especially intelligence analysis, band together in "old boy" networks to hide their ignorance and protect their positions, while those who are the professionals, long time experts and who do the actual work are excluded. These are big time costly mistakes.

This is actually a recipe for disaster, because such careerist bureaucrats, who often deceive the public about the value of their work, will soon clash with the operational intelligence professionals. Being inexperienced in intelligence, and often ignorant in international affairs, they become budget controllers, or terminology and spelling gurus, and waste time in petty futile arguments and obfuscation, thus turning swift operations and analysis into a nightmare. By the time they are replaced, they would have caused a lot of damage to the intelligence service. That is why nothing is more vital to an effective intelligence service than a strong, experienced and engaged director. In some countries the director of intelligence reports to a second class minister who is not among the highest on the government precedence list. President Herbert Walker Bush came to the presidency after having led the CIA. This gave him a first hand knowledge of how intelligence works. Robert M. Gates, a 27 year career intelligence professional with the CIA, and former Director of Central Intelligence, became Secretary of Defense under two presidents. In Israel, the director of Israeli intelligence reports directly to the Prime Minister, who is fed intelligence almost in real time.

In authoritarian regimes where intelligence is not subjected to the rule of law, oversight or accountability, rulers appoint individuals who will do what the ruler wants them to do, often for purposes that are unrelated to national security.

Across the board and as mentioned earlier, those working in intelligence are required to work with the same cooperative spirit as that of a sports team. If intelligence agencies keep the information they come across jealously guarded under the laws of secrecy and balk from sharing it with those who need it most both within government and private entreprise, then why do we need an intelligence service?

There has always been a tendency among intelligence agencies to build secret bureaucracies that are disconnected from the rest of government. Actually there are sometimes situations where intelligence services share their reports with foreign intelligence agencies, but not with other agencies of their own country! Not only that, while some services refuse to share information with other agencies of their own government, others refuse to receive information from other agencies of their own government! A former transportation intelligence chief proposed to share with the intelligence service of his country intelligence information that the service did not have access to. When he proposed that a Memorandum of Understanding be established to officialise the exchange, the intelligence service refused the whole idea.

"There is always a unique relationship between intelligence chiefs and their political masters. The political master has to rely on his intelligence chief for Threat Assessments, and for the cautious and professional conduct of the service. There must be an unusual degree of trust between them, and it has to be mutual. This cannot be achieved and preserved on a purely formal and official basis." [69] Suffices to say that both have to be knowledgeable about what they are doing and trust each other. Besides, their communication has to be directly between them without proxies in-between.

While intelligence services provide the bulk of intelligence, other sources of intelligence also play an important role, such as the police, airline and airport security officers, etc. Unfortunately, in real life many such organizations work separately, may get together occasionally, but for some reason love to keep secrets from each other. Reading all the literature that has been published so far points out most of the time to conflict and/or competition among their leaders.

This is especially the case in countries where the structural divisions within the security and intelligence community are built by the politicians purposely for fear of leaving these agencies with too much power. It is also believed that leaving the various security and intelligence agencies to compete among themselves will ensure better intelligence. This may sometimes be true, but it also duplicates efforts, creates clashes among them, and on the long run results in lack of preparedness facing the common threat. Just like the proverbial "too many cooks in the kitchen."

---

[69] Ibid., Efraim Halevy, "In defence of the intelligence services", The Economist print edition, 29 July, 2004.

Secrecy could be misused sometimes by certain bureaucrats to prevent their political foes from possessing all the information, hence have an advantage over them within high political spheres. Addressing the issue of "competition" and "competitive analysis" among and within intelligence and law enforcement agencies, Senator Richard Shelby considers "that each competing agency should have access to all the data possessed by any one of the agencies. From this perspective, then, at least some degree of informational centralization is essential. In fact, why a decentralized system composed of several partially informed agencies should necessarily be expected to perform better than a more centralized system composed of a smaller number of agencies whose analysts are more fully informed is not obvious."[70]

In their estimate, Bruce D. Berkowitz and Allen E. Goodman consider that "one of the signs that something was wrong with the traditional model was that intelligence officials would not rely on their standing organizations when a really important issue came along. Instead, they would establish ad hoc "task forces" and "intelligence centres." During the past decade, for example, the intelligence community has created new intelligence centres to cover critical issues such as proliferation, counterterrorism, narcotrafficking, and other special topics. The intelligence centres bring together the specific analysts and collectors needed to address a specific issue. The centres are also intended to connect intelligence consumers directly to intelligence producers. Indeed, establishing new organizations for high-priority assignments has become a reflex action."[71] The centres that Berkowitz and Goodman refer to are what is now known in the trade as "Fusion Centres, which we discuss in some detail in Chapter 9."

"Given these hierarchies, what particular features would be required for an alternative system - such as proposed by Treverton or Berkowitz and Goodman - to overcome the blind spots that seem to be generic to every hierarchical system? Most importantly, this alternative system would seem to require the creation of a master dataset of all intelligence information to which a very wide range of intelligence officials would have automatic access."

This means, as Berkowitz and Goodman note, "that compartmentation within the Intelligence Community would have to end.[72] "Compartmentation" requires the tight control of secret information, so that only those who are deemed to have a "need to know" are given access to particular kinds of data and collection methods. A significant problem with compartmented intelligence data is that only after the fact (such as following a surprise attack) can those who had actually had a "need to know" be identified. So, in the vision Berkowitz and Goodman

[70] Senator Richard Shelby's remarks in the Joint Inquiry Report are at: http://intelligence.senate.gov/107351.pdf Quoted in Thomas H. Hammond, "Intelligence Organizations and the Organization of Intelligence", International Journal of Intelligence and CounterIntelligence, v.23, number 4, pp.680-724, 2010.

[71] Bruce D. Berkowitz and Allen E. Goodman, "Best Truth", p.63. In Thomas H. Hammond, "Intelligence Organizations and the Organization of Intelligence"

[72] Ibid., p.156-157

presented of a decentralized intelligence community, the intelligence community's proclivity toward secrecy and compartmentation would have to be overcome: whatever the virtues of decentralization, it probably cannot work very well if intelligence data is tightly compartmented. Moreover, if abandoning secrecy and compartmentation within the Intelligence Community is essential, the implication is that the widespread access to intelligence information is also essential."[73]

"Indeed, any consistent pattern of intelligence community success in warning about surprise attacks may well be an indication that it routinely functions in a less hierarchical manner than implied by its formal structure and procedures. For example, specialized centres such as the Terrorist Threat Integration Centre (TTIC, created in 2003) and its successor, the National Counterterrorism Centre (NCTC, created in 2004), cut across established agency boundaries, and are thus likely to be significantly broadening intelligence community access to data held by a variety of separate intelligence agencies. In addition, other interagency committees, and even informal relationships within the community involving personal ties of various sorts, may also be flattening the intelligence community's hierarchies more than realized, and thereby reducing the blind spots to which formal hierarchies appear to be subject.[74] Presuming that these issues can be overcome, a single, complete, master dataset would seem to have two major benefits:

"One, a reduction in the number of blind spots because the structures of the Intelligence Community would no longer be quite so hierarchical; as a result, the data would now be processed in ways that might render visible some critical messages that were previously invisible.

"The second benefit involves one of the most important constraints on the intelligence community's analysts: the very limited amount of attention that can be allocated to each problem for which the analyst may be responsible. Unlimited access to the master dataset by a larger number of analysts might produce better results than a system built around a small number of highly specialized analysts, each of whom has only a restricted "need to know" access to various parts of the compartmented datasets. In effect, increasing the access to intelligence data can be seen as taking advantage of parallel processing in the intelligence community: a larger number of analysts could now be paying attention to the intelligence problems of current concern, and some of these additional analysts might even be just "free-lancers" from within the community who are pursuing their own hunches and conjectures on their own time and without any formal responsibility. Without wanting to denigrate specialists, "outsiders" in a field often have insights that the "insiders" may have missed."[75]

---

[73] Thomas H. Hammond, "Intelligence Organizations and the Organization of Intelligence", International Journal of Intelligence and CounterIntelligence, v.23, number 4, pp.680-724, 2010.

[74] Ibid., p.714

[75] Ibid., p.715

"In a section titled "Institutionalizing Imagination: The Case of Aircraft as Weapons," the 9/11 Commission Report remarked that "It is . . . crucial to find a way of routinizing, even bureaucratizing, the exercise of imagination."[76] Just prior to 9/11:

a) "an FBI agent in Phoenix had filed a report in July 2001 about potential terrorist interest in learning to fly airplanes,

b) "In late August 2001, another FBI agent in Minneapolis became involved in the detention and investigation of Zacarias Moussaoui[77].

c) "If these two agents had not had to rely on higher-level authorities to take action but instead could have queried, on their own initiative, a computerized master dataset in order to determine if their growing suspicions about al-Qaeda and airplanes were substantiated by other evidence in the intelligence community possession. Perhaps they would have discovered that they were both developing similar suspicions, which might in turn have helped attract the attention of the higher-level officials."[78] In fact, these higher - level authorities proved unresponsive, perhaps because they may not have even seen the communications from these agents.

"For example, the Phoenix and Minneapolis FBI agents, who did not normally specialize in counterterrorism but who had come across evidence potentially linking al-Qaeda to airlines and pilot training, would probably not have been preselected as having any "need to know" access to most kinds of counterintelligence-related data. In short, they probably would not have been given access to the centralized dataset. So, hierarchy and compartmentation, which have long been seen as essential to the preservation of secrets and their sources, also constitute fundamental barriers to the creation of an intelligence community that is not as subject to blind spots."[79]

The Security Intelligence Gap

As pointed out earlier, every country has - and will continue to have an ongoing intelligence gap. In some cases the gap is simply the result of good operational secrecy practices by the enemy, but it could also be caused by intelligence shortcomings. In other cases, the problem lies with either wrong analysis or

---

[76] See 9/11 Commission Report, p.344.

[77] Ibid., pp.273-276 for details

[78] The 9/11 Commission Report did state (p.272) that "If the [Phoenix] memo had been distributed in a timely fashion and its recommendations acted on promptly, we do not believe it would have uncovered the plot. It might well, however, have sensitized the FBI so that it might have taken the Moussaoui matter more seriously the next month."

[79] Hammond, p.716

assessment of the intelligence, or both. The other factor leading to such gaps is the one discussed above, i.e. the excessive compartmentalization that leads to withholding of information within the same government.

During a parliamentary testimony in a G8 country, the Parliamentary Committee on National Security was appalled at the way officials from the Department of Transport used the need for secrecy as a shield against questions put to them by the National Security Committee which were designed to determine whether the government was taking appropriate action to safeguard the traveling public.

This situation could certainly be witnessed in other countries, where the security of the public could occasionally be jeopardized as a result of the sometimes obsessive paranoia of secrecy. To ensure greater access to intelligence information, it is necessary to fight against the notion that sharing intelligence even with duly vetted members of parliament on the Committee could play into the hands of would-be terrorists. It is essential to be aware of the fact that unnecessary secrecy hides inefficiencies, provides cover-ups for poorly conducted intelligence operations, and generally fosters weak security.

Hiding information about security gaps at seaports and airports will not deter anyone seriously looking for those gaps, because anybody who works in and around a seaport or an airport long enough knows where the gaps could be.

To test its own system of security intelligence, especially by its emergency response services, it is incumbent on each government department, but also each stakeholder, to ask itself periodically: "Who is in charge if this or that emergency were declared?" That is instead of waiting for a real crisis to happen to find out that there are so many players who claim that they are the ones in charge. A situation as such is equivalent to having nobody in charge.

How to blind yourself and confuse the cards

When the Nazis invaded Poland in World War II; all the signs were there. How did the world miss it? Perhaps they just did not want to see or their intelligence was not taken seriously.

One has to caution from an intentionally misleading current among some analysts and special-interest groups such as the NEOCONs[80] who want us to believe the terrorists have no program except hate for the "Western way of life; and no political objective save to prevent the spread of democracy in Muslim lands; and a fanatical ambition to destroy freedom-loving Western societies."

---

[80] The Neo-Conservatives (NEOCONS), having successfully done their damage, they have conveniently disappeared from public view. While you could not avoid hearing them day in day out during the crisis they helped create, now they may pay you money to stay away from them!

In the case of the World Trade Centre terrorists, the answer that was forcefully fed by special pressure groups, but also the general public, and adopted by government and many in congress and popularized by much of the media is that "They did it because of who we are, or because "they don't think like us"; or "they hate us because they are without values or culture, uncivilized, anti-capitalist, and despise democracy and freedom. They are envious of our values, culture, civilization, capitalism, freedom, etc." "They" in this case is meant to encompass everybody who is Muslim or Arab.

Even though this is a widespread fallacy because the vast majority of both Muslims and Arabs are well disposed about America, its people and its culture. They may dislike some negative aspects in America, such as crime, violence, murder, and sexual promiscuity that are the common ingredients of movies and TV programs we feed them with, and which a large section of American public opinion also decries. But we do disregard the essential fact that the rage that the Arabs and Muslims demonstrate vis-à-vis the US is emanating as a result of what we do in their own backyards, and the type of horrible leaders and regimes over there we consider as our friends and allies. [81]

All and above, the overwhelming majority of Muslims are against the religious fundamentalists and extremists and would not welcome them as rulers. But they stay mum, and do not take action against them because of Western support to the corrupt leadership. The rather secular uprisings in Tunisia, Egypt and other Arab countries in January and February 2011 provide a loud cry against those types of regimes, but also against the certain dictatorship of the religious groups if they ever seized power. The tragic thing is that our leaders and many in other G8 countries have always known about this situation. They have actually known about that for several decades, but they chose to blind themselves and their own people, wrongly justifying their actions by the need to secure their supply of oil and gas.

Further self-blinding

Designating incompetent, corrupt, dictatorial, brutal, oppressive, and, at times, medieval regimes as friends and allies of Western democracies erodes the value of democracy and sets a bad reputation for the West in the world. It also undermines the illuminating ideals of Western democracy taught at Western colleges and universities founded in these countries, such as the American University in Cairo and the American University of Beirut.

A glaring example of voluntary self-blinding is none other than the former Bush administration's insistence on associating between the regime of Iraqi President Saddam Hussein in Iraq with Osama Binladen and Al-Qaeda in order to justify

---

[81] For an analysis by an "anonymous" former US intelligence analyst, see the book entitled "Imperial Hubris" by Michael Scheuer, Brassey's Inc. Publishers; Dulles, Virginia 2004. www.potomacbooksinc.com

removing Saddam Hussein from power and destroying Iraq. A ten year-old kid would have seen the absolute unlikelihood of such far-fetched association. The other glaring example was when CIA Director George Tenet and National Security Advisor John Negroponte seemed to have duped former US Secretary of State, General Colin Powell by getting him to declare, vial in hand, in front of the UN Security Council and media cameras that the regime of Saddam Hussein possessed nuclear capabilities.

This type of intelligence manipulation is of course inaccurate and not only pretty irresponsible, but also extremely dangerous, because it blinds us as to the underlying causes of terrorism, it radicalizes those who were not terrorists and pushes them to become terrorists. It leads to the destruction of countries and the killing of thousands of innocent people both at home and in the country under attack, all for the benefit of a few individuals, arms merchants and corporations, even though the overall discourse is masked with patriotic semantics and talk about good versus evil. It also ridicules and insults security and intelligence analysts. Under such conditions intelligence becomes a tool in the wrong hands and ultimately an instrument of national insecurity.

The combination of threat and technology has led to an increased collection of data on ordinary citizens. As David Omand, a former Security and Intelligence Coordinator in the British Cabinet Office, recently pointed out, the 'application of modern data mining and processing techniques does involve examination of the innocent as well as the suspect to identify patterns of interest for further investigation' (*The Guardian*, 25 February 2009).[82]

Intelligence is often used to justify rather than determine policy choices, says Professor Martin J. Smith.[83] As an illustration of how decision-making disregards intelligence is former National Intelligence Officer Paul Pillar's evaluation of the Bush Administration's decision to go to war in Iraq. Pillar said that "the Bush administration used intelligence not to inform decision-making, but to justify a decision already made. It went to war without requesting - and evidently without being influenced by - any strategic-level intelligence assessments on any aspect of Iraq."

Pillar went further than what intelligence officers normally reveal, by stating that "as the national intelligence officer for the Middle East, I was in charge of coordinating all of the intelligence community's assessments regarding Iraq; the first request I received from any administration policymaker for such assessment was not until a year into the war."[84]

---

[82] Martin J. Smith, Professor of Politics and Faculty Director of Research and Innovation (Social Sciences) at the University of Sheffield, "Intelligence and the Core Executive: Public Policy and Administration" (January 2010), number 25, (1), pp.11-28, p.23.

[83] Ibid., p.26

[84] Paul R. Pillar, "Intelligence Policy, and the War in Iraq." Foreign Affairs, March/April 2006, p.1. Reprinted by permission of Foreign Affairs. The Council on Foreign Relations, Inc. www.ForeignAffairs.com.

The question that begs itself ultimately is: Who is in charge of protecting a country from elected incompetent leaders, legislators and politicians who stubbornly refuse to be informed and become themselves sources of disinformation among their constituents. Waiting for another four years to vote them down is ultimately not in the national interest.

Democracy Challenged

One of the dangers of democracy in the twenty first century is that it can also bring to power administrations that are blinded by political, ideological and corporate self-delusioning, or simply self-interest. These administrations are often the instruments through which special interest groups fulfill the purposes of their agendas through the use, or rather misuse, of the democratic system. Some of these groups are after power, others after money, while curiously enough there are those for example who, like religious fundamentalists elsewhere, think in Biblical terms and use the powers they acquired through the ballot box and their positions as ministers or prime ministers to help speed the second coming of the Messiah! This is not what Western culture or the concept of democracy are all about.

The whole concept of democracy needs to be revised, updated and purified from much of the undemocratic clutter that has stuck to it since it blossomed in ancient Greece. As nations, we are at a turning point in our history, and this calls for a radical overhaul of the concept, the systems and the institutions of democracy in order to save it from the dictatorship of "democratic institutions". This calls first for action at home before we lecture others about its virtues; because all the others see is mostly the negative effect of its shortcomings and mis-application rather than its many genuine virtues and benefits. The main players in democracy today, namely the "elected representatives of the people" are quite often elected because of their glib talk and charisma or their degree of receptivity to manipulation rather than for their knowledge or experience.

Democracy as we define it today is not necessarily the most suitable system for nations during a certain period of their development. Such nations could be ready for genuine democracy after the concept and institution of democracies have taken root following years of training and education, and have become part of the local culture. In the case of many countries, such as Afghanistan for example, what they need today is honest, effective leadership and good governance within the traditional system they recognize, rather than through the illusory trappings of what mimics democracy.

Today, when the going gets tough and things fail to work, democratic countries turn to technocrats and professionals to redress things and run the show. To wit, when Italy under Prime Minister Silvio Berlusconi was falling into bankruptcy during the fall of 2011, the nation had to call in the economist Mario Monti to rescue the ship and take the helm; because, as a technocrat, he knows how things could fail and how to redress them. How many businesses, even mom and pop corner stores would hire a manager with the qualifications of an elected politician? They never do, because they know that all these politicians can do is parrot speeches that do not reflect their own convictions. Instead they look for somebody with experience, credibility and certainly one they can trust. Yet, despite our awareness of these elementary facts, we keep electing those politicians to run the affairs of state. Isn't it time that we learned something?

CHAPTER 4

THE THREAT OF TERRORISM

Violent action, blind or targeted, also fits under the definition of terrorism. It has been with us probably since we started existing as distinct societies. This is the same as the debate over the adage that "one's terrorist is somebody else's freedom fighter." The debate has not been settled, and may never be settled. Just ask the Irish, the Basque separatists, the Corsicans, the Palestinians, the Kurds, etc., then ask their opponents.

"In current counterterrorism rhetoric, terrorism is portrayed as a danger of such massive proportions that it threatens not only lives but "our way of life" and "civilization," a threat so great that…the norms of prosecution and punishment no longer apply" [85], as the (former) British Home Secretary David Blunkett stated after the Madrid train bombings in 2004.

"There are two interrelated assumptions in the claim that basic civil and human rights must be sacrificed in order to fight the threat of terrorism. First, there is the assumption that terrorism poses a unique and far graver threat than other threats, and second, there is the assumption that undermining civil liberties and legal protections is the most effective way to combat terrorism."[86]

"According to current counterterrorism rhetoric, non-state terrorism threatens many things: security, lives, values, freedom, democracy, and the existence of civilization itself, and poses a greater threat than the threats posed by war, invasion, accidents, natural disasters, and criminal activity. Several (Australian) government ministers have claimed that the magnitude of the terrorist threat is so great that it imposes a positive moral duty on governments to protect the individual's right to security even at the expense of many basic civil liberties.[87] i.e. if the "right to security" is so important that in times of threat it trumps other rights, then states clearly have a similar moral duty to fight the threat of accidents, crime, (drug trafficking) and other events even when doing so requires curtailing civil liberties."[88]

Countries that produce terrorists are mostly the ones responsible for this phenomenon. It is the doings of the leaders in these countries and their

---

[85] Jessica Wolfendale, "Terrorism, Security, and the Threat of Counterterrorism" - Studies in Conflict & Terrorism, 30:1, 75-92 (January 2007) - ARC Special Research Centre for Applied Philosophy and Public Ethics, Department of Philosophy University of Melbourne, Victoria, Australia. These phrases were used by George W. Bush and General Colin Powell, respectively, in public statements about the war on terrorism. (Quoted in Richard Jackson, "Writing the War on Terror: Language, Politics and Counter-terrorism", Manchester University Press, 2005, p.99 and p.111).

[86] Ibid., p.75

[87] Ibid., p.76

[88] Ibid., p.79

governments who are partially to blame; first, because it is their abysmal human rights record and their total disregard for the welfare of the population, that gives birth to the phenomenon. But then partially thanks to our support for these 'leaders'. We pay them tax-payers' money as bribes that are politely described as "financial aid." We also buy their services under the "terrorists rendering program" to interrogate and torture suspected terrorists because we do not want to be seen doing the dirty work.[89] Just think of deposed Tunisian President Zein El-Abdine Ben Ali, deposed Egyptian President Hosni Mubarak, Libyan Colonel Muammar Qaddafi, Syrian President Bashar Assad, and dozens like them whose turn to be deposed is coming.

If the same amount of money spent on combating terrorism were spent on combating organized crime and disease, and addressing the basic inequities that trigger terrorism, humanity could have possibly gotten rid of these scourges a long time ago; or at least minimized the threat they represent.

PRIORITIZING COUNTER-TERRORISM & COUNTER-PIRACY

Today the threat from terrorism remains as the major security threat to the transportation industry, particularly civil aviation, merchant marine, and mass transit. We should not discount though the threat originating from distraught or deranged persons, which calls for protective and preventive measures that are outside the domain of intelligence. In the case of the merchant marine, mounting modern-day piracy on the high-seas is a serious threat that has been going on for a long time without it being properly and expediently checked. Admittedly, addressing piracy requires a different approach than counter-terrorism due to the different environment in which it operates and the conditions surrounding its genesis.

"Just as there are many different threats to individuals and to nations, so there are many different means for countering these threats. Responding to the threat of disease will require different methods than responding to the threat of a hurricane, and some threats might require more or less state involvement in preventative measures. Countering disease might require a combination of education about disease transmission as well as effective medical monitoring and vaccine programs. Countering a hurricane will require efficient and prompt emergency services, housing that can withstand high wind-speeds and effective clean-up operations."[90]

---

[89] See Alain Chouet, "Au cœur des services spéciaux - La menace islamiste: fausses pistes et vrais dangers". (Inside the Intelligence Service Special Branch - Islamic threat; wrong leads and real dangers). Éditions La Découverte, Paris (2011). Just days before going to print, and by pure coincidence, the author came across the following excellent book by Alain Chouet, former Chief of the Intelligence Security Directorate with the French DGSE, whom the author had met several years earlier in Paris before either of them had retired. The issues about terrorism as well as many other points raised in this book are also echoed in Chouet's book in almost the same perspective. Chouet's book should be translated from French into other languages.

[90] Ibid., p.77

When thinking about how to respond to the threat of terrorism, one must assess the nature of the threat, its origins, its catalysts, its extent, what values it threatens, and the best means of averting or minimizing it, while anticipating possible future modus operandi on part of the terrorists. We may also want to assess whether we are part of the solution or rather the problem. This is called "detecting and identifying the trend.

In the 1960s and 1970s, we used to face a pattern of terrorism that is planned, commanded and controlled by some type of central organization with an ideological framework, a revolutionary committee, or even a foreign power.

Today, terrorism has gone the way the market economy has gone, namely through subsidiaries, franchises, part-time operatives, and a world-wide web on the net. Like the global economy, it has been decentralized, privatized, franchised and outsourced. Now we notice the change from centralised command-and-control to activation, or even self-activation of opportunity groups anywhere they can be found, without forgetting individuals who act on their own volition. This has become in some cases the critical element that defines where the next terrorist act could take place.

The role of the leadership is not anymore overall command-and-control. It is essentially ideological, or say inspirational. Otherwise, the operating cells are self-financing and operationally autonomous. Now of course we are confronted with the threat posed by a new type of moonlighting terrorists, which is certainly more challenging and calls for new, long-term approaches to combat it, or still better, prevent it.

The targets being hit today are almost indiscriminately global. They include civilians and state symbols anywhere, including the terrorists' own people and co-religionists. The elimination of Osama Binladen[91] will probably not put an end to terrorism. His death may have removed a powerful symbol, though it will not put an end to terrorism or to acts of revenge. A new approach is needed both to address terrorist acts from an intelligence and military perspective, but also by concentrating on the root causes of terrorism as discussed above.

Defining the threat environment

To understand the critical path to terrorism and how to pre-empt acts of terrorism while they are still in the planning phases, calls for an understanding of, and differentiation between the criminally inspired vs. the politically motivated threats. It is true that the end result of any terrorist act is the same, namely

---

[91] Binladen's name and surname have been transliterated from Arabic into English using a variety of spellings. The spelling we have used in this book reflects the way it is pronounced in Arabic.

destruction, mayhem and loss of life, yet the ultimate purpose of each is different. Some terrorist acts are home-grown, others imported or exported, and of course there are those that are criminally inspired.

Terrorist acts are also meant to score political points, achieve ideological goals, reach political and strategic objectives, or conduct a national liberation struggle; while of course criminal acts are meant to acquire personal or group material wealth. Throughout history, the quest by the major powers of the day to control natural resources and the maritime routes straddling small countries have almost always resulted in upheavals and revolutions in self-defence. To those powers, such actions count as terrorism, and they do not blink an eye as to the fact that they are the aggressors and that such a reaction had to be anticipated. All major and regional powers in history old and new have done that.

Therefore, proper understanding of the root causes that lead individuals and groups to undertake acts of violence helps a lot in preparing to prevent and pre-empt them before reaching the stage of having to fight them militarily. That is why it is of utmost importance to properly label the type of terrorism that is under investigation.

Investigating terrorism

While taking cue from the symptoms, law enforcement as well as intelligence officers must also address the roots of the problems at the same time they are investigating them. Is it difficult? Of course it is. Does it take a long time? Of course it does. Does it call for deep understanding of the complexity of issues at hand? There is no doubt about that. Do those involved understand that? You bet that many do not.

Investigating terrorism is similar to a criminal investigation, except that it is a crime in a political setting. It looks for the same indices, namely a motive, a perpetrator, and in the final analysis a beneficiary, i.e. "who stands to benefit from the crime?"

Today, acts involving the use of what is described as terrorist methods are uniformly labelled as 'acts of terrorism', and dealt with in the same manner irrespective of the motive, the victim, the perpetrator and the real ultimate beneficiary. This erroneous approach does a huge disservice to the investigation, but more so to how the incident will be handled and how similar future actions could be prevented.

This type of investigation should be conducted exactly like a medical diagnosis that calls for assessing the urgency of the matter, ascertaining the symptoms, understanding the causes and reviewing the medical history of the patient before prescribing the required treatment. This calls for diagnosing the ailment accurately, labelling it properly and dispensing the corresponding medication. Should all ailments be assigned the same label and given the same type of treatment, chances are that no patient will ever heal. Therefore, like diagnosing a patient's condition and determining the cure, it is essential that the nature of the adversaries and their objectives be properly labelled in order to know how to handle them or combat them efficiently and successfully.[92]

When we understand the 'why?' behind acts of terrorism, we can understand the reasons, the modus operandi, and how to defeat the action through prevention rather than only through confrontation. It is constantly reported for instance that "Israel faces constant threats from terrorism", though nobody cares to indicate why. The reader is left with the impression that it must be the result of some criminal genetic trait innate to the Arabs and the Palestinians against Jews.

There is a tendency to seek the easy way out when analyzing intelligence by lumping everything and anything under the generic "Islamic Terrorism" label for example. This is not just unfair, but it also camouflages the real bad guys, and wastes a lot of time and resources sometimes chasing the wrong people. Mind you, purposeful disinformation by all sides also plays a big role.

If you have a dripping faucet that is bothering you because of the sound the dripping water makes besides the loss of this vital resource, kicking the faucet does not stop the leak. You know what happens when kicking continues and intensifies. The faucet will break and more water will be gushing out of the pipes creating a flood. But knowing where the mains is hidden, and shutting it before the faucet is changed will guarantee that the problem will be solved. That is why problem-solving in the case of terrorism calls for going back to the 'whys?'

Understanding the nature of the adversaries

The causes of violence and terrorism are not all the same. Neither their objectives. When looking at what is happening in the Middle East for instance, many investigators and intelligence analysts even in some major countries have acquired their expertise almost entirely as desk analysts. Many of them have not resided or worked, or even visited their target countries, not to speak of knowing their languages.

Being constantly targeted by an off-the-shelf, ready-to-use analysis emanating from the "think tank" industry who normally lack access to intelligence, and who in many cases have their own agendas, it is tempting for the intelligence analysts and their political masters to adopt the positions these think-tanks provide, or which their bosses encourage them to adopt. So they tend to generalize in their

---

[92] For further information on this subject, please consult Stephen Marrin's and Jonathan Clemente's article entitled "Modeling an Intelligence Analysis Profession on Medicine", in the International Journal of Intelligence and CounterIntelligence, v.19, pp.642-665, 2006.

analysis and eventually their assessment by attributing the problem to Islam, to Muslims, to blind enmity towards the Jews or towards the West in general. That is they put everybody in the same basket. We should not also ignore the fact that sometimes the analysis or rather the assessment produced by the intelligence agencies is ignored or corrupted by design for political or strategic reasons at various later stages. Curiously enough, that same biased attitude is also demonstrated by the security and intelligence services of some Muslim countries.

In his Memoirs, former Pakistani President Pervez Musharraf commented that "the West rejects militant struggles for freedom too broadly. Too often (it) equates all militancy with terrorism"[93]

"Most counterterrorism legislation focuses on suspects' actual or likely intentions (rather than their acts) and at the same time lessens the burden of proof required to arrest and detain people. This combination means that the likelihood that innocent people will be arrested, detained, and tortured is very high."[94]

We all know that the root problems in the Middle East are not necessarily a question of religion, or a clash among religions, even if they are blindly dressed in the cloak of religion, and routinely presented as God's commands. The fact that nations behave in conflicting ways throughout their history is also greatly influenced by several other important contributing factors.

In a book review about Faisal Devji's book 'The Terrorist in Search of Humanity: Militant Islam and Global Politics', Julian Bourg, points out that "Devji emphasizes two different threads. On one hand, he challenges the tendency to centre the story of radical Islam on the Middle East by refocusing the analysis on the Indian subcontinent. This revision is valuable. Narratives of political Islam do tend to locate its historical emergence in the context of decolonization and the failure of secular pan-Arabism in the Middle East. An engaging chapter is dedicated to the travels of the "floating category" of the "Arab," appropriated, like the idea of the caliphate, by Indian authors since the nineteenth century...Reimagining Islamism as having roots elsewhere than the Middle East is helpful because it underscores its deep global origins and sheds light on the crisis zone between Kabul and Mumbai. Islam has always been global and decentred, more networked than hierarchical in ways that make it especially well suited to the landscapes of globalization.[95]

---

[93] Pervez Musharraf - "In the Line of Fire: A Memoir." Free Press, New York (2006), p.334.

[94] Jessica Wolfendale, "Terrorism, Security, and the Threat of Counterterrorism", Studies in Conflict & Terrorism, v.30, number 1, 75-92 (January 2007) p.85 - ARC Special Research Centre for Applied Philosophy and Public Ethics, Department of Philosophy University of Melbourne, Victoria, Australia.

[95] Faisal Devji, "The Terrorist in Search of Humanity: Militant Islam and Global Politics", Columbia University Press, 2009, v.10, p.223. Quoted in Julian Bourg, "On Terrorism as Human Sacrifice", Humanity: An International Journal of Human Rights, Humanitarianism, and Development, v.1, number 1, fall 2010, pp.137-154. By permission from the University of Pennsylvania Press.

As described by the Lebanese writer Elias Khoury in one of his books, *"modern civilization is built around 'non-memory." The flood of imagery shown by the visual media reminds us of a gigantic eraser: one image erases its predecessor, thus giving the impression that the world lives in an eternal present, and that there is no past!"*

That is why a good section of Western media in general talk about terrorism as if it were born only yesterday, or that it spawned all-of-a-sudden with no motive other than "they hate us because who we are and because of our way of life." In most cases this is the result of ignorance on part of the media, or, worse as a result of pre-meditated disinformation by political action groups with political designs which are also dressed in the cloak of religion to give them a divine imprimatur.

This is similar to how extremists from the East for example see the West: A mass of Christians allied with Jews and bent on subjugating Muslims to take away their resources, in this case oil. Both visions are not totally accurate. For an in-depth understanding of the world according to extremists, please see Appendix 2.

WHAT ARE THE CHALLENGES FACING US?

The first major challenge and rather impossible task is that of removing conjectural and uncorroborated matters of religious mythology from proven historical facts as a first step towards regaining control over established factual history. This in itself is actually more difficult than fighting terrorism. There are several other major points of contention that need to be addressed on a priority basis in order to stop, or at least freeze, the cancerous spread of terrorism:

1 - Disentangling good governance from the hold of blind religion

One of the greatest challenges people still face in most cultures and religions is how to draw a line between what's to God and what's to Caesar. A good part of Western societies have succeeded in drawing the line. However, for several cultures touching that line is simply inconceivable. People of all deep religious persuasions continue to live by the millennial beliefs they grew up with, and there are no signs that this is going to change soon. For them it is simply black or white.

When you mix beliefs that are rather based on man-made mythologies and folk tales with strategic, political and economic interests, then you add a touch of messianic zeal to the mix, this creates a situation that is often impossible to deal with. At least because each group has deeply convinced itself that God is on his side; and acting otherwise would be an insult to the Almighty and a sure road map to eternal damnation in Hell. This type of fundamentalism among competing religious groups, even in some of the G8 countries, leads some of the more extreme among them to justify the eradication of one people to accommodate another because their brand of religious belief urges them to do so in the name of God. Once these individuals seize power, albeit through the ballot box; they commit their countries' national resources and military power towards achieving that objective. By the end of the day the world becomes an unliveable place for the majority of humans.

2 – Western support to corrupt unrepresentative oppressive regimes

In order to uproot as many of the causes of terrorism and violent action as possible, there is a set of perennial existential problems plaguing countries and societies where extremist and terrorist tendencies originate that must be addressed. This should allow us to understand the **"why."** Knowing the "why", will allow us to know **"how"** to combat the resulting threat, and prevent it from migrating to other countries that are still not reading the proverbial "writing on the wall."

Despite all the glitter and appearances, scratch the veneer in all Arab and Muslim countries, and you will find the following major problems which are obviously deeply rooted. Some of which are very difficult to solve, but this is not an excuse for not trying:

➢ Rampant illiteracy
➢ Ineffective and antiquated educational systems
➢ Unsupervised and vindictive religious education
➢ Public health shortcomings
➢ Absence of an old age safety net
➢ High unemployment and lack of equal opportunities
➢ Vastly imbalanced national and regional wealth distribution
➢ Institutional and financial mismanagement
➢ Taxation without political representation
➢ Environmental pollution
➢ Issues of inclusion and exclusion within society
➢ Lack of participative culture
➢ Absence of a system of accountability and political checks & balances
➢ Solid belief among the population that sovereignty belongs to God, while the ruler acts as if he were the agent of God
➢ Leaders who rule but do not govern while diverting the nation's wealth to personal bank accounts in foreign banks
➢ Ongoing regional & international political, economic and strategic interventions by foreign powers for their own selfish reasons.
➢ The brain drain among highly qualified and well trained specialists to countries of immigration, thus depriving their countries from their badly needed skills.

Let us not forget also that it takes two to tango, and the onus to change is not only on the West, but equally on the Arabs and the Muslims themselves as discussed hereunder. Should that not happen, intelligence services in the world will have a very difficult time keeping control of the situation, and all governments will have an even more difficult time containing a situation that is bound to deteriorate. Until these challenges are met, the extremists and those who drift into terrorism will rule and endanger both their respective countries and the world at large.

In an article about the situation in Yemen following clashes between the government and insurgents in the north and the south (before the 2011 national uprising against Yemeni president Ali Abdallah Saleh), Rami G. Khouri, Editor at Large of the Lebanese daily "The Daily Star", pointed out that "terrorism traumatizes and harms four primary actors. The first is the terrorist himself. Most terrorists are reasonably smart and educated young men who have become crazy due to the circumstances of their lives and their societies' political, economic and social conditions, including interactions with foreign armies.

"The second is the society that breeds terrorists, including many in the Middle East. The disequilibria, disparities and distortions that plague those societies ultimately generate a handful of crazed men who become terrorists. Terrorists do not emerge from a vacuum. They emerge from terrorized societies.

"The third target of terrorism comprises those innocent civilians who are attacked by terrorists, whether in Arab hotels, Pakistani markets, New York City skyscrapers, or London buses. The attacked societies are terrorized and traumatized by the criminality that assaults them, and they usually have no idea why they were attacked or what to do in response. They are truly the innocent victims who pay the highest price.

"The fourth madness that often haunts the world of terrorism is the response of governments whose countries or citizens have been subjected to terror attacks. Terrorized, then crazed with anger and driven to seek revenge, governments in turn unleash their own immense military and police power to fight the terrorists and bring them to justice. This approach only rarely succeeds, and more often intensifies the first two problems mentioned above: local traditional societies around the developing world that are at the receiving end of Western powers' might eventually become crazed, distorted, ravaged lands full of tyranny, corruption, instability, abuse of power, and violence, and those traumatized societies in turn eventually breed more of their own criminal terrorists who attack at home and abroad. If we do not address these four dimensions of terrorism and its traumas, we will never resolve the problem."[96]

---

[96] Rami G. Khouri is Editor-at-large of The Daily Star newspaper published in Beirut, and Director of the Issam Fares Institute for Public Policy and International Affairs at the American University of Beirut, in Beirut, Lebanon. His article appeared on January 6, 2010 under the title "Wisdom in Yemen". Used by permission of Agence Global.

Finally, there is always the perennial and unhelpful blind support given to extremist or fundamentalist governments in Israel against the Palestinians. But also the failure of the Palestinian leadership to establish the legitimacy of the Palestinian cause through good governance and national solidarity. Without forgetting of course that the would-have-been natural allies of the Palestinians, namely the neighbouring Arab nations, are themselves in need of urgent rescue from their own leaders.

With so many crucial problems left unresolved, the recipe for an ever increasing radicalisation of the people of the region is a certainty. As we live in an ever interdependent world, we will all suffer the consequences. Nobody can claim ignorance of these facts. The world has been forewarned so many times. Is anybody listening?

3 - Home-grown terrorism: How to stop it

We are now faced with a daunting complication, namely the case of individuals who have been living in Western countries for many years, or were born there, and who carry on or initiate terrorist operations, or at least get themselves involved in providing support to extremist causes. In these cases there is as much work for the psychologists and students of human behaviour to do as there is for police investigators and intelligence analysts.

Some are so-called 'home-grown' jihadists born and raised in the UK, France, the U.S. or Spain for example. But others are foreign-born. Many are 'self-generated' jihadists who were never actively recruited by a terrorist organization in a traditional sense, but nevertheless contributed individually to the cause. Some have more direct links to established terrorist organisations, including Al-Qaeda, while others are manipulated by foreign governments.

A few of them were trained in a foreign country, but many were not. Some wanted to carry out mass-casualty attacks; others seemed more focused on supporting foreign jihads. The ones less directly involved in operational activity admired those who are, and generally immersed themselves in jihadist propaganda using the internet. Fraud, including identity theft, seems to have provided some jihadists with the easiest way of financing their activities. Some are university graduates, others dropped out of school at an early age. Some were associated with a street gang, smoked cannabis and drank alcohol. They were arrested for theft, indecent assault and/or robbery. They became further radicalised in prison, and soon became followers of one or the other extremist preachers they may have met while in prison, or following their release

Who are these home-grown youth and why do they do it?

According to the 2009 EUROPOL EU Terrorism Situation and Trend Report, contrary to public and media perceptions in Europe for example, of the 249 successful, failed or foiled terrorist attacks carried out in Europe in 2009, only one was characterized as 'Islamist'. The rest were all attributed to separatists, left-wing, right-wing, single-issue, or not specified types of terrorist actions, as detailed in the following table. Getting back to the roots of the problems that cause these young people to follow such radical ideologies and abdicate their moral responsibilities may occasionally take care of the problems.

Unfortunately though this is not as simple and easy as it sounds. To wit, the senseless brutal bombing in Oslo in 2011, and killing in cold blood of close to a hundred totally innocent young men and women vacationing on an island in harmless Norway. This massacre defies any sense of moral responsibility, besides raising the spectre of lopsided thinking and justification by an otherwise normal person for all appearances. Anders Behring Breivik killed these people and destroyed part of downtown Oslo while totally and irrevocably convinced that he was doing the right thing in defence of his faith and his country.

How to fight this type of home-grown terrorism is indeed a challenge, but there are sufficient cases of similar nature to enable authorities to study the phenomenon much more closely. This and other cases, which can be partially classified as mental cases, even though they are politically or religiously motivated, are addressed later in the book under the heading: The Potential threat that is never considered by intelligence agencies.

Member State	Islamist	Separatist	Left-wing	Right-wing	Single-issue	Not specified	TOTAL 2009
Austria					1	5	6
France		89			1	5	95
Greece			15				15
Hungary				4			4
Italy	1		2				3
Spain		148	23				171
TOTAL	1	237	40	4	2	10	294

Terrorist attacks in Europe in 2009[97]

Young people don't wake up one morning and say to themselves: "I think I am going to be a terrorist when I grow up." Something happens along the way, and the young man or woman finds himself or herself cornered into that situation. A lot of these young people are second generation youths who feel alienated from

---

[97] Source: EUROPOL TE-SAT 2010, The Hague, The Netherlands, p.12

their adoptive country and are therefore easily attracted by fundamentalist groups who look for young new recruits, just like street gangs who look for members. So who are the candidates for terrorism and why:

1. Youth in their late teens or early to mid-twenties whose assessment of the consequences of their rash teen's actions are not properly developed
2. Youth with perceptions of being disenfranchised
3. Youth alienated from old-fashioned authoritarian parents
4. Individuals detached from either or both their country of origin and their adoptive country
5. Individuals who grew up without proper guidance from parents and teachers
6. Individuals who led a youth of debauchery or crime, who suddenly want to redeem themselves
7. Anger vis-à-vis events surrounding the community
8. Non-radicals who decide to support a particular terrorist action for a sense of self valuation
9. Radical individuals on the fringe who are mentally fixated.

Most minority groups settling in countries of immigration after WWII consisted of individuals who basically became blue collar workers, or at best shop-keepers. As they became full fledged citizens of these countries and children were born to them, the children who identified to various extents with their country of adoption, became culturally in tune with its culture, though without losing their parents' culture completely. Professionally, they either continued in the footsteps of their immigrant parents, namely as members of the less fortunate classes, or succeeded through education in breaking from the mould and became skilled professionals just like their classmates and playmates within their adoptive country. But they still felt unequal to them.

In the 1960s it was leftist ideologies that attracted not only these young people, but most youth anywhere in the world, partially because it was the cool thing to do in those years. But also because it gave those young educated or semi-educated men and women a means to be accepted as members of the overall leftist fraternity. Leftist groups seemed to bring together native youth and minority groups together under the banner of socialist or communist ideals. This has worked particularly well in the case of Israeli and Palestinian leftists for example.

This succeeded up to a point, but then the leftist craze ceased to be cool and practically disintegrated by the end of the seventies, and almost disappeared with the melt-down of the Soviet Union. By then many children and grand-children of the former immigrants were integrated to a much better degree in society, and many of them rose to prominent positions, or became successful businessmen. Their religion or skin colour often became rather invisible.

Yet, some individuals and/or their families, and not necessarily only among poor or uneducated individuals, were never able to cross the socio-cultural divide and remained second class citizens at least in their own eyes. Though sometimes condescending attitudes towards them and occasionally subtle, if not outright visible discrimination, are pretty obvious to disregard. By then religion had become the rallying point the same way leftist ideologies and parties were earlier. Those individuals became a soft target either for recruitment by religious groups or simply volunteered to join in. Religion provided them with the social, political and ideological environment they could thrive in more than the overall atmosphere of the country they lived in. In their own eyes they had "arrived."

It would have been quite educating if the families, friends and former colleagues of the shoe bomber, the underwear bomber, the terrorists who have attacked transit systems in Spain and the UK, but particularly the 9/11 perpetrators, were visited by psychiatrists, psychologists or social workers and not just by police, intelligence and other instruments of law enforcement and repression.

One cannot ignore the fact that at least three or four of the 9/11 perpetrators did not fit the generic profile of a terrorist. As licensed pilots, albeit without much experience in some cases, they still were trained individuals who have lived what one may describe as a normal life in Western or westernized societies. The reports written by these specialists about how the perpetrators reached that stage could have provided invaluable lessons learned; especially for the benefit of the intelligence community. The amount of background information about these individuals and their socio-educational evolution would have opened the eyes and enriched those who design and supervise educational systems around the world.

Stopping Them

This is easier said than done, chiefly because of the diversity of motives that push some individuals to commit suicide attacks, and not others. That is beside the real impetus and objective that motivates their leaders, other than the declared bombastic rhetoric. One should not also minimize the role played by outside forces, such as intelligence agencies of certain countries in the region, as well as from outside the region which control some of those extremist groups, sometimes unbeknownst to them, and some other times knowingly.

"There exists a need to push for … anti-hate laws to be enacted within the governments of the Middle East. As suggested by Israel W. Charney: "Holy leaders... cannot be allowed to preach murder, sedition, terrorism or violent revolution."[98] To some this will appear as an affront to religion and to free

---

[98] Israel W. Carney, *"Fighting Suicide Bombing: A Worldwide Campaign for Life"* (Westport, CT: Praeger, 2007), p.158. Cited in Tod Strickland, "Toward Solutions: Understanding Suicide Attackers in the Contemporary Middle East", Canadian Military Journal, v.9, number. 4, 2009, p.18.

speech. However, such limitations are both reasonable and prudent. Institutions that would destroy democratic principles should not be afforded the protection of those same principles in the advancement of their goals."[99] Reasonable, but progressive limitations against messages of hate and destruction, and advocating the use of suicide tactics made in the name of God should be strongly considered. Of course such anti-hate laws would have been part of the solution had universal rule of law been part and parcel of governance in the countries that make up the Middle East.

One must also keep in mind that, as there are ideological Muslim extremists in the world, there are also Jewish, Asian and Christian extremists, each with its brand of 'divine inspiration'. One justifies the taking away of somebody's homeland in the name of God, the other justifies supporting them, and the third justifies getting rid of both.

In his book "In the Line of Fire: A Memoir", former Pakistani President General Pervez Musharraf underlines the fact that "the small fringe of extremists (in Pakistan and Afghanistan) holds rigid, orthodox, even obscurantist and intolerant views about religion, and strives to impose its rigid, dogmatic views on others. This fringe not only is militant, arrogant and aggressive, but can also be indoctrinated into terrorism." [100]

He also pointed out that "the turmoil in the Muslim world arises primarily because of unresolved, long standing political disputes that have created a sense of injustice, alienation, deprivation, powerlessness, and hopelessness in the masses. This situation is aggravated by the fact that by any measure, the Muslim countries have the least healthy social conditions in the world. Political deprivation, combined with poverty and illiteracy, has created an explosive brew of extremism and terrorism."[101]

General Musharraf concludes with a specific example by saying that "… gathering intelligence about al Qaeda is harder than conducting physical operations against it. All antiterrorist operations are intelligence-driven, but also require swift mobility by day and night and effective firepower."[102]

Countries that produce terrorists are the ones whose governments are significantly responsible for this phenomenon. It is not a question of inability to combat terrorism; it is the doings of these governments that gives birth to the phenomenon. That goes many years back and the way the Western world handled its relationships with the twenty two Arab governments and their heads of state

---

[99] Tod Strickland, "Toward Solutions: Understanding Suicide Attackers in the Contemporary Middle East", Canadian Military Journal, v.9, number 4, 2009, p.18

[100] Pervez Musharraf - "In the Line of Fire: A Memoir." Free Press, New York (2006) - p.278.

[101] Ibid., p.297

[102] Ibid., p.271

is a sure sign that things would deteriorate even further. The 2011 "Arab Spring" uprisings may have changed the formula, but that will take some time before it is clear how the situation will eventually evolve in the region.

According to Hartmut Behr and Lars Berger, the Barcelona Process gave authoritarian Arab governments a green light regarding anti-terror policies. "For a long time the so-called Barcelona process, launched in 1995, was treated as the central channel of European Union (EU) engagement with its southern neighbourhood. Its importance for our analysis lies in the fact that long before the manifestation of transnational Islamist terrorism through the attacks of 9/11, in Riyadh in 2003, in Madrid in 2004, and in London and Egypt in 2005, the fight against terrorism had begun to move to the top of the international agenda.

"The representatives of the Council of the European Union, the European Commission, member states of the European Union, and non-European Mediterranean countries issued a joint statement that mentions ... counterterrorism and its relation to political reform. (The European Union and Mediterranean) signatories pledged to "develop the rule of law and democracy in their political systems, while recognizing in this framework the right of each of them to choose and freely develop its own political, socio-cultural, economic, and judicial system" and to "respect their sovereign equality and all rights inherent in their sovereignty.

"By adding acceptance of "the need for a differentiated approach that takes into account the diversity of the situation in each country," Barcelona gave the authoritarian Arab governments the green light for any policy they deemed necessary to fight terrorism. This was especially worrisome given the ... broadening of the definition of terrorism to muzzle any form of peaceful political opposition. However, by framing the problem in this way, the EU fell into the rhetorical trap laid out by the authoritarian Arab governments of the false choice between authoritarian stability and Islamist chaos." [103] Keeping in mind of course what was mentioned above, that the blame for the chaos is squarely on the back of these Arab and Muslim governments, though without absolving the Islamists from their share of responsibility.

It should also be taken into account that the odd relationship that exists between the leading countries of the "free world" and the criminally responsible authoritarian governments in several parts of the world is also seriously to blame for the failure of reform-minded opposition in those countries. The actions of these

---

[103] Hartmut Behr and Lars Berger, "The challenge of talking about Terrorism: the European Union and the Arab Debate on the Causes of Islamist Terrorism", Terrorism and Political Violence, v.21, number 4, October 2009, pp.539-557.

governments are constantly monitored by Western intelligence agencies, which possibly share the information they collect with the leaders of those countries as part of the "rendition program"[104].

It is not surprising that even occasional inappropriate behaviour and misjudgement by Western officials feeds into the cycle of violence. Here is the Prime Minister of France, François Fillon accepting an all-expenses paid holiday from former President Hosni Mubarak, and actually goes to Egypt while the demonstrations against the rule of Mubarak are rocking the whole country. Then his Minister of Foreign Affairs at the time, Michèle Alliot-Marie, accompanies her father a few weeks earlier on a business trip arranged by a Tunisian businessman associated with former President Zein El-Abdine Ben Ali to spend her holiday in Tunisia while the country is boiling with demonstrations against the dictator. A couple of weeks later she proposed to offer French police techniques and advice - obviously in repression techniques - to Ben Ali so that he can deal with the nation in revolt. These glaring gaffes send an extremely loud message to the people in those countries about the total blindness of these foreign governments, which preach democracy, liberty, equality and fraternity. The government of France eventually redeemed itself by spearheading the support effort provided to the Libyan insurgency against the rule of Colonel Moammar Gaddafi[105].

About three or four years ago for example we managed to whitewash the destruction of a Pan Am aircraft in 1988 over Lockerbie in which the Libyan intelligence service was involved, and even liberated the main suspect on humanitarian grounds. In 1986 we side-stepped the bombing of a Disco in Berlin by Libyan agents in which a number of American servicemen were killed. We also 'forgot' about the bombing of the French UTA aircraft with Libyan involvement over the Sahara in 1984. Again in 1984 Libyan embassy personnel in London fired at London policewoman Yvonne Fletcher and killed her. Much earlier than that in 1978 Libya's intelligence service abducted and killed Lebanese Shiite clergyman, Musa Al-Sadr while on an official visit to Libya, then disposed of his body, etc. All of a sudden we proceeded a few years ago to beatify President Moammar Gaddafi of Libya after he stopped working on a would-be chemical weapons plant, which he would have never been able to complete and operate anyway. After putting the blinds on our eyes, we somehow discovered that, after all, he is a "wise man", because he allowed us to help ourselves to Libyan oil, since Iraqi oil was proving to be elusive at that time. As far as we are concerned, we simply followed the proverbial Japanese saying: "See no evil, hear no evil, speak no evil!"

---

[104] The "rendition program" is an innocuous name of a system by which countries that do not want to dirty their hands directly by torturing and maiming prisoners, outsource the "service" by subcontracting it to other countries whose leaders, who are responsible for the rise in terrorism in the first place, are flushed with our taxpayers' money in the name of combating terrorism.

[105] There are about 72 ways to transliterate the name and first name of Colonel Moammar Gaddafi from classical Arabic into English. We have chosen Gaddafi in this book, because this is how his name is pronounced in spoken Arabic.

After the insurrection staged against him by the Libyan people in March 2011 we rediscovered that he was an evil man. But that did not stop some former US officials and other shady figures in Washington from maintaining "business" connections with Gaddafi and his regime. One should not blame him, because he was following his self-created job description. The ones to be blamed are the governments who sent him their ambassadors, accredited his own ambassadors, received him with pomp and circumstance as if he were the emperor of Africa as he self-described himself. At the same time we blinded ourselves intentionally as to what was going on in Libya until the sounds and pictures of massacres and tortures of thousands of opponents in secret underground hideouts perpetrated by his sons and goons hit television screens following the seizure of Tripoli by Libyan rebels in August 2011.

The 2011 Libyan uprising is just one example of amazing reluctant pussyfooting and confusion among the Western allies as to how to proceed especially in light of the long honeymoon between Gaddafi, the US the UK, France, Italy and other European governments. The West did indeed clearly declare its support for the Libyan insurgents and managed to secure the somewhat hesitant support of certain influential members of the Arab League as a fig leaf to justify interfering in the Libyan situation. France declared its unequivocal support to the insurgents and sent its air force to target pro-Gaddafi forces. Then Britain followed suit and the US finally gave the green light for NATO to get involved. The insurgents were happy and the rest of the world approved. Everybody had an axe to grind vis-à-vis Colonel Gaddafi.

In the meanwhile, unconfirmed reports indicated that the US was negotiating a settlement with Gaddafi's emissaries in Mauritania.[106] After the insurgents captured the Libyan capital Tripoli and Gaddafi fled, the smell of the rendition deals that have been going on between U.S., U.K. and Libya's intelligence services, which were not really a secret, finally became public knowledge. The first public tell-tale sign about such "transactions" was the defection to the U.K. of Mousa Koussa, Libya's previous intelligence boss turned Minister of Foreign Affairs, who literally saw the writing on the wall and made a run for it to London to save his skin. His handlers were probably delighted to welcome him before he spilled the beans.

In Yemen, the population and the opposition chiefs rose against thirty-year President Ali Abdallah Saleh, who eventually fled the country after he was injured in a bomb attack. During all that time our hands were tied because President Saleh was our chief honcho in the "fight against terrorism." The search is probably on for a replacement.

The uprising in Syria against the ruling clique led by President Bashar Al-Assad, who represents a 1.4 million Alawis, a derivative of Shiite Islam, in a

---

[106] According to Antoine Sfeir, Director of Cahiers de l'Orient, TV5 French program "Kiosque", May 1st, 2011.

country that counts 23 million mainly Sunni Muslim and Christian Syrians was also another challenge. We used President Assad, reluctantly though, to be one of our rendition subcontractors. He was also quite acceptable to our allies in Israel because he kept solid control over the borders between Syria's occupied territories in the Golan Heights and Israel, thus preventing any Palestinians or others from even approaching the border area and threaten Israeli settlements and military positions on Mount Hermon, which straddles the border between Syria and Lebanon.

To make his point during the uprising in June 2011, President Assad dispatched a motley collection of "demonstrators" carrying Palestinian and Syrian flags, who were described by Syrian media as being Palestinians; to demonstrate along the Syrian-Israeli border fence. To be able to reach that fence, those "sudden" demonstrators had to cross miles of Syrian anti-tank positions and anti-personnel mine-fields, beside barrages of artillery and tanks. Assad made his point, and never repeated the routine again. But he had made it amply clear that he is indispensable as far as controlling the borders and protecting the Israeli Golan Heights. The Israelis made their point too, and, we are told, they killed over twenty demonstrators. The message was loud and clear, and our talk regarding getting involved in support of the Syrian national uprising, remained only that: talk. In the meanwhile the search is on for a future leader in Syria, who, like in Egypt, could secure a partnership between the Muslim Brotherhood with the army, on condition that they jointly undertake to protect the borders with Israel on the Golan Heights.

Encouraging, or at least pretending not to see the Israeli leadership in its onslaught on the Palestinians and justifying their takeover of what's left of their homeland for self-created security or divine command reasons is another totally misguided policy that is always camouflaged in innocuous terms such as "U.S. domestic imperatives." Little do we dare clarify what we specifically mean by that. At the end of the day there is no free lunch, and we end up having to pay the bill. Instead of genuinely supporting the people of these nations, and seriously settle the Israeli-Palestinian question for the benefit of both people, then reap the fruits in terms of long term projects, business contracts and political alliances, we end up on the receiving end of very angry people on all sides.

The confused and confusing message sent by the Western powers to all nations looking up to them for freedom and an example to follow in their struggle for democracy is a message of unreliability. The unreliability of Western support to democratic forces also provides an indirect strong support to all the undemocratic forces in the world. When quality people in those countries see the West fraternizing with murderous dictatorships they describe as "sharing democratic values", and are so much engulfed in shady dealings with these kinds of rulers and regimes, those who truly believe in authentic and genuine democratic values abstain from supporting the West. Some would get so disappointed that they could find themselves encouraged to feed into the stream of home-grown terrorism.

CHAPTER 5

THE QUEST FOR DECISIVE ACTION

To conclude this section, it may serve a purpose to say that there is an inordinate amount of literature being written and published about terrorism, how evil the terrorists are, and how to combat them using more and more sophisticated and intrusive technologies for which millions or billions of dollars are earmarked.

Since the first airplane hijackings and attacks at airports in the 1960s took place, everybody talks about protective and obstructive measures. It all boils down to spending more money to add more security layers, hiring more security guards, and buying more sophisticated equipment that basically strips innocent travelers and staff their dignity and privacy. As a corollary it also forces airline operators to reduce their ground and in-flight service personnel to balance their budgets.

As late as 2010, the author of this book gave presentations at two international conferences held in two different countries in the Middle East which were attended by senior aviation and maritime officials from these countries as well as foreign participants. One presentation was about the application of intelligence in the area of civil aviation, the other about the application of intelligence in the field of maritime transportation. Aside from the polite applause, nobody questioned his statements, nor did anybody ask him to further elaborate on his statements as to how to apply this or that, neither at the end of his presentation, nor later.

Only representatives from some European embassies eventually asked the speaker for a copy of his presentation. During coffee-breaks, most attendees were rather conglomerating around the booths of participating detection equipment manufacturers. There is money to be made there, both by the vendors and those who will make a commission off every purchase. When it comes to intelligence, there are no commissions paid, nor money exchanging hands.

This does not mean that explosive or weapons detection equipment is not required. Far from that. Yet we need to remember that detection equipment can only be useful as a last resort when the bad guys are literally at the gate. Intelligence, however, is the long-term tool to stop terrorists before they even leave their bases. While this is a more enduring way of preventing the rise of terrorism and protecting ourselves, it is rarely evoked today; maybe because it lacks the element of adventure or perhaps because it is actually more difficult to achieve.

Perhaps too because deep in the psyche of some, terrorism serves their grander strategic goals; and, to them, terrorism may not be that bad after all because it justifies the repressive and destructive counter-actions they excel at, and which they often use as an inflated excuse to maintain the very repressive policy against indigenous populations they rule over that leads to the rise of terrorism.

What will go a long way towards resolving the issue of terrorism is putting all the good will, determination and resources to help solve at least some of the basic and elementary problems that are the root causes of violence and terrorism, as well as looking at what it is that our domestic and foreign policies are doing that give birth to terrorism. Today nobody talks about that and therein rests the essence of the problem that faces us; that his why we chose to dwell in this book on the triggers of terrorism and piracy which are at the root of the threats we are facing. Addressing them in a timely fashion will help us mitigate the threat, if not eliminate it altogether. Keeping in mind of course that, to get out of this cycle of violence, which is becoming more acute by the day, calls for outstanding leadership from all countries without exception. Is there such leadership?

Misguided alliances

In her book 'The Mighty and the Almighty', former U.S. Secretary of State Madeleine Albright says: "In hindsight, it is always easy to identify mistakes (in foreign policy) whether by omission or commission. It is much harder to see clearly before the decisions are made, when the outcome is still in doubt and the players involved have yet to reveal their hands. In those circumstances, we need guidance; but for that, to whom – or to what – should we turn?"[107]

Despite all the sources and resources available to some major powers, both overt and covert, they still make some very basic incomprehensible assessments, or reach conclusions which prove that, despite the fact that they know everything; in effect they still did not understand anything.[108] "...In 1991, after the Persian Gulf War, the administration of the first President Bush expected Saddam Hussein to be driven from power by his own people. That did not happen"[109]. This type of analysis around which a war was planned and executed, proves that if the administration has turned to someone for guidance, it has certainly turned to the wrong people. It did, to wit, Ahmad Chalabi who became the darling of the White House and the Department of Defense, and misled them almost about everything related to Iraq. Worse still; the Western intelligence community is not stupid, but unfortunately, the analysis it produces is occasionally re-analyzed, re-

---

[107] Madeleine Albright, "The Mighty and the Almighty", Harper Collins Publishers, New York (2006), p.45 - By permission from the publishers.

[108] For a short background on the West and the Arab World please read "Why Tyrants Rule Arabs", By Gwynn Dyer - Toronto Star, July 20, 2004.

[109] Albright p.54

assessed and "reinterpreted" by the politicians to suit motives that are sometimes questionable, but which result into tragic and costly mistakes that affect their own countries and their own people.

Over the years, the usual suspects among Arab leaders inculcated in the minds of the world that Arabs cannot be governed other than by force. Hence the support we give to military dictatorships and authoritarian regimes that perpetuate this stereotyped outlook. It is these unrepresentative leaders of the Arab countries, i.e. our allies, who have interest in propagating disinformation to the effect that if they do not control, the country will go into the hands of the "Islamic extremists." But it is also these leaders who directly or indirectly encourage the extremists precisely to scare the world and the rest of the population with them. Yet we still go and support the unrepresentative governments against the people; all in the name of democracy. Go figure what is the definition of this democracy. Whenever there has been a window of opportunity that could signal a possible change, we rush to overturn the situation back to where it was. The uprisings in various Arab countries in 2011 provide an eloquent example.

Following the early 2011 revolt of the people in Egypt, we went and gave our support again to the military who may be fit to command and control, but are unfit to govern a civil society. The military are trained to give orders and receive orders, not to negotiate with parliamentarians, or to seek the desires of the nation. Besides, the military in Egypt, both the higher ranks and the institution as a whole, were directly involved in the nauseating corruption that the country has lived through for the past fifty nine years. The Egyptian people have never forgotten that these officers and their former mentors who were in charge of defending the country between 1948 and 1973, could only claim the fame of having lost every single war they were involved in.

The same amazing example of twisting things is that of Iraq. Iraq was attacked for two reasons. First to ensure the U.S. has direct control over the oil resources of the country before the Chinese or the Russians get to them. Saddam, the surrogate 'overseer' who had launched a war against Iran with our support and supply of poison gas (which was eventually used against the Kurds), became emboldened and attacked Kuwait. That proved to be too much for us and for the next door neighbour Saudi Arabia. The second objective was to basically destroy Iraq's military infrastructure, and return it to the "pre-industrial age", as President G.W. Bush declared. This was a gift to Israel, who always wants to ensure that any Arab country with strong economic potential around her be destroyed, lest one day they even dream of supporting an attack on Israel. Of course Israel can act any time as it pleases in light of its strategic interests, but it is still better when it gets somebody else like the US do it for her under an 'international' umbrella and at no expense to Israel. (For more on the future of Iraq, please see Appendix 4)

On the eve of his death King Hussein of Jordan suddenly removed his brother Crown Prince Hassan from the first line of succession, and appointed, his own son Abdallah (the current King Abdallah II), a military man, instead.

The reason for that unexpected change has never been explained publically. It is likely though that the dying King Hussein was put under pressure by the US and Israel to make the change. On one hand we were never too close to his brother Hassan, and the Israelis always want to ensure that Arab nations are under a short leash and controlled by people, they, i.e. the Israelis, trust. Despite his academic credentials Prince Hassan was not such a man despite his raucous relationships with the Palestinian population on both sides of the Jordan River. He is an Oxford University graduate, an intellectual cum philosopher, who believes in dialogue among religions, and is more at ease with like-minded international scholars than with Jordanian tribal society. On top of that, and more importantly, he is not a military man. Thus Abdallah became the new king, and his uncle, Prince Hassan graciously accepted his lot and kept busy with his inter-religious dialogue pursuits.

We must thus redefine our relations with questionable types of leaders and regimes we support in some countries, especially when we enter into bilateral intelligence arrangements with them. As far as these leaders are concerned, the definition and use of intelligence is oceans apart from the definition given in rule-of-law countries as mentioned earlier in the book. But who else but questionable people would agree to be partners in shameful inhumane rendition schemes. It is equally maddening that some Western governments are incapable of dealing with honest, competent, educated people in other countries, and seem to always concentrate on shady dealings with the most corrupt individuals in those countries.[110]

However we pretend not to see any of that. Our "democratic" governments have not realized yet that by ignoring what we "did-not-like-over-there" has had catastrophic effects over here. Predatory banking in the US brought financial catastrophe, while predatory foreign policy brought predatory terrorism.

Partnering between intelligence and foreign policy

In addressing terrorism, every country today talks about cooperation: cooperation among law-enforcement agencies, cooperation among intelligence agencies, etc. The new type of warfare, which has the new buzzword of "asymmetric warfare",

---

[110] These warning lines were written in 2009. By early 2011 "our staunch allies", such as the presidents of Egypt, and Tunisia were kicked out by the people of their respective countries, riots were taking place in Algeria, and Yemen. Massacres of civilians became a daily occurrence in Bahrain and Syria, and a quasi-civil war engulfed Libya and more to come. Is this not enough of a sign that our foreign policies, our support to failed dictators, and relying on shady individuals as advisors and leaders, along with self-blinded interference in other nations' affairs, push people to revolt and terrorism?

calls for a combination of police detective work, intelligence analysis and joint operational and analytical cooperation among ourselves and with allied agencies. This is not a job for minutes-takers and term paper careerists.

Most importantly though, there must be an ongoing partnership and not just coordination between the architects of foreign policy and the security/intelligence community. This should allow the security and intelligence community as well as the policy architects assess the repercussions of such a foreign policy both at home and abroad in real time <u>before</u> its course is charted. It should also allow intelligence to produce at least a "predictability factor" regarding the effects of political decisions made in other countries. Had this been the case, the collapse of the Soviet Union and the explosion of the Arab Revolt, aka Arab Spring of 2011, could have been at least envisaged on the radar screen. It is not sufficient to ask for an intelligence opinion, which may be followed or not. Intelligence must be an integral and permanent partner of the policy making process from design to conception to implementation.

Intelligence agencies must also be free to initiate, monitor, or investigate suspicious targets within reasonable parameters that are subject to accountability, as opposed to being hostages of delaying and damaging bureaucratic processes in the name of due process, or control against trespasses. If governments do not trust their own intelligence agencies, then they may as well shut them down. If the process of creating these agencies, staffing them at all levels, and the selection of their management is done properly, then everything should work well to the benefit of national security.

Cultural and operational differences between intelligence and law enforcement

Intelligence officers are not policemen. It is always repeated that there are cultural differences between intelligence and law enforcement. However, not often mentioned, there are also legal and operational differences. As described by Arthur S. Hulnick when discussing the differences between the CIA and the FBI, "given the pressures to cooperate on the targets that both must pursue, the differences must at least be understood. Several cases illustrate how the two can work more closely together, even though they are, and probably always will be separate."[111]

Intelligence agencies treat the protection of their sources religiously, so do law enforcement agencies for the same reason, but also because they must eventually make a court case that might be weakened by disclosure. "In terms

---

[111] Arthur S. Hulnick, (1997) "Intelligence and law enforcement: The spies are not cops problem", International Journal of Intelligence and CounterIntelligence, 10: 3, 269-286 p.275.

of organizational culture ... intelligence officers want to exploit their sources and law enforcement personnel want to make convictions. The two goals are not compatible; hence there must be some way to move from one to the other."[112]

Hulnick is of course comparing between the FBI and the CIA, and indicates that "when the FBI recruits a source, [that source] may well be targeted against one criminal event. The FBI wants the source to collect information that may be used eventually in court. That means that legal disclosure rules apply. The source's identity will eventually have to be revealed, as well as the methods by which the information was gathered." As for the CIA, Hulnick points out, that the agency "has no desire to let the source appear in court, thus "blowing their cover," nor does it want the identity of their sources revealed. It is no wonder that there are serious differences between intelligence and law enforcement in regard to operations and methodology."[113] As Baker points out, "As far as law enforcement is concerned, intelligence that cannot ultimately be introduced in court as evidence borders on the worthless."[114]

It was 9/11 that brought the existing wall between intelligence and law enforcement to the fore, which led to major changes in how US intelligence and the FBI work internally, with each other and with other players in the intelligence field. Senator Richard Shelby, Republican Senator from the state of Alabama, then Vice Chairman of the Senate Select Committee on Intelligence (and previously Chairman), presented some extensive thoughts on these issues in an "Additional Views" section printed as part of the Joint Inquiry's Report.[115]

"Senator Shelby reviewed the story of the "Phoenix memo" - cited in Chapter 3 - sent to high-level FBI counterterrorism officials by a Bureau agent in Phoenix, Arizona, who had become curious about Middle Easterners, some of whom with known sympathies to Islamic radicals, who were then undergoing pilot training in the area. As Shelby summarized these events:

"Headquarters personnel, however, decided that no follow-up was needed, and no managers actually took part in this decision or even saw the memorandum before the September 11 attacks . . . [It] is astonishing that so little was made of it, especially since it drew readers' attention to certain information already in the FBI's possession suggesting a very specific reason to be alarmed about one particular foreign student at an aviation university in the United States."[116]

---

[112] Ibid., p.276

[113] Ibid., pp.276-277

[114] Baker, p.43. Cited in Arthur S. Hulnick "Intelligence and law enforcement."

[115] Senator Shelby's remarks may be read in the appendix to the Joint Inquiry into Intelligence Activities Report: http://intelligence.senate.gov/107351.pdf. Quoted in Thomas H. Hammond, "Intelligence Organizations and the Organization of Intelligence", International Journal of Intelligence and CounterIntelligence, v.23 number 4, pp. 680-724, 2010.

[116] Joint Inquiry Report, p.44

"Senator Shelby emphasized the problems of gaining access to this information and then sharing with other agencies. He noted that a large body of significant data was already possessed by the intelligence community, stemming from law enforcement investigations into such events as the 1990 New York City assassination of Rabbi Meir Kahane, the 1993 World Trade Centre bombing, the abortive plot to blow up various harbors and tunnels in New York City (the "Day of Terror" plot), the 1996 Khobar Towers attack in Saudi Arabia, the 1998 U.S. embassy bombings in Kenya and Tanzania, al-Qaeda's "Millennium Plot" to attack the Los Angeles airport, and the attack on the USS Cole in October 2000 in Yemen.[117]

But, he observed, the problem was that "Most of this information … remained locked away in law enforcement evidence rooms, unknown to and unstudied by counterterrorism analysts within the intelligence community."[118] Shelby suggested that such information might have proved quite useful:

"That this information possessed potentially huge relevance to the Intelligence Community's CT [Counter-Terrorism] work is beyond question. Indeed, until the late 1990s, at least, U.S. law enforcement offices probably had more information on Al-Qaeda - its key members operating in the West, its organizational structure, and its methods of operation - than the CIA's CTC [Counter-Terrorism Centre]. Two CT specialists from the Clinton Administration's National Security Council later described court records from 1990s terrorism trials as being "a treasure trove" that contained "information so crucial that we were amazed that the relevant agencies did not inform us of it while we were at the NSC."[119]

"In a report section titled "Tyranny of the Casefile", Senator Shelby argued that "the FBI was fundamentally a law enforcement organization: "its agents are trained and acculturated, rewarded and promoted within an institutional culture the primary purpose of which is the prosecution of criminals."[120] As a consequence, he continued, "Within the Bureau, information is stored, retrieved, and simply understood principally through the conceptual prism of a 'case' - a discrete bundle of information the fundamental purpose of which is to prove elements of crimes against specific potential defendants in a court of law"[121] This has systemic effects, he suggested:

"The FBI's reification [i.e. substantiation] of "the case" pervades the entire organization, and is reflected at every level and in every area: in the autonomous, decentralized authority and traditions of the Field Offices; in the priorities and preferences given in individual career paths, in resource allocation, and within

---

[117] Ibid., p.90

[118] Ibid., p.90

[119] Ibid., p.91

[120] Ibid., p.99

[121] Ibid., p.99

the Bureau's status hierarchy to criminal investigative work and post hoc investigations as opposed to long-term analysis; in the lack of understanding of and concern with modern information management technologies and processes; and in deeply entrenched individual mindsets that prize the production of evidence-supported narratives of defendant wrongdoing over the drawing of probabilistic inferences based upon incomplete and fragmentary information in order to support decision-making."[122]

He then argued that:

"Particularly against shadowy transnational targets such as international terrorist organizations that lack easily identifiable geographic loci, organizational structures, behavioral patterns, or other information "signatures," intelligence collection and analysis requires an approach to acquiring, managing, and understanding information quite different from that which prevails in the law enforcement community. Intelligence analysts tend to reach conclusions based upon disparate fragments of data derived from widely distributed sources and assembled into a probabilistic "mosaic" of information. They seek to distinguish useful "signals" from a bewildering universe of background "noise" and make determinations upon the basis of vague pattern recognition, inferences (including negative inferences), context, and history. For them, information exists to be cross-correlated - evaluated, and continually subjected to re-evaluation, in light of the total context of what is available to the organization as a whole. Intelligence analysts think in degrees of possibility and probability, as opposed to categories of admissibility and degrees of contribution to the ultimate criminal-investigative aim of proof "beyond a reasonable doubt."[123]

Senator Shelby next analyzed several of the 9/11 events from the perspective of the FBI's "case file." He began by noting that the Joint Inquiry Staff (JIS) had found that the FBI knew that convicted terrorist Abdul Hakim Murad "had been involved in an extremist Islamic plot to blow up twelve U.S.-owned airliners over the Pacific Ocean and crash an aircraft into CIA Headquarters."[124] However, he noted that:

"Murad was not charged with a crime in connection with the CIA crash plot, apparently because it was merely at the "discussion" stage when he was apprehended. Because the CIA crash plot did not appear in the indictment, however, the FBI effectively forgot all about it. As the JIS has recounted, the FBI's case file for the Murad case essentially ignored the air crash plot, and FBI agents interviewed as part of our inquiry confirmed that Murad's only significance to them was in connection specifically with the crimes for which he was charged: "the other aspects of the plot were not part of the criminal case and therefore not

---

[122] Ibid., p.99

[123] Ibid., p.101

[124] Ibid., p.101

considered relevant." Convinced that the only information that really matters was information directly related to the criminal investigation at hand, the FBI thus ignored this early warning sign that terrorists had begun planning to crash aircraft into symbols of U.S. power. Thus, rather than being stored in a form that would permit this information to be assessed and re-assessed in light of a much broader universe of information about terrorist plans and intentions over time, the Murad data-point was simply forgotten. Like all the other tidbits of information that might have alerted a sophisticated analyst to terrorists' interest in using airplanes to attack building targets in the United States, the episode disappeared into the depths of an old case file and slipped out of the FBI's usable institutional memory."[125]

This approach, Shelby concluded, "is entirely unsuited to virtually any long-term strategic analytic work, and is patently inappropriate to counterterrorism analysis against the loose, interconnected and overlapping networks of Islamic extremists that make up the modern jihadist movement."[126]

Finally, Hulnick points out that "counterintelligence isn't the only problem pressing the CIA and the FBI to collaborate more effectively. Terrorism, the illicit narcotics trade, proliferation of weapons of mass destruction, industrial espionage and global organized crime all have begun to loom large as problems that require both the attention and cooperation of law enforcement and intelligence operations. The "centre" concept in intelligence operations has developed, in which multi-agency units are focused on counterintelligence and foreign espionage, counterterrorism, counternarcotics, with a new unit working against global organized crime.[127] These centres bring together representatives of various intelligence components, with the FBI as the law enforcement element, so that information can be shared and operational plans reviewed on an inter-agency basis."[128]

Reinstating quality into the intelligence service

There are several other very important factors that must be taken into consideration to ensure a qualitative edge in intelligence analysis, evaluation and interpretation.

There is a tendency in some intelligence agencies to constantly preach for neutral analysis, i.e. opinion-less intelligence analysis. What "armchair analysts" preach about producing neutral analysis, supposedly to maintain objectivity and neutrality of the analysis, is misleading and not useful as far as decision-making is

---

[125] Ibid., p.101-102

[126] Ibid., p.64-65

[127] John Buntin, "Cops and Spies", Government Executive, April 1996, p.40. Cited in Arthur S. Hulnick "Intelligence and law enforcement."

[128] Hulnick, p.274

concerned at the political level. Neutral analysis means nothing; especially that the observed trend nowadays is to "democratically" elect Presidents, Prime Ministers and Ministers, many of whom do not know much about world issues, and worse still, refuse to be informed. Providing these types of leadership with neutral analysis will confuse them even more. What they need is possibly multiple, but prioritized assessments that reflect the repercussions of each on national security and foreign policy, so that they have a clear and simple choice.

We need to reduce excessive staff mobility within the security and intelligence establishment. Upward mobility should not necessarily be achieved by jumping from one area to another over short intervals. To be efficient and effective, intelligence services must have a high retention capacity. Services that have a high turnover of skilled intelligence officers and analysts will never be able to retain the long term expertise they desperately need to be able to function effectively on a long term basis.

It was said earlier that monitoring trends is one of the most important functions in an intelligence service. The only way to be able to do that is by making everything possible to keep badly needed assets such as operations long-term analysts who have established the requisite depth of knowledge and experience on a given subject or subjects. However, one finds an extremely high retention capacity in administrative and support functions, which is not a bad thing, but unfortunately not in the crucial intelligence and analytical functions.

For no known reason, some intelligence services create two tier employment streams; a management-track stream among operational staff, and no-career streams for those badly needed, highly experienced rare commodities, namely qualified analysts. Some agencies even put a cap on the salaries of the intelligence analysts, which puts them well below their counterparts in the operational sections and freezes their careers at that level. Not only that, they assign these analysts to work under the supervision of management-stream young or old intelligence officers who frequently have no clue as to the issues or regions under the microscope. This blind practice pushes the best among the seasoned analysts to leave, which is the best gift these services offer the enemy. In the long run this is tantamount to suicide.

"Intelligence analysts are urged never to suggest or recommend policy. This is not to say that intelligence analysts have no policy views - they all do. For the most part, intelligence professionals present the facts in a clear, concise and unbiased manner." [129] Once they reach more senior ranks, then the bias starts to be built to guarantee a cushioned retirement, or the bias is forced on them by politicians

---

[129] To read more on this topic, see Michael Scheuer, "Imperial Hubris: Why the West is Losing the War on Terror", Brassey's Inc. Publishers; Washington, D.C. 2004, p.237. www.potomacbooksinc.com

whose knowledge of the facts on the ground in other countries are pretty flimsy. And this is where the damage starts being done, because in many cases they distort the facts to suit other ulterior motives.

Nothing is more vital to an effective intelligence service than a strong and engaged director. A good intelligence agency is like a good orchestra. If you bureaucratize an orchestra, the artistic creativity contributed by each musician and each section will diminish. The director of intelligence is to his people what the orchestra conductor is to the musicians. The conductor is in charge of the music, not budgets and human resources. This must be left to the orchestra's administrative officer. If you were to pick an accountant or a human resources specialist to conduct the Royal Philharmonic Orchestra, you can kiss music and attendance goodbye.

It is very important to highlight the fact that security is a long term commitment and not a seasonal or occasional activity. It is expensive and does not allow for cutting corners. Those who did cut corners paid a very heavy price both financially and in terms of people killed and property destroyed.

In the final analysis, proper intelligence is a game of specialists and professionals not cliques, cronies and nepotistic practices. To leave intelligence in the hands of public servant amateurs from the very first stage of recruitment, to training, to supervising, is a sign of gross negligence. The worst part is when knowledgeable intelligence officers are forced to serve under supervisors of such qualities, which is a sign of abject irresponsibility.

Today terrorists and criminals have the initiative, everybody else reacts to them. The day the initiative is seized by law enforcement and intelligence in particular, terrorists and criminals will have a very difficult time operating with impunity.

Finally it is unfair to the members of the security and intelligence community to find themselves having to do the cleanup work and be blamed for lapses in intelligence as a result of a misdirected foreign policy in which they were not consulted. Or, when they are consulted, their advice is not taken seriously. Aviation and Maritime industry professionals, beware!

PART II

APPLYING INTELLIGENCE
TO AVIATION & MARITIME SECURITY

CHAPTER 6

AVIATION & MARITIME SECURITY INTELLIGENCE

Introduction: The aviation and maritime security environments

Definition, standardization and implementation of civil aviation security requirements and recommended practices regarding Acts of Unlawful Interference are set in the International Civil Aviation Organization (ICAO) Annex 17. That is among other measures including ICAO's 37th Assembly Declaration on Aviation Security adopted in 2010 requiring Member States to take actions to enhance international cooperation to counter threats to civil aviation. In the maritime industry, security is regulated by the International Maritime Organization (IMO) through its Safety of Life at Sea (SOLAS) regulations and the International Ship and Port Security (ISPS) Code, as well as the Flag State and Port State Control security measures and regulations.

Threats to civil aviation include threats to airlines, aircraft, individual passengers and both ground and flight crew, baggage and cargo containers, checked-in luggage and carry-on baggage, airports, terminals, runways, navigation facilities, airport periphery, airside and curbside threats, runway approaches and cargo facilities. They also include threats to general aviation, Fixed Base Operators (FBOs), ground handling companies, caterers, refuellers and other airport services.

Threats to the maritime industry include threats to ships/vessels, ports, port facilities, passenger terminals, national and international waterways including their locks and approaches, international straits and multinational rivers, navigation facilities, waterside and landside moorings, seaplane operations, and finally threats to Mobile Offshore Drilling Units (MODUs).

While ICAO's and the IMO's security functions essentially revolve around terrorist threats, the responsibility of civil aviation authorities around the world go beyond the stipulations of Annex 17 and the ISPS Code and include criminal threats, which are as lethal as terrorist acts against the security and safety of civil aviation and maritime transportation. As well, they also involve criminal elements, some of whom are beyond suspicion, from within the countries involved.

SOURCES OF THREAT TO CIVIL AVIATION

Direct threats

These are what one might call 'common threats' such as attempts at hijacking aircraft for ransom or prisoner release purposes as was pretty common during the 1970s; hijacking of aircraft and their use as man-controlled bombs, such as the 9/11 attacks; the use of aircraft to convey terrorist supplies that terrorists or hijackers could have access to on board aircraft; surreptitious transport of terrorist supplies via freight and cargo; destroying aircraft on the ground or upon take-off or landing by means of MANPADS (Man-portable air defence systems); armed attacks against passengers and airline check-in counters staff at airports; detonating rigged-vehicles stationed in front of air terminal departure or arrival gates by remote-control, or storming those gates using trucks, etc.

Physical preventive measures implemented at ports and airports have proven their efficiency, though at a high cost for cargo and passengers, as well as for law enforcement agencies and the staff working at these facilities. The same is true of port facilities, vessels berthed, at anchor, or at sea, as well as of inland waterways and international seaways. These costs and complications could be partially reduced through timely and precise actionable intelligence. Timely, precise intelligence and success at detecting and arresting the would-be terrorists, pirates or criminals before they go into action would almost certainly take care of the problem before it happens, and better still before it is even attempted.

We still need to keep in mind the different legitimate "philosophies" among countries and among allies when it comes to black-listing of individuals who may pose potential threats to civil aviation on a no-fly list. The European Union challenges the indiscriminate collection of personal data without concrete suspicion, and considers that it does not automatically lead to greater security. Not that Europe is not concerned about security or that Americans do not care about civil liberties, but the European Parliament aims at closely scrutinizing counterterrorism policies on the basis of evidence, not assumptions.

It must be noted here that the window of opportunity to catch a terrorist at the airport is pretty tight and too close time-wise to detect. Umar Farouk Abdulmuttalab, the would-be "underwear bomber" whose name was on the No Flight List, was apprehended way too late; not before he boarded the flight in Amsterdam, but when he attempted to light the fuse of his explosive device after the aircraft landed in Detroit, Michigan. That is why intelligence has to be on the ball and ahead of everybody else. Besides, adding names to a list is one thing and quickly determining if the individual presents a risk, and taking the appropriate measures to deny him/her boarding is another. Such individuals must be stopped before they even reach the airport from which they plan to depart.

Direct threats though are not the only threats to civil aviation. There are a number of indirect threats resulting from air travel practices that should also be taken into consideration, namely:

Threat-transfer resulting from airline code-sharing arrangements

Code-sharing arrangements linking national carriers with foreign air carriers may present a source of threat to the security of aviation resulting from passengers or cargo connecting to a national carrier. At most airports today, in-transit passengers have to go through manual and x-ray security checks. Some countries require any passenger, in-transit or not to submit his/her identity particulars before starting their trip. These practices have diminished the likelihood of threats resulting from airline code-sharing arrangements, but will not eliminate them completely. In the case of flight bookings close to departure time, the chances of missing the potential terrorist during the physical security inspection process become elevated.

Since certain foreign carriers may pose a potential threat to national security, a mechanism must be put in place whereby intelligence and security agencies receive early notification of national air carrier's intention to enter into a code-sharing arrangement with a foreign carrier. This should allow these agencies enough time to consult with allies and partners in the security and intelligence community and produce a timely intelligence Threat Assessment before the code-sharing arrangement is approved by the civil aviation authorities.

Threats related to bilateral agreements

Whenever a new bilateral agreement is being negotiated between two governments, or when foreign carriers request a Foreign Airline Operating Certificate (FAOC) to serve national destinations, it is imperative that the information be relayed to the appropriate intelligence and law enforcement agencies early in the game in order for them to prepare an intelligence assessment regarding potential threats, both resulting from criminal activity as well as terrorist activity.

This on-site security inspection in the country of origin where the operating base is located would be in line with the safety inspections rendered periodically to foreign airlines, airports and ports to ensure their adherence to international safety and labour standards, and proper implementation of workplace safety regulations.

Transferred threats

There has been previous reporting on certain airlines and maritime shipping lines representing a risk in terms of transferred-threat. The reason being that either the airline, or the shipping company is known, or widely suspected of being used by narcotics traffickers, or people smugglers, or is accessible to terrorist elements, or is controlled by organized crime figures. Again, information about the airline, the shipping company and even a specific ship, must be relayed to the appropriate intelligence and law enforcement agencies as soon as possible for the same purpose.

The aviation industry fights back

The case of threats to civil aviation has been going on since the 1960s, even though it has abated thanks to radical security measures at ports and airports. A wide array of local, regional and international protective and preventive measures has been taken since. Some proved decisively successful, others not as much, or not at all. Since this book is intended for professionals, all these physical security measures at ports, airports and aboard aircraft and ships are well known to them. Hence we find it repetitive to list them yet again. Over the years more and more cooperative intelligence has helped to improve the situation, especially when intelligence had the opportunity to do its job properly. In this book we argue for yet more direct involvement by all the players concerned, both in government and the industry, working together in the context of intelligence as permanent partners, not on an *ad hoc* or selective basis. We are all in it. The following chapters will show us how to do that.

SOURCES OF THREAT TO THE MARITIME INDUSTRY

The UN Office on Drugs and Crime (UNODC), issued a report on April 8, 2010 in which it "warned that of the more than 440 million maritime containers that move around the globe each year, accounting for 90 per cent of international trade, only 2 per cent are inspected, creating opportunities for crime syndicates and terrorists to use them, a gap UNODC and the World Customs Organization (WCO) are trying to fill with the Container Control Programme."[130]

One should be thankful that threats against ships and the maritime industry have been relatively limited, but then there are ample examples that point to a dramatic increase. Aside from the attack on the French tanker Limbaugh, everybody in the business remembers the attack on the USS Cole, both of which took place in the Arabian Sea. One cannot of course ignore the wave of piracy that has been going on for many years in the South China Sea, the Straits of Malacca;

---

[130] UNODC Annual Report 2010, p.30.

and the now almost daily attacks by Somali pirates in the Gulf of Aden, around the Horn of Africa, in the Indian Ocean, and along the southern coasts of Yemen all the way to Oman.

A new spate of violent ship hijackings in the Gulf of Guinée on the Atlantic side of the African continent could turn the region into a new piracy hotspot. "In 2011, the region has registered a substantial increase in hijackings with 18 ships attacked since March in an area where no incidents were reported in 2010. The first six months of 2011 saw 266 piracy attacks globally, compared with 196 over the same period in 2010. However, it is also noted that hijackers were seeing a slightly lower success rate in taking over ships, due to the vigilance of international anti-piracy naval forces operating in the Gulf of Aden."[131]

If certain threats to the maritime industry have not materialized yet, it does not mean that they are unlikely to happen. This calls for preventive and protective action the same way such measures are taken by the aviation industry. Keeping in mind of course that more radical measures are called for on the high-seas in the case of maritime transport. What kinds of threats endanger the maritime industry? There are several of the

1. Direct threats from terrorists
2. Threat transfer resulting from shady ownership, operating and chartering arrangements, and fly-by-night ports of registry
3. Threat transfer resulting from shipping companies known to be a threat risk
4. Threat transfer resulting from berthing or transferring cargo at ports where security standards are questionable
5. Threat transfer resulting from ships that disappear while on a scheduled course at sea, and suddenly reappear in a totally different zone without prior notification
6. Threats from pirates to national and international waterways.

Threats to ships

While access to ships and harbours is pretty much controlled nowadays, the size of the operation in so many ports is so large and involves so many players and logistical operations that it is pretty difficult to control every corner of it. Yet, many of the major ports have succeeded in keeping a handle on security in their ports. Even though it is still possible to intercept and board a ship on the high seas, this becomes impossible when it comes to aircraft in flight. Even if protection against potential terrorism in a maritime environment is nowadays much more under control, protection against smuggling, especially drug smuggling, still calls for a lot of work and interagency cooperation.

---

[131] "West Africa becoming piracy hotspot", South African Press Association and Agence France Presse, September 17, 2011.

Countering threats to ships, ports and port facilities from an intelligence perspective is not different from that in an aviation environment; the potential terrorist threats to ships could be any of the following, or a combination thereof:

1. Hijacking or seizure of the ship, and/or of persons on board
2. Tampering with cargo, baggage, ship's stores, essential equipment or systems (including security or communications systems)
3. Unauthorized access to the ship including presence of stowaways
4. Smuggling weapons, explosives, or equipment, including chemical, biological or radioactive materials, including undetected trans-shipments from one ship to another
5. Use of the ship to carry those intending to cause a security incident and their equipment. (Such as motherships in attacks by pirates)
6. Use of the ship itself as a weapon, or as a means to cause damage or destruction
7. Attacks from seaward whilst at berth or at anchor
8. Attacks whilst at sea.

So far threats to ships have concentrated around cargo ships and tankers, or the occasional yacht. Threats to cruise ships on the other hand have not happened since the hijacking of the cruise vessel Achille Lauro in 1985 by Palestinians while sailing from Alexandria to Port Said. The most recent attempt has been the chase given in February 2008 by Somali pirates to the m/s Nautica, which was carrying over a thousand passengers and crew in the Gulf of Aden. In 2005 pirates opened fire on the m/v Seabourn Spirit about one hundred miles off the Somali coast. In this case as in that of the m/s Nautica, the faster cruise ships managed to escape. Hijacking a cruise ship with several hundred passengers or more and almost the same number of crew poses a real logistical dilemma for would-be hijackers. One can imagine the nightmare it would create regarding the safety of those on board, but also the leverage it could offer the hijackers in terms of exorbitant ransoms.

Threats to ports and port facilities

Access to major ports today is pretty difficult, and an attack on port facilities may not produce the same "wow" effect as attacks against an airport or air terminal. But it could result in major destruction, disruption of loading and offloading operations, and potential loss of life if it were to happen. Terrorist threats to ports and port facilities could include the following targets:

1. Damage to, or destruction of the port or a vessel alongside, by explosive devices, arson, sabotage, suicide bombing or vandalism
2. Hijacking or seizure of port, vessel alongside, service vessels or of persons on board
3. Tampering with cargo, baggage, vessel's stores, essential port equipment or systems (including security or communications systems)

4. Unauthorized access to the port including presence of stowaways on board a vessel alongside
5. Smuggling weapons, explosives, or equipment, including chemical, biological or radioactive materials
6. Use of a vessel alongside as a weapon or as a means to cause damage or destruction
7. Blockage of port entrances, access to canal locks, approaches to the port etc.

Threats to international straits and waterways

Many countries have, or share, a substantial network of inland waterways, large lakes, international waterways such as the Suez Canal in Egypt, the Bosphorus in Turkey, the Isthmus of Corinth in Greece, the straits of Gibraltar between Morocco and Spain, the straits of Bab El Mandeb between Yemen and the African coast, the straits of Hormuz between Oman and Iran, the Panama Canal, the St. Lawrence Seaway in North America, or a combination of several maritime domains. A number of such facilities have one or several locks of various sizes, others do not. Depending on their layout, geographical location, usage, internal political stability or lack thereof, presence or absence of adequate security and monitoring equipment, all these characteristics must be taken into consideration when planning the security outlay of these mega utilities, and of course the required intelligence.

The importance of these specific regional and geographic characteristics in planning the security of ports and port facilities is highlighted in a report on "Port Security in the Caribbean Basin" tabled by the US Government Accountability Office (GAO) in 2007. Parts of this report are summarised below to provide a live example.

"To determine the threats and security concerns in the Caribbean Basin related to port security, GAO representatives interviewed officials from U.S. federal agencies, international organizations and associations and various stakeholders involved in port security in the region. To determine the actions taken by Caribbean Basin countries to implement international port security requirements, i.e. the ISPS Code, and the challenges they face, GAO representatives visited several Caribbean nations and reviewed information provided by agencies and organizations working in the region. To determine the activities under way by U.S. government agencies to enhance port security in the Caribbean Basin, GAO representatives met with agency officials and reviewed pertinent documents. Finally, to identify the potential economic impacts of port security in the Caribbean Basin, GAO representatives met with officials from the countries visited, as well as from U.S. agencies and international organizations, and reviewed various analyses by a government agency (the agency is not identified, but it could be the CIA or the FBI), and nongovernmental researchers."

Referring to intelligence, the GAO report points out that "while intelligence sources report that no specific, credible terrorist threats to maritime security exist in the Caribbean Basin, the officials GAO spoke to indicate that there are a number of security concerns that could affect port security in the region. Caribbean ports contain a variety of facilities such as cargo facilities, cruise ship terminals, and facilities that handle petroleum products and liquefied natural gas. Additionally, several Caribbean ports are among the top cruise ship destinations in the world. Given the volume and value of this maritime trade, the facilities and infrastructure of the maritime transportation system may be attractive targets for a terrorist attack." The GAO report reveals that its "prior work on maritime security issues has revealed that the three most likely modes of attack in the port environment are a suicide attack using an explosive-laden vehicle or vessel, a standoff attack using small arms or rockets, and the traditional armed assault."

"Beyond the types of facilities and modes of attack to be considered, official GAO representatives identified a number of overarching security concerns that relate to the Caribbean Basin as a whole. Among these concerns are: (1) the level of corruption that exists in some Caribbean nations to undermine the rule of law in these countries, (2) organized gang activity occurring in proximity to or within port facilities, and (3) the geographic proximity of many Caribbean countries, which has made them transit countries for cocaine and heroin destined for U.S. markets. Other security concerns in the Caribbean Basin mentioned by U.S. agency officials include stowaways, illegal migration, and the growing influence of Islamic radical groups and other foreign terrorist organizations."

Each of the departments involved in security in general provided GAO with additional information to be added to the report. The Department of Homeland Security for instance identified drug smuggling, information about cargo movement and integrity. The Department of State made several technical comments, but underlined the fact that "compliance with the International Ship and Port Facility Security Code (ISPS) does not necessarily mean that a port is secure from a terrorist attack. The State Department noted that it and its contractors have witnessed open gates, poor screening of vehicles, and inadequate physical protections at ports with cruise line activity. The State Department stated that these deficiencies, coupled with poorly trained security personnel, can make cruise line terminals and cruise ships vulnerable to attack."[132]

THE CASE OF SOMALI PIRACY ALONG THE HORN OF AFRICA AND THE GULF OF ADEN

Piracy attacks which have plagued the Horn of Africa since the early 1990s have increased dramatically and threaten one of the world's most important

---

[132] GAO – "Maritime Security in the Caribbean", Washington, DC June 29, 2007.

trade routes; as almost one third of the world's containerized cargo and nearly half of the world's bulk cargo is carried through the Gulf of Aden from the Indian Ocean en route for the Red Sea and the Suez Canal to markets in Europe and the Mediterranean and vice-versa. (See Appendix 6 for more details on the origins of piracy around the Somali Coast). The phenomenon of piracy in modern times is not a monopoly of the Somalis only as mentioned earlier in this chapter. The waters of the Straits of Malacca between Indonesia, Malaysia and Singapore have constantly been the theatre of piracy attacks for many years well before the contagion spread to the East African coasts.

The interception of foreign ships on the high seas by Somali pirates and others is still going on with increased impunity. The original reason having been partially the continuing practice of unregulated fishing, and dumping of toxic waste in the disputed areas by foreign vessels, but also because the governments of these intruders, several of them involved in the civil war going on in Somalia, were not willing to consider a more muscled approach to the problem under the pretext of international law constraints.

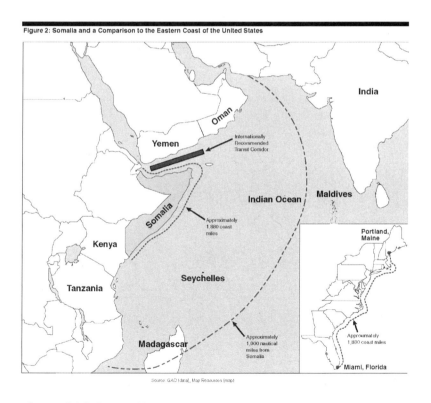

Figure 2: Somalia and a Comparison to the Eastern Coast of the United States

Source: GAO (data), Map Resources (map)

Source: GAO Counter Piracy Report

The profit-making business of Somali pirates

The Dutch Maasmond Maritime Shipping News Clippings reported from Amsterdam on March 17, 2011 that "the International Chamber of Shipping (ICS) said oceangoing pirates inflicted between $7 billion (U.S.) and $12-billion in damage on the global economy in 2010.

By time of publishing, "ransom payments have shot up over the last five years and now average around $5.4 million per ship, from around $150,000 to $300,000 previously, according to Dieter Berg, head of the maritime division at reinsurer Munich Re. By using bigger "mother ships" equipped with more sophisticated equipment pirates have been able to carry out an increasing number of attacks and range further away from the immediate Somali coastline."[133] "Mr. Shri S. Hajara, Chairman and Managing Director of the Shipping Corporation of India, said that he felt that the actual (overall) payment would amount to about $15 million, considering the payments made to mediators too."[134]

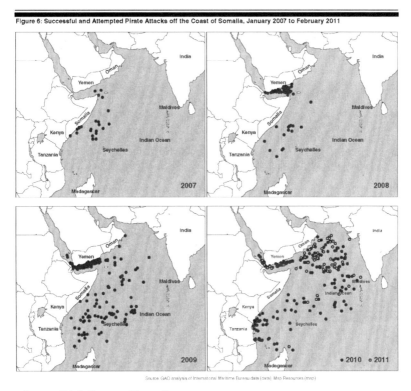

Figure 6: Successful and Attempted Pirate Attacks off the Coast of Somalia, January 2007 to February 2011

Source: GAO Counter Piracy Report

---

[133] "Piracy becoming Criminal Enterprise", Source: Maasmond Maritime Shipping News Clippings, March 15, 2011.
[134] "Legal regime to help fight piracy sought", The Hindu, February 25, 2011.

In a widely distributed statement, S. Venkiteswaran, Senior International Maritime Advocate said "our firm is experienced in doing negotiations (but) now it's a big racket. In this business there are a lot of players who make money, big money. Along with private security agencies who claim to be experts in delivering ransom and freeing ships, insurance companies are also charging millions for piracy policies from ship owners. India has more at stake because a substantial number of seafarers around the world, even on foreign-flagged ships are Indian. Piracy is already costing the global economy several billion US dollars annually, and if not nipped in the bud now, it will turn into a global monster. "I don't think it is controlled in Somalia or any pirate infested area, the control centre could be somewhere else. Once the ransom is received, fifty per cent of it goes to the financiers; thirty per cent goes to the commander of the mother ship and his crew and the attack squad commander. Ten per cent of the ransom is given to elders and ten per cent to Security guards."[135]

In the middle of all this, the Somali government "jailed an American, three Britons and two Kenyans for illegally bringing $3.6 million in cash into the country, allegedly to pay ransoms for two ships seized by pirates, the Journal of Commerce reports. The six men were arrested on May 24, 2011 shortly after they landed in a small plane at Mogadishu airport and were waiting to transfer the cash to another aircraft that was to fly it to another part of the war-torn African country. The two men charged with carrying the cash received 15-year sentences and were fined $15,000 each, and the other four, including the pilot, got four years and fines of $10,000. Three of the defendants, including the pilot, were employees of a Nairobi, Kenya-based security firm. This is the first time westerners have been sentenced for breaking this law."[136]

"IBN reveals that excess insurance costs due to Somali piracy at up to $3.2 billion per year, while re-routing "slow and low" ships costs upwards of $3 billion. Cargoes stolen and diverted from Kenya and Yemen, (or) Suez Canal fees lost by Egypt as vessels reroute, (as well as) lost fishing and tourism to Mauritius, the Maldives and Seychelles add up to $1.25 billion a year. The report also describes how the business of piracy is conducted in Somalia. "Elders in the pirates' family tree form a de-facto government. Their role is hostage negotiations and liaison with the outside world. Businessmen and international financers provide the capital for their operations. The Commanders marshal resources, recruit subordinates, and organize operations. They decide on the target based on the type of ship and cargo, owner and port of origin. All this information is often acquired from ports. A 30-member security squad protects the commander and ferries supplies to the attackers. At least a 24-member attack squad comprising of fishermen and others go out on mother ships for hijacking other ships.

---

[135] "The profit making business of Somali pirates", Maasmond Maritime Shipping News Clippings - Rotterdam: IBN April 20, 2011.
[136] "Six foreigners jailed in Somalia over pirate ransom" - PortNews June 22, 2011.

"The pirates are mere foot soldiers of a thriving multi-million dollar piracy industry in Somalia. And this industry has well-entrenched international connections too. Somali pirates are not just brute buccaneers, but part of a thriving business model with international connections."[137]

Somali pirate attacks hit record level

"Attacks on shipping by increasingly sophisticated Somali pirates in the Gulf of Aden and the Indian Ocean reached record levels in the first nine months of the year, the International Maritime Bureau says. Indian ship owners, who have been increasingly hit as pirates have extended their raids up to 1,500 nautical miles east of the gulf, deep into the Indian Ocean, say the piracy scourge is costing the global shipping industry more than $9 billion a year. U.S. risk management company Aon reports there has been a 267 percent year-on-year increase in attacks in the Arabian Sea.

Figure 5: Total Hostages Captured by Somali Pirates, 2007 to 2010

Source: GAO analysis of International Maritime Bureau data

Source: GAO Counter Piracy Report

"IMB Director Pottengal Mukundan says there were 352 attacks on shipping worldwide in the January-September period; up from 289 in the first nine months of 2010. "But what's significant," he said, "is that the number of hijackings is down." Pirates have only seized 24 ships so far in 2011, compared to 35 in the equivalent period last year. This has been attributed to more vigorous action by

---

[137] "The profit making business of Somali pirates", IBN April 20, 2011.

naval forces -- and more ships carrying armed guards, a practice once considered too provocative to be effective. IMB credits this reduction in hijackings to policing and interventions by international naval forces, correct application of the industry's latest Best Management Practice – including the careful consideration of the crews' retreat to the ship's 'citadel' – and other onboard security measures. "Somali pirates are finding it harder to hijack ships and get the ransom they ask for.

"Various naval forces are deployed off Somalia and across the Indian Ocean. These include the European Union's Operation Atalanta, NATO's Operation Ocean Shield and the U.S.-led Combined Task Force-151, as well as independent flotillas from countries such as China, Iran, India and Russia."[138]

The NATO Shipping Centre (NSC) is the link between NATO military forces and the merchant shipping community. Manned by uniformed NATO members, the NSC is the primary permanent point of contact in NATO for the shipping community. The NSC is the primary advisor to merchant shipping regarding potential risks and possible interference with maritime operations. In addition to its current counter-piracy mission, the NSC supports NATO, national and multinational Naval Cooperation and Guidance for Shipping (NCAGS) operations and exercises. The NSC is part of the Allied Maritime Command Headquarters Northwood in the UK. The NSC is currently engaged in two NATO operations: Ocean Shield and Active Endeavour.

Operation Ocean Shield is NATO's counter-piracy operation in the Arabian Sea, the Gulf of Aden and the Somali Basin. The NSC collaborates with the United Kingdom Maritime Trade Operation (UKMTO) in Dubai and with the European Union's Maritime Security Centre - Horn of Africa in order to track merchant vessels as they transit these perilous waters. Beyond tracking ships and responding to pirate attacks, including the warning of individual ships that may be in the vicinity of an attack, the NSC is a proponent of the recommended self-protective measures found in BMP4 and works to encourage all merchant vessels transiting the operation area to employ the Best Management practices that have been recommended by the BMP4 signatories. The NSC provides current information on piracy to mariners through its website including current alerts on pirate attacks and the location of Pirate Action Groups, the disposition of known pirated vessels (motherships), and alert map, weekly situation updates and much more.

"While such forces have been extremely active in counter-piracy efforts, the area of ocean to be patrolled, more than 1 million square kilometers, makes it an impossible task to monitor all shipping and prevent all possible attacks," the International Institute for Strategic Studies, a London think tank, observed in an analysis. "As a result, the shipping industry is turning to private security firms to fill the gap." France and Spain allow armed detachments on their vessels. British-

---

[138] Maasmond Shipping News Clippings, Rotterdam, November 12, 2011.

flagged ships have also been allowed to carry armed guards against pirates. Up to 200 British merchant vessels regularly sail through the waters where the pirates lurk. The British say armed guards - previously discouraged by London - would only be permitted to operate while passing through dangerous waters.

"The change in British thinking on this issue reflects a wider shift by governments, shipping companies and maritime organizations, including seamen's unions, toward providing armed guards on their flag vessels. When the piracy crisis in the Gulf of Aden emerged five years ago, with sea bandits from lawless, strife-torn Somalia striking largely in coastal waters in speedboats using rocket-propelled grenades, the general consensus was that armed guards would risk worsening the problem. But now the stakes are infinitely higher. The pirates, organized mainly along clan lines, have evolved into highly sophisticated groups. They use "mother ships," usually hijacked modern fishing trawlers, to penetrate deeper into the Indian Ocean for extended voyages and capable of launching multiple attacks. There are believed to be 7-10 gangs financed by moneymen in the Persian Gulf with agents in London's shipping insurance fraternity who identify targets with the most valuable cargoes for ransom. These costs are then passed on to consumers."[139]

The maritime industry reacts

The pirates have become well organized, use modern technology and range ever further from shore in their search for likely targets. For many ship-owners and operators transporting valuable cargoes, paying a ransom has been the easiest, and cheapest, option. The amazing part is that "ransom payments are legal under British law, as they are covered by insurance. The logic being, that stopping ransom payments would lead to hostages being killed in an attempt to extract payment. Without taking concerted action to curb the rapidly escalating ransoms, the piracy business will inevitably become more sophisticated, more violent and more costly to the shipping industry and the global economy."[140]

According to Howard Snaith, maritime director with INTERTANKO, whose members own the majority of the world's tanker fleet, said that the pirates "have the whole of the Indian Ocean pretty much pinned down." The fight against piracy has been hampered by legal ambiguities over the appropriate venue to prosecute captured suspects. A UN envoy proposed special courts to be set up rapidly in the Somali enclaves of Somaliland and Puntland, and in Tanzania, to try captured pirates. Pirates have also been using torture to force crew members to operate captured mother ships."[141]

---

[139] Ibid., Maasmond Shipping News Clippings, Rotterdam, November 12, 2011.

[140] "Somali pirate ransoms skirt U.S. directives", Maasmond Shipping News Clippings, Rotterdam, August 10, 2011.

[141] "Somali piracy threat worsening by the week", Maasmond Shipping News Clippings, Rotterdam, February 24, 2011.

"The International Transport Workers' Federation (ITF) "signalled its revulsion at the increasingly widespread and brutal piracy epidemic and said it is moving closer to having to advise seafarers to consider avoiding working in all the affected areas – including the Indian Ocean. The global union federation, which numbers 201 maritime trade unions representing 720,000 seafarers worldwide, took the step after a week-long consultation sparked by the increasing number and range of Somali pirate attacks, and by their now routine use of extreme violence and death threats against the mariners they are holding hostage.

"ITF seafarers' section chair Dave Heindel commented: "The world has lost control of piracy. Yet there is a way that control can be regained: by actively going after pirates, stopping them and prosecuting them. Not this ludicrous situation of taking away their guns and setting them free to strike again. The only real deterrent will be the capture and punishment of these criminals under law."[142]

The Somali Foreign Minister said during a keynote speech at a counter-piracy conference in Dubai in mid-April 2011 that "the victims in Somalia suffer a double tragedy the rest of the world does not, namely their food, medicines and fuel, which have to be delivered with armed naval escort, and they pay much higher prices for these basic necessities than the rest of the world when small ships and dhows can get through."[143].

STOPPING SOMALI PIRACY

The maritime industry fights back

In most cases where pirate boats or skiffs attack a commercial vessel, all the ship crew could do in self defence is to follow the "Best Management Practices" (BMP) recommended by the IMO[144] with support from various maritime industry organizations. They could also disable the ship's engines, then muster and hide in difficult to find locations aboard their ship. They were initially encouraged to hose the pirates with water from the deck, which is a pretty dangerous thing to do because the pirates are armed with machine guns and rifle propelled grenades. Many ships still rely on a combination of water hoses and long range acoustic devices, which so far did not prove to be effective. Keeping armed guards on board, mostly mercenaries, former security or disguised military personnel has not proven to be decisive, though it proved to be occasionally effective in repelling the pirates.

---

[142] "Seafarer Boycott of piracy areas now possible", ITF Press Release, February 25, 2011
[143] "Maersk Line's piracy costs to double", GulfNews, April 25, 2011.
[144] IMO Best Management Practices (BMP4), August 2011

In the case of piracy in and around the Gulf of Aden and other sea lanes around the Horn of Africa and in the Indian Ocean, several countries, independently, through the Djibouti Code member countries, through the NATO alliance, or through the European Union's Naval Force Counter-piracy Operation (EUNAVFOR)-Operation Atalanta, have sent their fleets and/or their air force to combat this rather resurrected threat of yesteryears to lives and to international shipping. The term 'combat' may seem inadequate since all they are doing is simply manage a situation they are unable, or unwilling to put an end to.

In the few instances where the pirates were caught by these navies criss-crossing that area, the pirates were first released and their weapons seized. Only at a later stage were they apprehended and taken to the ship's country for trial. The reason given for releasing the pirates is that international regulations prohibit keeping them under arrest. It is quite ironic that we are bombing the hell out of everybody else - where there is, or could be oil for instance. However, when it comes to basically wretched but dangerous pirates we abide by the laws of peace.

Because of the kneejerk reaction to piracy since day one, the latter have gained confidence in their ability to challenge all the military and naval forces in the region. The hijacking of a merchant vessel while at anchor off the port of Salalah, Oman on August 20, 2011 has brought to light a disturbing trend wherein pirates with particular chutzpah are now not only attacking ships sailing in the high seas but entering areas near the ports to carry out their operations.[145] The chutzpah and disregard for all the international show of force did not stop there though. On 12 January 2012, having just completed the escort of a World Food Programme ship carrying food-aid into Somalia, and while operating close to the Somali port of Mogadishu, the EU NAVFOR Flagship, the ESPS PATINO was fired upon with light calibre weapons by pirates who also tried to board the PATINO. The ship's force-protection team returned fire and eventually subdued the attackers.

Riad Kahwaji, founder and CEO of the Institute for Near East and Gulf Military Analysis based in Dubai, said tens of millions of dollars in ransoms may be helping Somali pirates create a sophisticated intelligence network that is helping them expand their reach.

"To go this close to the shore of Oman when there are at least two task forces, this shows boldness and confidence," Kahwaji told Gulf News. "Obviously, there are people on shore providing the pirates with intelligence." A superior underground information pipeline would explain why "dozens of destroyers, corvettes and patrols in the Gulf of Aden and seas off Oman are not able to pick them up," he said. "There is serious intelligence failure on behalf of the alliance forces." Paid informants on shore, Kahwaji speculated, are feeding the pirate network with real-time data detailing the manifests of ships, departure times and even the intended destinations of commercial vessels.

---

[145] "Hijack of vessel berthed at Salalah", DNA India August 24, 2011 & ECOP Maritime August 25, 2011.

EU NAVFOR
PRESS RELEASE

Pirate attack on the EU NAVFOR Flagship

At first light on 12 January 2012, having just completed the escort of a World Food Programme ship carrying food-aid into Somalia and while operating close to the Somali port of Mogadishu, the EU NAVFOR Flagship, the ESPS PATINO, was approached by one skiff with a group of suspected pirates onboard.

The suspected pirates opened fire with light calibre weapons and tried to board the PATINO. The ship's force-protection team returned fire in self-defense and the ship's helicopter was launched.

The skiff broke off the attack and the men surrendered to the helicopter after throwing their weapons, ladder and fuel barrels overboard.

Five of the six men who were in the skiff had received injuries, two of which required medical treatment onboard the SPS PATINO.

Investigations are ongoing to check whether the suspect pirates' report that a seventh man who had been in the skiff and who was lost overboard during the attack are correct.

EU NAVFOR Somalia
EU NAVFOR Somalia - Operation ATALANTA's main tasks are to escort merchant vessels carrying humanitarian aid of the 'World Food Program' (WFP) and vessels of 'African Union Mission in Somalia' (AMISOM), and to protect vulnerable ships in the Gulf of Aden and Indian Ocean and to deter and disrupt piracy. EU NAVFOR also monitors fishing activity off the coast of Somalia.

For any further questions, do not hesitate to get in contact with us.

Best regards,

European Union Naval Force Somalia
Operation Atalanta Public Affairs Office

Tel: +44 (0) 1923 9 58611
Mob: +44 (0) 7762 7 84746
Fax: +44 (0) 1923 9 58608

For official comments on the above please contact EU NAVFOR Spokesperson: Harrie Harrison, Commander RN
Tel: +44 (0) 1923 958693 Mob: +44 (0) 7540 417378

Internet: http://www.eunavfor.eu

E-Mail: media@eunavfor.eu

You are receiving this email because you are opted-in to receive updates from the European Union Naval Force in Somalia - Operation Atalanta. If you do not wish to receive these emails, you can unsubscribe now.

Pirates, he said, "are getting a lot of intelligence to help them do what they want. There is enough money to build a sophisticated system of control." To defeat the pirates, Kahwaji said authorities need to strike the central nervous system of the pirates. "You have to have counter-intelligence, a serious joint effort," he said. "They need to track the chain of intelligence and see how it is moving, then take it out."[146]

The idea of having 'intelligence' tuning in against the Somalis does not seem to have taken sufficient root yet, though, admittedly, the situation in Somalia is such that no amount of technical intercepts and signals intelligence managed from remote locations could be that helpful at this stage.

Since the Somalia and Gulf of Aden piracy situation manifested itself, several new important players, along with their military intelligence capabilities were also set up to provide specific maritime counter-piracy intelligence. Whether this intelligence is shared with each country's national intelligence agency is not clear. The assumption is that they should, and the intelligence agency will then share the information with the Department of Transport, which in turn will use the intelligence to sensitize the maritime industry stakeholders as recommended in previous chapters.

---

[146] "Piracy wave set to hit households in the GCC", Gulf News, Dubai, September 2, 2011.

In the words of Admiral Mark Fitzgerald, commander of U.S. naval forces in Europe and Africa "the entire Indian Ocean is becoming a problem of piracy," he told a forum at the International Institute for Strategic Studies in London. "We can't put ships out everywhere and just start randomly looking. So we really need intelligence based operations to go after that kind of threat."[147]

The Security Council keeps renewing the "authorization for States and regional organizations fighting piracy off the Somali coast to enter the strife-torn country's territorial waters and undertake all necessary measures that are appropriate in Somalia, provided they cooperate with the Somali Transitional Federal Government"[148]. The resolution effectively contradicts itself since, not only there is no government in Somalia, whatever is designated as 'government' is partially formed by those who manage the activities of the pirates and benefit from it.

While Somali or South China Sea piracy on the high-seas does not fall under the definition of terrorism, combating piracy effectively involves a multi-pronged solution that includes applying the military interdiction option, the protection option, the prevention option, as well as the problem-solving option all being applied concurrently.

For some reason, governments and diplomats seem to operate at a different speed from the industry. Instead of facing the situation of piracy heads-on, they held an anti-piracy conference that called for another anti-piracy conference! "One of few new proposals to emerge from the anti-piracy conference held in Dubai in April 2011....was to hold another anti-piracy conference, this time under the auspices of the United Nations.

Following the Dubai conference, Casey Christie published an article under the title "It's Time to Strike Hard at Pirates Who Threaten Seafarers' Lives", which was published by "Concept Tactical Worldwide" on April 28, 2011. The writer said: "The main focus of the event was on the economic impact piracy is having on world trade. This is, of course, significant but in my opinion far less important than the lives of the men and woman on board the vessels being targeted. Why is it that when a plane is hijacked no one talks about money lost yet when an oil tanker is taken it's all about the value of the cargo? Perhaps it is because of the picture one creates when the words oil and tanker are put together. You would be forgiven for just seeing in your mind's eye a colossal ship with millions of dollars of oil on board. However we must not forget that there are human beings on that oil tanker and they are a lot more precious than any amount of oil."[149]

Instead of seriously and decisively passing on the attack, the International Maritime Organization (IMO) issued a Press Release in May 2011 announcing "a Memorandum of Understanding (MOU) to allow the IMO fund the building of a

[147] Admiral Mark Fitzgerald, IIS March 25, 2010.

[148] UN Security Council Resolution SC/10092, November 23, 2010.

[149] Maritime Executive, "It's Time to Strike Hard at Pirates Who Threaten Seafarers' Lives", April 27, 2011.

regional training centre in Djibouti, to promote the implementation of the Code of Conduct concerning the Repression of Piracy and Armed Robbery against Ships in the Western Indian Ocean and the Gulf of Aden (Djibouti Code of Conduct). The objective being to formulate a regional coordination process for maritime security training and to endorse the regional training centre and to establish the mission and objectives of the regional training centre in Djibouti; the coordination process for regional maritime training; and the process for the programming of regional training.[150]

Africa and the Africans are probably subject to more training programs than anybody else. The problem is not the lack of skilled people. The real problem is that the applicability of what they learn is not ensured, and the whole project becomes a make work scheme that will also put a good deal of money in the pockets of some high placed individuals in the region. Exactly like the Euro-Mediterranean Dialogue between members of the European Union and the heads of state in the southern Mediterranean. Ask the former presidents of Egypt and Tunisia where had the money they received from the Europeans gone.

On May 26, 2011 the Danish daily Copenhagen Post published an article about a "new deal with the Seychelles island nation to help with the prosecution of pirates. Denmark, it was reported, "has reached an agreement with the Republic of Seychelles that the island nation will accept, jail and prosecute pirates who are captured. "Convicted pirates" it added "will thereafter be incarcerated in either of Somalia's autonomous regions, Somaliland or Puntland. The agreement, which was announced by the foreign minister and defense minister, is described as being "the latest development in Denmark's strategy to help fight piracy in the Somali basin and off the east coast of Africa. Until recently, pirates caught were set free on land due to the lack of an international procedure for their prosecution. According to the Danish Minister of Foreign Affairs, the arrangement with the Seychelles ensures that "it will be possible to prosecute pirates in the region they come from instead of dragging them by the dozen back to Denmark to prosecute them there."

The Minister underlined the fact that "Denmark should not carry the burden alone, but should naturally share it with a group of other NATO countries." But then he added something interesting when he said that "the government is considering whether to deploy surveillance airplanes to search the seas and whether to give NATO Danish mandate to precision-bomb land-based pirate camps in Africa."[151] This last revelation, still-born as it is, was probably the first time an official has talked about a substantive part of the overall solution to the problems of piracy along the Somali coast, and to the real problems that contributed to it within Somalia itself.

---

[150] International Maritime Organization (IMO) Opens Djibouti Centre, Press release May 31, 2011.
[151] "Seychelles to take pirates", Quoted by permission from The Copenhagen Post, May 26, 2011.

Somali Pirates surrendering
Source: European Naval Force Somalia - Operation Atalanta – By permission

On June 15, 2011 Assistant Secretary Andrew Shapiro with the U.S. Department of State, announced before the House Committee on Foreign Affairs' Sub-Committee on Terrorism, Nonproliferation and Trade Hearing on "Confronting Global Piracy" that "combating piracy emanating from a failed state will require concentrated and coordinated assistance to states in the region – including those parts of Somali society with which (it is possible to) work – to build their capacity to deal with the social, legal, economic and operational challenges to effective law enforcement. "Realistically", he said, "there will be no end to piracy at sea until there is some degree of political stability and economic recovery ashore in Somalia, including local governmental authorities with the ability to enforce law and order both on land and at sea. "We believe" he added, that "supporting the re-establishment of stability and adequate governance in Somalia represents the only sustainable long-term solution to piracy."[152]

Andrew Shapiro is correct here, though he is way too late. In 2010 this author wrote not once but twice to two different departments within NATO and other maritime organizations about this situation. The correspondence referred to the comments made by the new NATO Secretary General Anders Fogh Rasmussen about piracy on the high seas, and pointed out that to the general public and to professionals in the field it does not make any sense that pirates of that calibre can defy the whole world and all the navies and military aircraft deployed in the region for so long. Then added that notwithstanding whatever political or international maritime law expediency arguments that have been raised by governments and by NATO or EUNAVFOR, the arguments do not hold water in

---

[152] US Congress Hearing on "Confronting Global Piracy", June 15, 2011.

this particular situation, and are totally meaningless in that part of the world, and rather an indication of indecision and weakness. Besides, they will certainly not solve the problem.

What should have been done from day one

What this author proposed in the correspondence was that "from day one, what should have happened was to place intelligence assets on the ground in Somalia and other key countries, while enforcing a one to ten mile safety zone along the coasts of Somalia for fishermen to do their business. The rest would be a "no-sail zone", similar to the "no-fly zone" created during the Iraq conflict. A warning notice should have been broadcast across Somalia in the various dialects of that country, as well as through a universal Notice to Mariners worldwide.

The notice should have clearly indicated that ANY ship, boat, skiff, or whatever that ventures beyond the safety zone, will be given one warning shot across the bow, and if the vessel does not identify itself satisfactorily and turn back, it will be destroyed and sunk lock-stock-and-barrel, no questions asked. This should have ensured that piracy, as well as illegal fishing and toxic waste dumping in that area would have been stopped immediately right after the first incident. It is not too late to do that, though we cannot proceed with such actions now before we ensure that all hostages held by the pirates have been liberated, and before taking measures to guarantee that no more hostages are taken. There will be battalions of lawyers crying foul because they consider this to be trespassing into their hunting grounds. But why should mariners die, and shippers and shipping lines suffer, just to please some unscrupulous lawyers, and of course the pirates?"[153]

The whole battlefield in Somalia is and remains a police, a military, a coast-guard, and a humanitarian operation all in one. The current, or rather perennial, drought and famine situation in Somalia and the Horn of Africa could have served as an opportunity for certain qualified and capable countries from among the Arab and Muslim world to get involved on land in Somalia, albeit with indirect world support, such as the work undertaken by the United States Africa Command (AFRICOM)[154]. They could thus provide a ground presence both to

---

[153] The author has sailed through the Straits of Hormuz - Arabian Sea - Bab El-Mandeb - Suez Canal corridor several times in both directions between 2009 and 2012 and watched the protective measures taken by the ships' master in preparation for the crossings. He was also informed that naval vessels were monitoring the region from a distance, and, at one time, did indeed see a military helicopter escorting the ship while in a particularly dangerous stretch between Yemen and the coast of Somalia.

[154] The United States Africa Command, also known as U.S. AFRICOM, is one of nine Unified Combatant Commands of the U.S. Department of Defense. It is devoted to achieve a more stable environment where political and economic growth can take place through the delivery and sustainment of effective security cooperation programs that assist African nations build their security capacity to enable them to better provide for their own defence. An important part of this approach is to learn from African partners what is important to them through joint interactive activities, such as conferences, exercises, training, and familiarization programs. All the joint multi-national programs described in this book should provide a very effective means for collective conflict management, without forgetting of course their importance as far as proper intelligence analysis and assessment are concerned. One should not forget that the major premise for success is the proper selection of the local partner(s) and avoid substituting one corrupt regime by another as has often been the case.

protect the humanitarian efforts, and to slowly squeeze the 'bad guys' on the terrain. Unfortunately the Arab and Muslim countries that could do it are neither interested, nor do they have the inclination to get seriously involved. Besides, several of these countries are themselves facing domestic upheavals and civil war-like situations they are unable to handle.

In the meanwhile merchant maritime and ship crew safety and security continue to be threatened, and taxpayers ultimately end up forking out the ransom money in one way or another. That without forgetting the trauma caused to the hostages if they are not summarily killed by their kidnappers, and the heart-breaking anxiety caused to their families.

OVERLOOKED THREATS

Narcotics smuggling: A serious threat that is rarely considered by intelligence agencies

The moment the expression "threat to aviation security" is mentioned, we all automatically think of terrorist threats. We hardly consider threats from organized crime and drug smuggling rings as being "threats" in the same category. A number of major cities in Europe and North America have become a haven for violence and murder as a result of drug trafficking gangs controlling certain neighbourhoods and suburbs. Despite the efforts of law enforcement agencies and the occasional visit by the minister of the interior in a given country, these areas tend to almost be outside the jurisdiction of the government. The financial and logistical support required to fight this criminal activity is not made available at the required level and for the length of time it requires.

Had the governments provided the same resources they dispose of to combat terrorism to fight against organized crime and drug-related crimes, the situation could have been brought under control by now. The good-will on part of the authorities may be there, but it falls very short of the means that the fight calls for. The politicians do not view this threat with the same perspective they have when they think of terrorism despite the fact that there is no comparison between the occasional terrorist attack and the ongoing daily terror in the cities. Besides, politicians think first of votes, and those dangerous neighbourhoods are lost to the candidates anyway. So why bother?

When the word 'drugs' or 'narcotics' is mentioned, people automatically think of criminal activity. It is thus perceived as simply a matter of concern only to customs and the police. Narcotics crosses the line between foreign and domestic intelligence and between intelligence and law enforcement

Organized crime may have access to certain areas of operations within ports and airports, which would facilitate the movement of contraband, people, and logistics related to national security. It is not enough to target something at a location unless you have the intelligence teams to provide guidance for better use of the resources. Surveillance teams are an extremely important requirement; and air assets are a must. But without the ongoing contribution of intelligence, it would be twice as difficult and as expensive to put an end to organized crime activities at both ports and airports. It is also almost always the case that more than one senior government official 'above all suspicion' is implicated. Their main role is to alert the smuggling operators of any police bust. When required, intelligence agencies must have the freedom to initiate surveillance on such suspect individuals without court order, either to confirm their innocence or to have them arrested. Narcotics are as lethal as terrorism if it is not more so.

Sensing the importance of intelligence support to combat transnational organised crime, John William Coyne and Peter Bell noted that "while not a new phenomenon, the rapid expansion of transnational organized crime activities and interests, its increasingly complex structures and ability to maximize opportunity by employing new technologies at a rate impossible for law enforcement to match complicates law enforcement's ability to develop strategies to detect, disrupt, prevent and investigate them.

"In an age where the role of police has morphed from simplistic response and enforcement activities to one of managing human security risk, it is argued that intelligence can be used to reduce the impact of strategic surprise from evolving criminal threats and environmental change. If law enforcement is to improve its outcomes against transnational organized crime, what is clear from the review is that a multifaceted approach is needed that will involve traditional justice responses that are aligned with a strategic response. If this is to occur then law enforcement leaders need more imaginative intelligence products than the extant quantitative intelligence assessments received today especially if they are to develop an entrepreneurial response."[155]

Customs and the police do engage in undercover operations of course and collect intelligence. But by definition intelligence agencies also collect intelligence. Curiously enough the intelligence players within these organizations do not talk to each other much of the time. Or, to be fair, they talk to each other, but they do not work closely together. Customs and police in many countries do not share intelligence related to major drug cartels including those involved in financing terrorism, and if the intelligence service asks for it, chances are that they will not share it with them.

---

[155] John William Coyne and Peter Bell, "The role of strategic intelligence in anticipating transnational organized crime", International Journal of Law, Crime and Justice (May 2011), v.39, number1, pp.60-78.

By the same token, when intelligence agencies, which have access to more sophisticated intelligence collection or interception capabilities in general come across intelligence related to drug smuggling, they hide behind the lackadaisical excuse of "it is not within our mandate" and abstain from sharing it with their counterparts working for customs or the police. The excuse they advance is that they do not want to jeopardise their sources. All of that of course is not just nonsense, but could approach criminal negligence.

If terrorism is bad, seeing a nation's youth injected with drugs is worse than terrible. Yet the resources thrown at countering drug smuggling dwarf in front of the financial resources, as well as human resources and logistics thrown at counter-terrorism and espionage or counter-espionage. But descimating the youth of the country is deemed of secondary importance.

The potential threat that is never considered by intelligence agencies

There is yet another type of threat that is often not referred to as a threat, not just by the general public and people in the industry, but also by intelligence agencies. That threat is the threat coming from individuals who suffer from serious mental disorders who attempt to hijack airplanes or cause serious trouble on-board. These types of potential threats do not make it to the No-Fly List.

Mental health has never been the domain of intelligence services or law enforcement agencies in terms of collecting intelligence or issuing Threat Assessments under that category. Yet, examples abound of mentally-challenged individuals constituting threats to the aviation industry, and incidents have been recorded.

In 2006 a special Threat Assessment centre was created in the UK by the Home Office, the Department of Health and Metropolitan Police Service to jointly assess and manage the risk to politicians, members of the British Royal Family, and other public figures from obsessive individuals to pre-empt incidents in which mentally ill people attack or harass such personalities. The centre, called the "Fixated Threat Assessment Centre", was created in 1982 after a mentally disturbed intruder broke into the Queen's bedroom while she slept at Buckingham Palace, sat on the foot of her bed, asked her for a match to light his cigarette, and held a 10-minute conversation with her. The word 'fixated' in the name of the unit indicates that the main motivational drives behind the stalking of public figures are pathologically intense fixations on individuals or causes, these being obsessive pre-occupations pursued to an abnormally intense degree.[156]

---

[156]"Fixated Threat Assessment Centre", Wikipedia. Also consult Paul E. Mullen, David James, J. Reid Meloy, Michele T. Pathé, Frank R. Farnham, Lulu Preston, Brian Darnley and Jeremy Berman (2009): "The fixated and the pursuit of public figures". Journal of Forensic Psychiatry & Psychology, v.20, Issue 1, 2009, www.informaworld.com/smpp/con tent~db=all~content=a903475075

To help protect passengers and crew, especially aboard aircraft, it should be incumbent on psychiatrists and mental institutions that have solid reason to believe that a given patient could constitute a threat to civil aviation or any other target to act. This means they should be given a direct contact point with a predetermined federal law enforcement agency, such as the FBI or the TSA in the USA, or Scotland Yard in the UK, or the Bundesgrenz Polizei in Germany to which they can report their fears or confirmed suspicions. The reason the qualifier "direct" is used here, is to shorten the communications path, as well as the chances of divulging what is basically protected personal information. These agencies would then communicate the required details to the intelligence agency of the country involved, as well as the airlines' security departments. This should allow at least some vigilance regarding that source of threat. There will certainly be those who will cry about "divulging personal information", though in such cases public safety and security should be paramount

In their book "Best Truth" Berkowitz and Goodman provide an arresting illustration of what can happen when there is no special centre or other office for some problem or group. Their example focused on the then little-known Japanese religious cult, Aum Shinrikyo, which had released homemade nerve gas in a Tokyo subway in 1994, killing twelve and injuring 5,000: "One reason why the Aum went undetected is that it did not fit into the structure of any intelligence organization. No agency had an "Office of Northeast Asian Techno-Terrorist Quasi-Religious Cults." The threat did not match any of the established boxes on the intelligence community's organization chart or production plan for collecting and analyzing information on terrorism, and so it fell through the cracks."[157]

"The intelligence community needs a more effective mechanism for detecting, assessing, and monitoring these unlikely threats. There is no one structure which is always best. Are any of these organizational schemes better than the others? In truth, an argument can be made for almost any organizational structure. It depends on the immediate situation. An organization will usually be organized effectively for one type of problem, less effectively for others. Similarly, centralizing an organization may improve efficiency by eliminating redundancy. Such "excess capacity" is often what allows an organization to meet requirements that are not important now, but which may become important in the future. Or, to use the modern parlance, an organization that has been "right sized" for one assignment may be utterly "wrong sized" for another....No single scheme can meet the rapidly changing demands for information and improvements in the means for producing it."[158] A threat is a threat is a threat, whether it is from terrorists or mentally challenged individuals. The end result is the same.

---

[157] Bruce D. Berkowitz and Allen E. Goodman, "Best Truth", p 87-88. Quoted in in Thomas H. Hammond, "Intelligence Organizations and the Organization of Intelligence", International Journal of Intelligence and CounterIntelligence, v.23 number 4, pp.680-724, 2010.

[158] Ibid., pp.680-724

CHAPTER 7

ORGANIZATION AND MANAGEMENT OF THE TRANSPORTATION SECURITY AND INTELLIGENCE FUNCTION

Transportation security; and especially the important intelligence function within transportation security must be treated and managed as a whole, albeit with distinct modules by mode of transportation under one centralized umbrella. In other words, transportation security must be multi-modal, but managed by one team of security and intelligence professionals at the top, and threat information touching any module must be shared by all the modules among themselves.

There is a certain tendency post 9/11 to concentrate security in one integrated department such as the U.S. Department of Homeland Security, which has created a huge multicultural and multidisciplinary bureaucracy where expertise ends up being diluted, and generalists tend to reign. This is really going overboard with centralization. Certain aspects of security intelligence call for centralization, others will be more efficiently run when they are not totally centralized.

It is argued here that each department should keep control of its own security as it knows its backyard best. But each department's security function will still continue to be involved with everybody else as will be discussed hereafter when we talk about integrated Threat and Risk Assessment Centres. The Department of Transport for instance should be responsible for overall transportation security; the Health Department should be responsible for public health security, etc. Having everybody mixed with everybody else in a huge security pool may be counterproductive at the end, especially once the race starts as to who will reach the top echelons of the department's hierarchy, and who they will pull along with them.

Learning from the experience of others

The U.S. National Counter Terrorism Centre (NCTC) gathers information from across the government, pulls it all together, and assesses terrorist threats facing the United States, then develops a plan for the government to combat them. Quoting from a study financed by the U.S. Congress, the authors report the fact that the NCTC "is struggling because of flawed staffing and internal cultural clashes."

"The 196-page unclassified report entitled "Forging a New Shield' found that the centre's planning arm did not have enough authority to do its main job of coordinating the White House's counterterrorism priorities. "The report is the result of an eight-month study by the 'Project on National Security Reform', a non-partisan research and policy organization in Washington, D.C. The study was financed by Congress and draws on more than 60 interviews with current and former government and congressional officials, including nearly a dozen officials at the NCTC.

"The result", the study concludes, "is a lack of coordination and communication among the agencies that are supposed to take the lead in planning the fight against terrorism, including the CIA and the State Department. The findings come just weeks after the (NCTC) was criticized for missing clear warning signs that a 23-year-old Nigerian man (Umar Farouk Abdulmuttalab - the underwear bomber) was said to be plotting to blow up a Detroit-bound commercial airliner on 25 December 2009.

"NCTC's planning operation is supposed to be staffed by representatives of various agencies, but not all of them sent their best and brightest", the report said. It also cited examples in which "the CIA and the State Department did not even participate in some plans developed by the centre that were later criticized for lacking important insights those agencies could offer. As a result, the centre's planning arm "has been forced to develop national plans without the expertise of some of the most important players," the report determined.

The Study points out that "the NCTC was part of the overhaul of the government after 9/11, including the creation of the Directorate of National Intelligence. Now, years after the attacks, the entire reorganization is coming under scrutiny, raising fundamental questions about who is in charge of the nation's counterterrorism policy and its execution. "The fluid nature of modern terrorism necessitates an agile and integrated response," the report concluded. "Yet (the U.S.) national security system is organized along functional lines (diplomatic, military, intelligence, law enforcement, etc.) with weak and cumbersome integrating mechanisms across these functions."

"The centre noted in a statement that the study found the centre had "made progress" in linking national policy with operations, adding that the report's recommendations "provide an extremely thoughtful and useful critique of how counterterrorism actions are or are not fully synchronized across the U.S. government."

"The report found that the centre's planning arm struggled with "systemic impediments" like overlapping statutes, culture clashes with different agencies, and tensions with two formidable players: the State Department's counterterrorism office and the CIA.

"Under President Obama, the report determined, counterterrorism issues have become more decentralized within the National Security Council's different directorates, leaving the NCTC's planning arm to collect and catalogue policies and operations going on at the CIA, the Pentagon, and the Departments of State and Homeland Security, rather than help shape overall government strategy.

"Since NCTC was created in 2004, its planning arm has been largely focused on a comprehensive review to assign counterterrorism roles and responsibilities to each federal agency, producing then revising a document called the National Implementation Plan. But pointedly, NCTC does not direct any specific operations. Since the completion of that longer-term project, the study's authors found that NCTC's 100-person planning arm had become more involved in immediate counterterrorism issues: working on various classified projects involving Afghanistan, Pakistan, Yemen, and threats to the United States at home.

"The study called on (President) Obama to issue an executive order to define the nation's counterterrorism architecture in order to address some of the problems and improve coordination. It also recommended giving the centre's director a say in the choice of counterterrorism officials at other federal agencies, a step the 9/11 commission had recommended but was not adopted." [159]

This particular experience is cited to help those intent on improving the organization and management of intelligence especially that related to the aviation and maritime sectors, learn the very real obstacles and omissions that will probably face such projects and address them before finalizing their plans.

When the requirement to post air marshals aboard certain flights in the USA or traveling to the USA immediately following the 9/11 terrorist attacks against the World Trade Centre in New York City took place, a civil aviation security intelligence officer working for a Western country pointed out to his superiors some countries such as Jordan and Israel that have been doing that for many years. He suggested that those two countries should be contacted for the purpose of learning from their particular experience. Then it would be possible to adopt or disregard what's inapplicable under his country's laws.

The response he got from the Director of Transportation Security Intelligence was shocking, as he was told: "Now you want to justify a trip for you to this or that country". He got exactly the same reaction when a couple of years later the ISPS Code implementation phases were being undertaken as he suggested that a reconnaissance visit be made to the Suez Canal Authority at Port Said, Egypt as well as the Bosphorus Straits Authority in Istanbul, Turkey; both being critical international waterways in the middle of a turbulent part of the world. Learning from others does not necessarily mean only learning from other Anglo-Saxon

---

[159] Also consult the report produced by the Project on National Security Reform entitled "Toward Integrating Complex National Missions", February 2010 www.pnsr.org/data/files/pnsr_nctc_dsop_report.pdf and the NCTC "2010 Report on Terrorism" http://nctc.gov/witsbanner/docs/2010_report_on_terrorism.pdf

countries. The world is wide and large and every country has its own experiences, especially when they are situated in areas deemed rightly or wrongly to be particularly dangerous.

Management of transportation security intelligence

From a strategic perspective, management of intelligence and threat information pertinent to the various transportation modes requires a dynamic and versatile organizational structure, competent management, flexible methodologies, and proper balancing between operational efficiency, national security but also commercial viability in order to:

1. Manage intelligence sourcing

2. Optimize the dissemination of threat information

3. Establish an implementation mechanism that ensures speed, ongoing accountability and compliance with security requirements

4. Identify classified and unclassified deliverable products (i.e. classified and unclassified reporting)

5. Monitor and follow up on operational and security trends in the industry around the world to be able to support the department's ongoing trend-monitoring over an extended period of time.

Unfortunately, traditional government departments, transport ministries included, are still, inflexible, often staffed with, or managed by paper pushers and public servants who are either not encouraged to take initiatives, or are afraid to do so for fear of harming their career and future retirement pension. This applies at all levels of government, management and other. While security and intelligence organizations, which constitute the leading force in charge of protecting countries from terrorists and dedicated criminals work within tight parameters, the "bad guys" do not lack initiative, guts, courage and often self-sacrifice to do what they set out to do.

Currently departments of transport in most countries do have a security capability, though the level of sophistication and operability of the security function may vary from country to country. Ideally the Department or Ministry of Transport, which is a major player when it comes to both the national transportation system and its security, would have what could be referred to as a Transportation Security Directorate.

Security and intelligence functions of the Transportation Security Directorate

The Transportation Security Directorate is expected to perform the following functions in order for it to carry out its critical preventive and protective intelligence mandate successfully:

1. Design, manage and support all physical and site security operations for all modes of transport

2. Acquire intelligence information from other government sources such as the intelligence and law enforcement agencies

3. Share with intelligence and law enforcement agencies threat information obtained through its own interaction with the aviation and maritime stakeholders

4. Undertake analysis of threats and emergency situations and provide value-added gained through its intimate knowledge of its own diversified fields of activities

5. Produce and disseminate, or contribute to Threat Assessments related to the security of the transportation system depending on how production and dissemination of Threat Assessments are handled in the country

6. Contribute to Risk Assessments performed by the various aviation, maritime and other transportation stakeholders

7. Keep senior management informed of proven threats and emergency situations

8. Ensure ongoing liaison (Inter-departmental, intra-departmental, as well as on an international basis with similar organizations overseas)

9. Coordinate the departmental personnel security screening formalities with the national intelligence service and law enforcement agencies depending on how this function is designed in a given country

10. Manage occurring security-related crisis through its Operations Control Centre, which includes representatives from intelligence and law-enforcement agencies

11. Produce occasional classified and unclassified studies and papers reflecting its own experience, as well as that of other countries in the area of transportation security

12. Manage and supervise Joint Regional Transportation Security Committees (As will be discussed in Chapter 9)

13. Train the next generation of security operations managers

14. Provide periodic security training and awareness programs to its own staff and to members of the intelligence and law enforcement agencies involved in transportation security

15. Organize and attend national and international transportation security conferences

16. Introduce on-going facilitation programs to counter-balance the disruptive effect of security measures at ports, airports, etc.

17. Perform periodic quality assurance inspections to ensure that security measures are working, but are also changed or modified periodically to avoid the blinding effect of routine.

18. Initiate periodic live and desk-top security simulation exercises and participate in simulation exercises initiated by other government departments.[160]

Managing intelligence: The view from the Department of Transport side

The optimization of the Transportation Security Directorate's security operations with respect to management of its actionable intelligence requirements and production of short and long-term Threat Assessments calls for the following actions:

1. Internally:
Streamline the acquisition and analysis of intelligence, updating threat trends, take the lead within the department in following the evolution of the threat and manage the minute by minute response from a transportation security perspective, as well as produce event reporting and dissemination of actionable Threat Assessments within the headquarters of the Department of Transport and among its regional offices across the country.

---

[160] The immense benefits of simulated exercises have been proven with pilot, ship master and train operators training. Simulation exercises also develop the skills necessary to work effectively with the co-pilot (first-officer) even if they had met only a few minutes prior to the flight. Another integral part of simulation training is in Crew Resource Management (CRM), which emphasizes effective communication, cooperation and teamwork so that during a crisis, the pilots become better decision makers and more synergistic in their response.

2. At the national level:

Require the various security intelligence organizations and law enforcement agencies to include specific transportation-related intelligence in their counter-terrorism and criminal intelligence collection requirements mandate as well as supporting them to achieve the desired results.

3. At the regional level:

In addition to the headquarters-to-headquarters relationship between the Department of Transport and the security intelligence community, there is a pressing need to institutionalize and structure the working relationship not only between the department's regional offices and the regional offices of the security intelligence organizations; but also include local, regional and federal law enforcement players (Ministry of the Interior - National Defence - Coast Guard - port and airport authorities - as well as industry stakeholders and corresponding players in neighbouring transborder countries).

Transportation security and intelligence: A two-way street

To get a better understanding of the functions of transportation security, intelligence and law enforcement agencies need to be familiar with the composition and workings of the Transportation Security Directorate within the Department of Transport, as well as the workings of airlines, shipping companies, ports and airports. By understanding these functions, law enforcement and intelligence agencies will be in a better position to determine **what** intelligence to collect, **where** to collect it from, and **how** to analyze it to provide meaningful assessments.

It is time for those responsible for security, to understand that the world does not exist for security; it is rather security that exists for the world. To bring reality within their scope, security and intelligence professionals need also to understand and appreciate the realities, the operational constraints, and financial limitations in which the transportation industry operates.

As the security and intelligence community is called upon to understand how the transportation industry works, the industry itself needs to understand how security and intelligence work, what they can and cannot achieve, as well as the realities and constraints under which they live. By understanding how the aviation and maritime industries operate, the intelligence agencies will be able to narrow the margin of doubt and incomprehension. This dual role constitutes the second pillar of this book.

While the aviation industry is generally pretty much vocal and is constantly lobbying governments for a host of matters of interest to its operations, the maritime industry is sometimes not aggressive enough vis-à-vis governments and the public the way the airline industry is; or at least that's the impression one gets. The latter, along with its main industry representative IATA, are constantly on the back of the governments, while also keeping the pressure on ICAO. The fact that air transportation operates from airports that are within the vicinity of cities, or sometimes almost right downtown; renders the industry highly visible to everybody. Talk about air travel is in every newspaper, on every TV channel, practically on a daily basis. Ships, most of which are cargo transporters or tankers, operate, with few exceptions, mostly from vast ports and remote areas that are not in full view of the public. Since ocean-going ships do not serve anymore for scheduled passenger transportation, aside from cruise ships of course, they are not as visible as airplanes. To read about the maritime industry one has to subscribe to industry publications, whether paper or electronic. Maritime transportation is rarely in the news, unless some major accident or piracy attack is reported about.

To be effectively proactive, the maritime industry must knock at the doors of the security and intelligence agencies too. One would just cite the Somalia piracy situation and how long it has been dragging. Had the industry been more proactive and more vocal, governments and international organizations such as the International Maritime Organization (IMO) would have acted much more quickly and firmly from the outset, and the problem could have been taken care of more efficiently and determinately right from day one. Remember: It is like the popular American saying: "Cows don't give milk. You have to take it from them!"

Balancing between national security, operational efficiency and commercial viability

To ensure a balance between operational and economic imperatives on one side, and the requirements of security on the other side, the exchange of intelligence and implementation of security measures must be a joint ongoing endeavour as evidenced hereafter:

1. The aviation and maritime industries are committed to maintain and improve safety and security as they facilitate the movement of passengers and goods while controlling costs. They cannot do that in the midst of security requirements imperatives without mutual understanding, cooperation and support between industry professionals and security and intelligence professionals.

2. Heavy-handed and sometimes irrational security measures have a heavy impact on passengers' convenience and civil liberties. They also severely impact operations, on-time performance and the costs of running the airline, the shipping company, the port, or the airport.

3. Terrorism against aviation, and piracy on the high seas have devastating consequences on these two industries in terms of loss of life, diminished productivity, higher liability and insurance costs.

4. Actionable intelligence information is not always available. Intelligence information must also be corroborated and confirmed as much as possible. As pointed out earlier in the book, there is simply a flood of information that comes to the attention of intelligence agencies, most of which could turn out to be hearsay, purposeful disinformation, personal interpretation, or pure nonsense.

    By understanding how the transportation industry operates, these agencies will be able to narrow down the margin of doubt. This can be done either by hiring transportation specialists among their intelligence officers and analysts, or by running some of the more plausible intelligence they receive by their transportation security counterparts.

    That is also why one may find former intelligence officers working for Transportation Security Directorates. You may also encounter active intelligence officers physically working on temporary secondment within the premises of the Transportation Security Directorate. They have the experience, are properly trained, have the required security clearances, and know how to handle intelligence. If these were former transportation professionals before joining their country's intelligence service, so much the better because they understand the inner workings of both the transportation mode they come from and the world of intelligence. There are not that many people with such indispensable credentials around, but they do exist. The trick is to look for them.

5. Depending on the country and its intelligence service, a good deal of the intelligence that comes to the service's attention is not collected by its own efforts. It is rather shared by other countries' intelligence services subject to a government-to-government bilateral arrangement. This type of intelligence is known in the trade as "third-party" intelligence, and may not be shared with anybody without the express written approval of the agency that produced the original raw intelligence.

    Respect of the "third-party" rule weighs heavily on the workings of all intelligence agencies everywhere. That is why they are particularly sensitive as to sharing this information. That is also why for the intelligence agency to be able to work hand-in-hand with the transportation security officers, that the latter be properly vetted, cleared and indoctrinated security-wise. In most, if not all cases, company security officers are former police, military or intelligence officers. Hence, they possess a heightened awareness as to the exigencies, and pressing requirements of security measures. Divulging classified information and "third-party" intelligence is as harmful to intelligence agencies as divulging industry shortcomings and trade secrets to competitors.

6. Some intelligence is not shared by intelligence agencies, or requires to be sanitized before it is shared, because revealing it might reveal the source of the intelligence, and/or how, or from whom it was obtained. In a few countries where the rule of law is strictly upheld and individual liberties and human rights are sacrosanct, protecting individual rights and identities is given utmost importance. This is one more reason why intelligence agencies are understandably reluctant to share information liberally, and are wrongly thought to hoard information. They do not.

7. As discussed in Chapter 5 it so happens that sometimes police and intelligence services in a given country do not share a close working relationship: i.e. they do not share intelligence. There are solid reasons for that other than the desire to keep knowledge in-house. Police agencies need to divulge information and evidence to submit to courts to be able to press charges. Intelligence, however, wants to protect the sources of the intelligence, so it withholds the information from their police counterparts so that they do not divulge it in court and jeopardize their own investigation; unless of course the case is tried in camera, i.e. not in public.

   This situation does not exist in all countries. Some countries have created mechanisms that encourage, facilitate or impose such cooperation under strict rules. Some other countries do not 'worry' about these problems. That explains why it was mentioned earlier in the book that there are a variety of intelligence cultures around the world.

8. Finally, both the aviation and maritime industry themselves must also understand how both intelligence and the regulatory bodies function and interact in security matters.

On October 30th, 2007 Dalhousie University organized a public event under the "Critical Infrastructure Protection Initiative". During a panel discussion focused on the challenges of sharing sensitive information across organizations responsible for protecting critical infrastructure Gordon Helm, Manager of Port Security and Maritime Operations for the Port of Halifax in Nova Scotia, Canada expressed one of his greatest concerns, namely "striking a balance between security and efficiency, since the Port of Halifax plays a key role in local, national and continental economies. The Port acts as a strategic hub linking Halifax to Chicago in the North American transportation network. This is a complex operation involving cargo infrastructure, power generation, tourism and the Navy with the potential for significant repercussions in the event of a natural or manmade disaster. Information that is collected in isolation may seem insignificant; however, important patterns can emerge when information is shared in real-time and viewed in conjunction with information from other sources.

"Helm gave the hypothetical example of someone in a van trying to access a restricted area inside a port while claiming to be lost. On its own, this may seem inconsequential. However, by relaying a record of this incident (i.e. establishing a documentary and evidenced trace to create a pattern and trend analysis) along with security camera footage to other organizations at the Port, a later attempt to penetrate a secure area at another facility in the same way is recognized as a threat and handled quickly and effectively before the threat materializes. In order to create and distribute what he calls a "fused picture," Helm described how the Port Security Command and Control System acts as a nerve centre that collects and analyzes information submitted voluntarily by various organizations via a fiber optic network.

"A fundamental problem for Helm is getting organizations to agree to share information. For competitive reasons, private companies do not want to disclose information. For legislative and policy reasons, government organizations cannot disclose information. Helm's challenge is to create a viable system that provides a value-added network so organizations see the benefits inherent in being a part of such an alliance. According to Helm, this integration of public and private collaboration is a unique situation in North America."[161]

Collection and coordination of intelligence about threats to transportation security

Generally speaking, the approach to airport/airline security is essentially focused on intercepting individual terrorists and/or would-be hijackers, guns, knives, explosives, Improvised Explosive Devices (IED) components, or any instrument or substance that could be used as a weapon. Threat information of an immediate nature normally originates from intelligence agencies, from law enforcement organizations, other government departments, but also from the transportation industry itself.

To ensure that the Directorate of Transportation Security receives adequate, pertinent and precise actionable intelligence, it must ensure that security and intelligence agencies, which are the source of most threat intelligence, understand the specific requirements of the Directorate. Equally important, is that intelligence agencies must be formally tasked to collect targeted intelligence specifically related to threats to the transportation sector.

Being of the essence, the specificity of this intelligence requirement must be spelled out in detail in an official document, such as a Memorandum of Understanding (MOU), governing the relationship between the Department of Transport and each of the security intelligence and law enforcement organizations involved. The details of the types of threats to the transportation sector identified

---

[161] Stewart Fraser, "Balancing Security and Efficiency", The CIP Exchange: Forum for Critical Infrastructure Protection, Dalhousie University, Halifax, Nova Scotia, Canada, fall 2007.

as targets for intelligence collection can be worked out jointly between the Transportation Security Directorate and each one of these organizations according to its specific mandate.

As pointed out earlier, the Department of Transport itself is a significant source of threat and intelligence information through its regional offices, the emergency operations centre, industry stakeholders, local and regional law enforcement agencies, as well as other federal government departments at the local and national levels, such as the Coast Guard, the armed forces, the department of foreign affairs, the department of national defence, the various police forces, etc.

To comply with the universal and logical requirement of narrowing the circle of those who handle intelligence information, normally a prime contact point is identified within the Transportation Security Directorate. This point or individual(s) will be the only interlocutor(s) with the various intelligence and law enforcement agencies in matters related to exchange of intelligence and production of Threat Assessments. (See Chapter 8 for a more in-depth discussion of Threat Assessments.)

The applicability of the Israeli *modus operandi*

When Richard Reid climbed aboard a trans-Atlantic flight with a British passport issued in Belgium, no luggage, a one-way ticket and a bomb in his shoe, we made everybody take off their shoes. Now that Umar Farouk Abdulmuttalab has gotten past security with no luggage, a one-way ticket paid in cash, and a bomb in his underpants, we're going to check everybody's underpants with body scanners. But no scanner ever invented can look into another person's mind. Only when we start talking to passengers will be able to get into their heads. And that is where the real danger lies.

"Israeli reasoning regarding aviation security is that "things do not hijack planes, terrorists do." Therefore the Israelis are focused on intercepting individuals. Security at El Al airline and at Israeli ports and airports depends on intelligence and intuition, i.e. the "human factor." Israeli airport security, much of it invisible to the untrained eye, begins before passengers even enter the terminal."[162]

"Israeli officials constantly monitor behaviour, alert to clues that may hint at danger: bulky clothing, or a nervous manner. Profilers make a point of interviewing travelers, sometimes at length. "They probe for anything out of the ordinary, anything that does not fit. Only when the profiler is satisfied that a passenger poses no risk is he or she allowed to proceed to the check-in counter. By that point, there is no need to make him remove his shoes, or to confiscate his bottle of water."[163]

---

[162] "Israeli Style Security could head west", Transit Security, August 28, 2006.

[163] Ibid., "Israeli style security could head west", Transit Security, August 28, 2006.

But before any of that takes place, the passenger's name is run into the computer data-bases of the numerous Israeli intelligence and security agencies, particularly if the name is, or sounds like it could be Muslim or Arab in particular. Though, occasionally Mizrahi Jews, i.e. Jews of Arab origin, who have kept their Arab name and did not change it to an Israeli or European sounding name, would also be flagged by the system. The same process applied to air passengers is also followed aboard cargo and cruise ships, where the passenger and crew lists are communicated electronically in advance to the border security agencies. Passengers and crew are interviewed one-by-one prior to disembarkation at Israeli ports, and a second more detailed interview may be mandated either by random selection or by prior determination.

The Israelis' strong point is that they do not rely excessively on shared intelligence as much as they rely on their own widespread sources and human intelligence. That is beside the fact that Israel's centralized decision-making on intelligence matters tends to be more efficient.

Another special contributing factor to the Israeli modus operandi is that their security, intelligence and military personnel have practically all gone through the same compulsory military service training with the Israel Defense Forces (IDF), which moulds them not just during and after completion of their military service, but also afterwards, as they are recalled periodically to serve under uniform afterwards. Hence their ongoing networking is of tremendous importance to their respective professional activities. Furthermore, Israel is essentially targeting a visible minority that it regards almost as a disposable item, namely Arabs and Muslims in general and Palestinians in particular. [164]

In a special report by Stephanie Gutmann, entitled "Doing Security the Israeli Way" and published by the Spectator, Gutmann reported that "CNN spent an hour interviewing Isaac Yeffet, former head of El Al security."

She points out that 'the secret to [the Israelis'] successful airport security is a screening system based on ethnic profiling. The heart of the Israeli strategy is the idea that the most sophisticated scanner in the world is an intelligent, alert human being and that the most important terrorist behavior database is the shared assumptions, memories and life learning we call "common sense. It revolves around a simple principle", Guttmann says: "Look at people, not things."

"I've been through Ben Gurion Airport many, many times", she said. "As a female Caucasian with a Jewish last name, you'd think I wouldn't have any trouble with "racial and ethnic profiling." Yet I've been questioned extensively more than once. In every instance, it had nothing to do with what I was carrying or whether I was a little darker than usual. It had to do with my behavior."

---

[164] Also see: Oren Barak and Gabriel Sheffer; Israel's "Security network and its impact", International Journal of Middle East Studies, Volume 38 (2006), pp.235-261.

"Israeli strategy is built on multiple face-to-face contacts between passengers and airport personnel. A mile or so away, on the road leading to the terminals you encounter...a checkpoint. A young soldier approaches your vehicle, peers in, and asks a few questions, innocuous things like "How're you doing? Where are you going today?" The substance of the answers (e.g. "I'm going to Casablanca") is far less important than what psychologists call your "affect" - your demeanor, whether your gaze is steady or if it ping-pongs around, whether you are sweating heavily, whether your clothes seem appropriate to the surroundings or just subtly...well...off."

She then quotes former El Al security Chief Rafi Sela, who told the Toronto Star that "The whole time, they are looking into your eyes - which is very embarrassing. But this is one of the ways they figure out if you are suspicious or not." Certainly other factors, demographic factors - stuff other people would call "profiling" - does affect this encounter."

"Early one morning" she added, "I was held for slightly longer at this checkpoint because I arrived at the airport in a hired car service driven by a young male Israeli Arab [i.e. a Palestinian]. There were several more questions than the times I had driven up by myself or in a car driven by a non-Israeli Arab [i.e. a Jewish driver]. On this occasion the soldiers also opened the trunk and poked around a bit among the luggage. Since the driver and I were forthcoming, cooperative, calm, and direct we were soon sent on our way."

"Another time when I received much more scrutiny was a day when - I admit - I was upset about a few things. They checked my passport and wanted to know why I kept flying back and forth to England. I told them I was visiting my brother, but it took a long time to convince them I had no bad intentions. The second screening occurs while you wait in line to check your baggage. You are then approached by a uniformed young person (they are usually Israeli reservists) and "chatted with" again, the same sort of "where are you going?" stuff - even such friendly questions as, "Did you enjoy your trip to Israel? Where do you live in the United States? Do you go to a synagogue there?" People are often taken aback by the synagogue question but it is not an effort to identify Jews; rather it is simply a conversational gambit to prolong the contact, a way to get in close and feel the vibes"

Gutmann concludes by saying that "they're not looking for everything they look for in North America. They just look at you. Even today with the heightened security in North America, they will check your items to death. But they will never look at you, at how you behave. They will never look into your eyes. And that's how you figure out the bad guys from the good guys." 165

---

165 Stephanie Gutmann, "Doing Security the Israeli Way", Spectator, January 15, 2010.
http://spectator.org/people/stephanie-gutmann/article.xml Also see Rafi Sela in an interview with Transit Security: "Israeli Style Security could head West", August 2006.

The Israeli version of airport and port security which gives a kind of person-to-person attention to each passenger, thorough as it may be, works well within a rather minor aviation environment. What works in one country does not necessarily work in another. If the Israeli system were applied in North America or at extremely busy major international hubs such as London, Frankfurt, Bombay, etc., the whole air transport system, which involves millions of daily passengers, will literally come to a standstill.

To enhance aviation security, in October 2003 the Department of Homeland Security's (DHS) Transportation Security Administration (TSA) began testing of the Screening of Passengers by Observation Techniques (SPOT) program used by the Israelis to identify persons who may pose a risk to aviation security. The SPOT program utilizes behaviour observation and analysis techniques to identify potentially high-risk passengers.

"To better understand how SPOT incorporated expertise on behaviour analysis for aviation security, TSA also interviewed current and retired officials of Israel's El Al Airlines whose security processes TSA cites as providing part of the basis of the SPOT program. At the end of the exercise, TSA noted that "Although SPOT is based in some respects on El Al's aviation security program, El Al's processes differ in substantive ways from those used by the SPOT program. In particular, El Al does not use a list of specific behaviors with numerical values for each, or a numerical threshold to determine whether to question a passenger; rather, El Al security officers utilize behavioral indicators as a basis for interviewing all passengers boarding El Al passenger aircraft, and access relevant intelligence databases, when deemed appropriate. According to these officials, El Al also singles out certain passengers for further questioning based on their nationality, ethnicity, religion, appearance, or other descriptive characteristics, but these are not the only bases on which a passenger may be questioned. The scale of El Al operations is considerably smaller than that of major airlines operating within the United States. In Israel, El Al operates out of one hub airport; in contrast, there are 462 TSA-regulated airports in the United States."[166]

"Between 2010 and 2011 The Department of Homeland Security (DHS) has completed an initial study to validate the scientific basis of the SPOT program. In May 2010 the US Government Accountability Office (GAO) reported that the Transportation Security Administration (TSA) deployed this program, which uses behavior observation and analysis techniques to identify potentially high-risk passengers, before determining whether there was a scientifically valid basis for using behavior and appearance indicators as a means for reliably identifying passengers who may pose a risk to the U.S. aviation system. TSA officials said that SPOT was deployed in response to potential threats, such as suicide bombers, and was based on scientific research available at the time.

[166] "Aviation Security, TSA Taking Steps to Validate the Science Underlying its Passenger Behavior Detection Program", GAO-11-461T, April 6, 2011 p.2.

"DHS' Science and Technology Directorate completed a validation study in April 2011 to determine the extent to which SPOT was more effective than random screening at identifying security threats and how the program's behaviors correlate to identifying high-risk travelers. However, as noted in the study, the assessment was an initial validation step, but was not designed to fully validate whether behavior detection can be used to reliably identify individuals in an airport environment who pose a security risk. SPOT officials advised that it is not known if the SPOT program has ever resulted in the arrest of anyone who is a terrorist, or who was planning to engage in terrorist-related activity.

"DHS' validation study found that SPOT was more effective than random screening at identifying individuals who possessed fraudulent documents and identifying individuals who law enforcement officers ultimately arrested. However, DHS noted that the identification of such high-risk passengers was rare in both the SPOT and random tests."[167]

In its June-July 2011 issue, Aviation Security International reports that "a deterrence argument is weakened by the fact that 16 individuals with terrorist involvement have travelled through 8 SPOT airports on 23 different occasions undetected by the Behaviour Detection Officers (GAO, 2010)." The authors "suggest that this apparent lack of effectiveness is not surprising given that there is little scientific evidence that humans can detect intent to deceive on the basis of nonverbal behaviour observation and analysis techniques."[168]

Perhaps we should end this chapter with the following story that has made it on the internet. It is related to security of passengers onboard aircraft. In a popular Arabic blog site, surfers were asked to relate a particularly interesting experience related to their work. An unidentified person responded with the following story related to aviation security in Egypt, which appeared in Arabic and translated hereunder

"I work in the aviation industry and one day I was on a SWISS [i.e. Swiss Air] flight preparing to take off for Zurich. Suddenly I heard a commotion in the cabin involving an Egyptian military officer, a major to be precise, who was traveling to Switzerland for some military training course. The aircraft was still on the ground and beside the officer sat an Iraqi lady."

Egyptian officers, it must be clarified, are apparently not allowed to travel in groups on commercial carriers for safety purposes following the EgyptAir flight

---

[167] GAO's "View of the SPOT program" - Aviation Security GAO Report # GAO-11-807T, July 13, 2011, and "TSA Has Made Progress, but Additional Efforts Are Needed to Improve Security" - GAO-11-938T, September 16, 2011. Also see "The Screening of Passengers by Observation Techniques Programme: Analysing the issues", Aviation Security International, June-July 2011.

[168] "Screening of passengers not successful", Aviation Security International, June-July 2011.

990 crash in 1999 in which a large number of senior Egyptian army and air force officers (are said to have) perished when their flight mysteriously ditched into the Atlantic very close to the U.S. coastline. That was before 9/11 of course.

"The major was talking on his cell phone with a colleague of his, who was also on his way to attend the same course but traveling on a different airline as per the instructions. During the conversation, which was naturally carried out in Arabic, the major told his colleague "Let's pray to God to ensure that our mission is successful." The moment the Iraqi lady sitting beside him heard this sentence, she screamed at him "What do you want to do to us? Shame on you, what do you want from us?" The woman had suspected him of being a terrorist planning to hijack the aircraft.

"The major was dumbfounded because he could not understand why she was so upset. Hearing the commotion, a flight attendant rushed to find out what was going on. She reassured the Iraqi woman that everything was alright, but she reported the matter to the captain. The latter of course immediately notified the tower that he suspects a possible terrorist threat developing aboard the aircraft.

"Naturally all hell broke loose after the fatidic two words: "terrorist threat", were uttered. Of course "we had to rush to the aircraft" said the blogger, who seemed to belong to one of the security details at the airport, and along came people from the Office of State Security, Military Intelligence, General Intelligence, Passenger Police, State Criminal Intelligence, Cairo Airport Security, and staff from the Military Facilitation Services Office at the Airport.

"I am not going into the details of all the security measures undertaken in order to evacuate the terminal and the aircraft to ensure the safety of the passengers, because some of these measures are classified, and I cannot talk about them. Of course the first thing was to disembark the passengers. However the major refused to leave the aircraft saying he did not do anything wrong. He eventually relented when he noticed the tension and the exaggerated commotion caused by the presence of fire trucks, ambulances and special forces around the aircraft, and agreed to disembark.

"The aircraft was then towed to a remote secure area called "hijack area", so that if something happened, i.e. an explosion, it would not cause too much damage. It was then thoroughly searched, i.e. each centimetre of it, not just the passenger cabin as well as the luggage hold, the engines, the air conditioning units and the cockpit, etc.

"Once the aircraft was declared safe and that no threat existed on board, the control tower briefed the captain about the result of the search and he was cleared to take off. The captain, acting within his rights spelled out in international Civil Aviation regulations refused to let the major return to the aircraft. The major was incensed; and despite his rage, and the attempt by the various security entities mentioned above to convince the captain to change his mind, the aircraft finally took off for Zurich four hours later without the major."

To make his story more popular, the blogger added the names of some apparently well known figures in Egyptian football who were traveling on the same flight including that of a lawyer known to him, qualifying these additions as being "of interest to those who love football, as well as lawyers or law graduates like him," i.e. the blogger. This detail actually serves as a good evidence to corroborate the story.

Commenting on the attitude of the SWISS captain, the blogger said: "Of course the captain was Swiss, otherwise everything would have been normal. These people", he continued, "have a different way of thinking. I have the right to prevent you form traveling, and you have the right to sue us, you win the case, and we pay you the compensation, but they don't jeopardize the safety of the airplane." The blogger concluded by saying: "Practical, rather than emotional thinking, and pretty accurate too."[169]

---

[169] Swissair at Cairo Airport, http://forums.myegy.com/thread100097.html, Posted by "Calimera" on August 29, 2010 and accessed on December 31, 2011.

CHAPTER 8

MANAGING THREAT AND RISK ASSESSMENTS

The Threat Assessment is one of the key intelligence early-warning products through which the Directorate of Transportation Security informs the stakeholders in both the public and private sectors about the presence or absence of a threat, the estimated or actual level of that threat, and, when available, information about an estimated timeframe. It is the most important intelligence product it shares with the stakeholders on an ongoing basis. Depending on the country, Threat Assessments may be communicated to the Directorate of Transportation Security by the country's intelligence service as a finished product; or the intelligence made available to that Directorate, and it falls to it to prepare the Threat Assessment, but also the overall Risk Assessment for dissemination to the stakeholders. The latter scenario is perhaps more efficient because it allows the Transportation Security Directorate to include value added to the assessment before it disseminates it.

Another type of Threat Assessment that is performed by intelligence agencies consists of client-driven periodic analyses which deal with long-term departmental security requirements as well as immediate threats, tactical intelligence sharing or special events requirements. They are meant to assist clients in their Risk Management responsibilities. Keeping in mind that intelligence is not about withholding information, but how to share it, a Threat Assessment will inform the stakeholders if there are measures to be taken by their organizations, or not. It should also help them evaluate the risk of such occurrence hitting their operation or facilities, the likelihood of it happening, the possible consequences, and what protective and preventive measures should be taken.

Generally speaking, Threat Assessments should be mandatory not only for counter-terrorism and counter-intelligence purposes, but also before adopting or implementing key foreign or domestic policy measures. As a matter of fact, in certain cases a Threat Assessment may be strongly recommended to protect the country from ill-thought policy decisions made by its leaders, politicians and legislators.

When preparing a Threat Assessment, normally the intelligence community would start by looking at events, organizations, or individuals of concern at home, in certain parts of the world, or both at the same time. When we say home, it does not mean only looking at the "usual suspects" within the various communities, but also within our own body politic in terms of 'what is it we are doing, or not doing at the government and legislature levels, that may cause the terrorists target our country.

The Transportation Security Directorate communicates internally and with other partners and industry stakeholders in a variety of means, we might wish to call "deliverables." These could be reports, briefing notes, memoranda, etc.; but the most important is probably the Threat Assessment, or Threat and Risk Assessment as it is sometimes referred to.

In the case of transportation security, Threat Assessments produced by the Department of Transport are disseminated to specific individuals and divisions within the department and shared with outside stakeholders wherever warranted and whenever possible, all on a need-to-know basis. Where there is reason to believe that a threat may be imminent, specific intelligence needs to be shared with senior management on an urgent basis, especially where they may have to order closure of the country's airspace, deny an aircraft overflight or landing rights on national territory, or stop a ship from proceeding inside territorial waters.

As was mentioned in Chapter 4, acts involving the use of what is described as terrorist methods are uniformly labelled as 'acts of terrorism', and dealt with in the same manner irrespective of the motive, the victim, the perpetrator and the real ultimate beneficiary. This erroneous approach does a huge disservice to the investigation, but more so to how the incident will be handled, those responsible tried in court, and the innocent freed, but also similar future actions prevented. Hence the need to properly label each incident.

Production of joint Threat Assessments

It used to be the practice to create ad hoc joint task forces to manage certain security and intelligence operations as the need arises. Today, the ongoing multiple threat environment and the way to combat it have changed, as the weakness of ad hoc joint task forces became more and more evident.

In many cases, members of the task force started their work with little or no in-depth comprehension of the background or causes of events. It also took them a long time to build the necessary specialized expertise required to address the problem. Besides, and this is a major handicap, in many cases the individuals involved had never worked together before. Worse still is that by the time they consolidate their working bond, they are disbanded.

Today the tendency is to maintain permanent inter-agency and inter-departmental Integrated Threat Assessment Centres. These centres are expected to ensure that those involved maintain an ongoing handle on intelligence, terrorism, as well as major criminal trends. They also build on ongoing hands-on expertise among the diverse players. Examples of such organizations would be The US National Counter Terrorism Centre (NCTC), the British Joint Terrorism Analysis Centre (JTAC) as well as the British Cabinet Joint Intelligence Committee (JIC).

National Threat Assessment centres

An effective security system begins with a comprehensive Threat Assessment. While many individual departments and agencies produce such assessments, their ability to share information and conduct effective analysis has been inconsistent in the past. To address this gap, some governments have established a National or Integrated Threat Assessment Centre.

The centre's primary objective is to produce comprehensive Threat Assessments, which are distributed within the intelligence community and to first-line responders, such as law enforcement, on a timely basis. Its assessments, based on intelligence and trend analysis, evaluate both the probability and potential consequences of threats. They also allow the government to coordinate its response to specific threats in order to prevent or mitigate risks to public safety.

These centres are designed to be the only source of community-wide Threat Assessments for the government. They also evaluate threats in preparation for domestic and international special events such as summit and G8-G20 meetings, major sports events such as the Olympic Games, etc. It is not very likely, one could add, that these permanent inter-agency Threat Assessment centres also keep watch as far as major criminal trends such as piracy on the high seas and international drug cartels are concerned, and just concentrate their work around criminal trends suspected of links to terrorism.

National Threat Assessment centres bring together key partners from across the security intelligence community. The centre analyses security intelligence provided by its various partner agencies at home and overseas, including from Intelligence Fusion Centres as will be discussed in Chapter 9, and pieces together a picture of potential threats. Participating departments may include: the national intelligence service, signals intelligence, correctional services, customs and immigration, national defence, the department of transport, the national police, the cabinet security office, and the department in charge of public safety/security and emergency preparedness. Individuals representing these departments bring the information and expertise of their respective organizations to the centre. When required, the centre can also draw upon the specialized knowledge of other government agencies, such as the department of agriculture, the departments of health, environment and natural resources. However each country may have a variation around that theme.

Based on the intelligence available as well as assessments exchanged from international partners with whom the country maintains bilateral security intelligence arrangements, the centre produces Threat Assessments that are then distributed to members of the security intelligence community, provincial emergency authorities, and first responders. Rarely would they share the Threat Assessments with the private sector stakeholders, and if they do, it is probably a bit too late in the game.

Some countries prefer a rather less centralized system whereby each department maintains a Threat Assessment Centre of its own but which remains organically linked to the other players in the security intelligence field. The logic behind their preference is that each department has a greater grasp of its operational environment especially because of its presence in the field of its operations, while intelligence professionals working within an intelligence service are isolated from the specific workings of the department concerned.

Transportation Intelligence analysts working within their own Department of Transport have specific responsibilities based on a combination of geographic and subject matter expertise. Some are specialized in the aviation industry, others are specialists in the maritime domain, and some are closer to the workings of overland transport including mass transit. The same applies to their counterparts from other departments, such as the intelligence service, the police, customs, immigration, defence, foreign affairs etc.

Experience has shown that national, or integrated, Threat Assessment centres managed by and located within the premises of the country's intelligence service, may be too cumbersome and staffed by junior departmental representatives who, being on secondment, they cease to become involved in the daily activities of the departments they represent. In these cases they may end up acting as messengers rather than analysts. Being rather detached, they lose touch with what's happening operationally in the transportation sector for instance. Besides, departmental representatives must be hand-picked for their ability to play collegially in a multi-discipline environment to prevent turf wars and inter-departmental upmanship, barring that the work being done may end up spinning in a vicious circle and not implemented as it should.

The Threat Assessment process

The essence of an ongoing workable and efficient Threat Assessment is first class actionable intelligence, vigilance, and an ongoing solid working inter-relationship between all the stakeholders involved. It is up to the targeted entity however to evaluate the degree of risk to which it could be exposed by that threat, its vulnerability, and the measures it plans to implement to mitigate the risk, which should be spelled out and updated periodically in the Security Plan of each stakeholder.

The value of a Threat Assessment is directly proportional to its timeliness, precision and reliability of the source producing it. Unfortunately many of the Threat Assessments that are produced are neither particularly precise nor absolutely reliable. They are rather quite general and often inconclusive as to whether there is a threat or not. Thus they are often qualified with a caveat that testifies to their uncertainty when that is the case. The reason that many Threat Assessments tend to be general in nature is that the intelligence on which they are based is in itself general and often uncorroborated. In the absence of better intelligence and the pressure to produce 'something', they are occasionally disseminated even though they may be of no use, or not actionable.

It is misleading, to say the least, to call these products "Threat Assessments." Perhaps threats that are not based on verifiable actionable intelligence should rather be referred to as "Threat Overview", "Threat Perspectives", "Threat Environment", or "Threat Advisory" as long as they are just that; a general analysis of a particular situation that has the potential of triggering a threat, or several classes of threat that are based on uncorroborated intelligence rather than on actionable intelligence.

If the information to be disseminated were based on actionable intelligence, that is narrowed down to reasonable specifics, then and only then should it become eligible to be referred to confidently as a Threat Assessment. In this case, those who will receive these assessments will immediately recognize them as a serious warning, and thus give them the importance they deserve and the attention they call for.

In most cases the descriptive name given to the document continues to be a Threat Assessment. We should perhaps warn that receiving Threat Assessments that are actually threat overviews on a daily basis would numb the senses of urgency among the recipients, who, after some time, will become "colour-blinded" and may end up treating the advisory with less alertness. Therefore, differentiating between Threat Assessments by using different descriptive titles, and possibly enhance documents or electronic messages using colours, signage and warning signals simultaneously, may be a more efficient way of hilighting a real threat more seriously and give it immediate attention.

Risk Management in an aviation or maritime environment

The overall philosophy regarding risk is that it can never be eliminated, but it can be managed. Risk is (also) a function of both probability and consequence.

There is often a debate among security and intelligence professionals as to who should perform a Risk Assessment. Should the Transportation Security Directorate perform both the Threat and the Risk Assessments? Or should it just concentrate on producing the Threat Assessment, and leave the Risk Assessment to the stakeholders, such as the port and airport authorities, airlines, shipping companies, etc., because they understand their operating environment better than anybody else, and will be the ones to manage the risk?

At the end of the day it may be both, but with various degrees of involvement. It is argued here that the onus should mainly be on the stakeholder to assess the risk to its own operations. The stakeholder knows the intricacies of its business and operations, and is better placed to assess its own vulnerability, while the Transportation Security Directorate should also take the Risk Assessment seriously into account in light of the country's overall national security. It must be mentioned here that there is a tendency to consider Risk Assessments as a quantifiable science where probabilities of occurrence are established through mathematical and statistical formulas. This may provide a degree of lighting along the runway for a safer landing, but it does not replace years of professional experience handling the country, region and issues that combine to create the threat potential in the first place.

As mentioned earlier while discussing the Threat Assessment process, the Risk Assessment performed by the stakeholder must be part of the overall reporting it shares with the Transportation Security Directorate regional security office in whose territory the stakeholder operates. The regional security office will share the Risk Assessment with its headquarters, and the latter will share it with the security and intelligence agency that originated the intelligence about the threat if warranted. This way everybody is in the know.

Mark B. Salter, Associate Professor at the University of Ottawa, School of Political Studies, looks at Risk Assessment from a totally different perspective. In his article 'Imagining Numbers: Risk, Quantification, and Aviation Security', published in "Security Dialogue,"[170] Professor Salter considers that "the public imaginary has become fixated on the inconveniences of travel and not the increased securitization of everyday life. Simultaneously, the technique of quantification of abstract risk categories renders the imaginary as real, invoking the authority of statistics and probability. Following on from critique of the usage of statistical methods in social control", Salter argues that "imaginary risks are made real dangers through the use of quantification as a particular professional strategy of the managers of unease."

"Since first becoming a high-profile target for terrorists and hijackers in the late 1960s, aviation security has waxed and waned in the public imagination. Tolerance for security procedures and delays at airports decreases as the memory of attacks fades, while demands for a secure and efficient sector are made continuously by industry members and the businesses that depend on global mobility." He considers that "Aviation security is a dramatically important vector of global

---

[170] Mark B. Salter, "Imagining Numbers: Risk, Quantification, and Aviation Security", Security Dialogue 2008 v.39 pp.243-266.

security that is under-represented in security studies."[171] But since the attacks of 11 September 2001, more scholarly attention has been paid to aviation and airport security.

Salter refers to Didier Bigo's work on "Security and Immigration" by examining "how the networks of police and intelligence agencies evolve through the development of technical knowledge and expertise, which then constitute the threats that those selfsame agencies must control."[172]

"Unfortunately" says Salter, "contemporary security analysis of aviation takes place within a realist, empiricist frame that simply reinforces the state-centric assumptions of power politics. It ignores the networked nature of threats and the complex web of state and non-state security actors that actually provide security. Within this realist perspective, airplanes and airports are perceived as being highly symbolic targets that are particularly vulnerable physically.

"But, by the same token", Salter continues, "apart from high level international treaties on the criminalization of attacks against civil aviation, aviation security is predominantly seen within a national security or policing frame.[173] Civil aviation is assumed to be a technical and commercial activity with no inherent political value – other than the symbolic value attached to flag carriers or to hijackings. A realist myopia persists, which includes assumptions that terrorists are rational actors but cannot be negotiated with, that states are unitary actors chiefly responsible for aviation security, and that terror against aviation is chiefly a 'criminal' and not a 'political' act."

"A parallel can be found in the way that the Risk Management paradigm reorients police attention away from the actual lack of public security in the civil aviation network in a complex, open, interdependent society towards the social consequences of security management. For example, an airline carrier might cease operations in an unstable part of the world because it wishes to avoid the risk of hijacking or terrorist attacks. It may accept the risk of metal cutlery and glass within the first-class cabin. It may mitigate the risk of hijackings similar to those of 9/11 through reinforcing cockpit doors and pressuring the government to provide funding for such refurbishments. It may transfer the risk of a catastrophic attack

---

[171] According to Salter, "Aviation security is engaged within the 'air transportation management' field and the 'terrorism studies' field, both of which are entirely state-centric. Air transport management experts, often from airlines, airport firms, consultancies, or specialist aviation universities, focus on aviation security from a problem solving perspective: public vs. private security screeners, effective technologies, the role of human factor analysis, appropriate screening procedures, etc. Within terrorism studies, aviation security is seen as a subset of national security. Neither perspective is particularly "critical" in questioning the status quo (see Salter, "SeMS and Sensibility: Security Management Systems and the Management of Risk in the Canadian Air Transport Security Authority", Journal of AirTransport Management 13(6): pp.389-398). Quoted in Mark B. Salter, "Imagining Numbers."

[172] Didier Bigo "Security and Immigration: Toward a Critique of the Governmentality of Unease", Alternatives: Global, Local, Political (2002), v.27 (special issue): pp.63-92. Quoted in Mark B. Salter, "Imagining Numbers."

[173] Joseph S. Szyliowicz, "Aviation Security: Promise or reality?" Studies in Conflict and Terrorism 2004 v.27 number 1 pp.47-63. Quoted in Mark B. Salter, "Imagining Numbers."

through war insurance, issued by a national government or commercial insurer. More importantly, risk is used by airports and air carriers to pressure governments to spend more on aviation security.

"The presentation of risk is used by governments to justify the expansion of airport screening, no-fly, air marshal, surveillance, and other policing programs. Risk is also used to manage passenger and stakeholder expectations. Several air carriers now announce that it is their policy that passengers remain seated, that the washrooms in the first-class cabin are reserved for first-class passengers for security reasons, and that crowding near the cockpit is prohibited. While these controls are framed in the language of risk, they are justified through the appeal to the maintenance of security (not the reduction of risk).

Risk analysis in the area of aviation and maritime security has become a source of good business. "Within the aviation security field", Salter remarks, "several competing consultancies have established models of risk analysis for terror attacks, which are promoted at regional and international industry conferences. Both the International Civil Aviation Organization (ICAO) and the International Air Transport Association (IATA) are moving towards 'enterprise Risk Management' and 'security management systems' that are based on quantifiable security and ROI (return on investment) results."

"The expression of surveillance in quantitative terms, then, becomes the key for the development of data from which to draw conclusions about empirical security threats. In short, with the paradigm of risk, 'one does not *start from* a conflictual situation observable in experience, rather one *deduces* it from a general definition of dangers one wishes to prevent. These preventive policies thus promote a *new mode of surveillance*: that of systematic predetection"[174]

"Within the field of aviation security, average wait times and throughput of passengers through a screening point and numbers of items seized become the focus of policing, rather than the actual security impact of dangerous individuals or prohibited items.[175] The mechanism of security thus erases the actual object of security and places governmental emphasis on the management of insecurity." In support of his argument, Salter cites the following example: "The banning of liquids/gels – or, more precisely, the strict limiting of liquids/gels – is another example of the security mechanism. The international norm of 100ml of liquids/gels is based on an assumed failure of screening – 100ml of explosives would likely not cause a catastrophic crash. This limit emerged from within the Israeli aviation security community and has been adopted around the globe. An exception to this general adoption demonstrates the importance of expertise: Australia's aviation

---

[174] Robert Castel, "From Dangerousness to Risk", in Graham Burchell, Colin Gordon & Peter Miller, editors, The Foucault Effect: Studies in Governmentality. Chicago, IL: Chicago University Press (281-298) p. 288. 1991 Quoted in Salter, "Imagining Numbers", p.255.

[175] Mark B. Salter, "SeMS and Sensibility: Security Management Systems and the Management of Risk in the Canadian Air Transport Security Authority", Journal of Air Transport Management, 2007 v.13 number 6, pp.389-398.

security authorities have refused to impose a liquid ban on the grounds that *their* [author's italics] risk analysis demonstrates that other security screening procedures will detect this threshold of explosives."[176]

Managing risk assessments

The basics of risk management consist of either, accepting the risk, transferring the risk, managing the risk, or mitigating the risk. The challenge of course will always be: How much is enough?

While assessing the risk to its facilities, the stakeholder would normally assign to it three types of factors: An importance factor, i.e. how important is the asset socially and economically; an occurrence factor, i.e. what is the likelihood of an event occurring; and a vulnerability factor, i.e. whether the facility is defenceless or could be protected even partially. It will be up to the stakeholder at the end to weigh the risk qualitatively through probabilistic analysis, and quantitatively either by using a risk score, or scale, or by assessing the various rings of protection available around his facility.

As the intelligence community shares intelligence with the stakeholders through the Department of Transport, the stakeholders, in turn must share the Risk Assessment they perform in-house with their intelligence suppliers also through the Department of Transport. The intelligence agencies will thus be in a much better position to make recommendations to the government regarding the possible overall impact of the threat if it materializes on national security as well as on the national economy.

Governments and international organisations such as ICAO and the IMO have been working over the years to find the right balance between intensifying security controls at ports and airports on the one hand and facilitating legitimate trade and movement of passengers on the other hand.

In the cargo area for example it is not possible to check every shipment and every container entering or leaving a country. To minimise the risks involved, Risk management comes to the rescue as a facilitation tool to set security priorities in order to determine where the greatest areas of exposure to risk exist, and allocate limited resources effectively to maintain a proper balance between controls and facilitate the movement of cargo.

Risk management should not be a static process but an interactive process in which information is continuously updated, analysed, acted upon and reviewed. The risk management process consists therefore of the following elements: a) determining the strategic and organisational context in which risk management

---

[176] Mark B. Salter, "Imagining Numbers: Risk, Quantification, and Aviation Security", Security Dialogue 2008 v.39 pp.243-266.

will apply; b) identifying, analysing and prioritising risks; c) assessing risks by taking appropriate and proportionate measures to cover the identified high risks; d) monitoring and reviewing the process on a regular basis.

The second element of the risk management process is the important risk analysis phase. This is the phase during which the systematic use of available information is relied upon to determine how often defined risks may occur, and the magnitude of their likely consequences. Risk analysis will identify risks that could result in establishing risk profiles. These profiles will be the basis for the next step in the process, namely taking the appropriate measures to cover the risk. Risk profiles will identify known risk areas, actual incidents and the corresponding (high) risk indicators. Risk profiles establish also an action plan of checks, carrying out the appropriate controls, and allocating the available resources.

Examples of risk areas can be found in the information or intelligence about the passenger, or about a cargo shipment, the country of origin or point of departure, and chosen route of transport. Risk areas can be specific destinations, specific countries of origin, sensitive goods such as nuclear material, narcotics etc. as well as other factors which, taken together, increase or reduce the level of risks.

Key principles of risk management

The key principles of risk management have been studied, applied and updated appreciably over the years. The US Coast Guard in particular has established some unclassified, very practical principles and rules regarding the performance of Risk Assessments for Ports that are less cumbersome than other much more complicated studies in the field. Because of their simplicity and their applicability to both the aviation and maritime sectors, we thought of summarizing them to serve as an example to follow.

"The final goal of Risk Management is to achieve an adequately low and consistent level of risk. The goal for transportation security is to ensure that if the level of threat increases; either the consequences or vulnerabilities decrease to offset that increase. For example, a port (or airport) may decide to increase security checks after receiving a bomb threat. In another case, a vessel may be required to shift to a berth further away from buildings during a shortage of security personnel, (or an aircraft moved to a remote runway or diverted to a second level or third level airport).

"The key to risk-based decision making is to correctly assess the value of risk. This requires four separate assessments:

- Criticality assessment
- Threat assessment and scenario selection

- Consequence and vulnerability assessment
- Determining mitigation strategies and implementation methods

Step 1: Criticality assessment

"A criticality assessment is a process designed to systematically identify and evaluate important assets and infrastructure in terms of various factors, such as the mission and significance of a target. For example, nuclear power plants, key bridges, major transportation hubs, and major computer networks might be identified as "critical" in terms of their importance to public safety, national security, and economic activity.

"In addition, facilities might be critical at certain times, but not others. For example, large sports stadiums, shopping malls, or office towers may represent an important target only when in use by large numbers of people. Criticality assessments are important because they provide a basis for focusing the mitigation strategies and implementation methods on the most important items by identifying which assets and structures are more crucial to protect from an attack. Criticality assessments consider such factors as the importance of a structure to the missions of the port or the airport, the ability to reconstitute this capability, and the potential cost to repair or replace the asset. Criticality assessments should also give information on impacts to life, economic security, symbolic value and national defense. Criticality assessments provide information to prioritize assets and determine which potential targets merit further evaluation.

"A Criticality Assessment will help identify activities and operations critical to a port. This will assist in target selection. Examples may include supporting a cruise line industry, or providing waterway access for commuter ferries. Identify those specific infrastructure targets that support critical operations of the port. All identified targets should be included in the evaluation. In addition, it is important to consider the role or mission of the target in the operation of the port. Broadly, we consider five mission or operation areas to be of interest:

"These are Public Health, Commerce, Safety/Defense, Transportation and Communications. The effect of destruction considers which consequence factors are affected by the loss of the target. The next consideration in determining criticality is the ability to recover from destruction of the target. If an individual bridge is considered, but it is one of four parallel bridges crossing the same waterway, the ability of the port to recover from its destruction is likely to be better than if it is the only means. Finally, consider the number of mission areas affected, the degree of the effects and the ability to recover and make an overall assessment of the criticality. Criticality should be rated according to the following scale: Critical/Moderate/Marginal.

"Some targets may need to be considered individually; for example, large facilities such as Port Authorities may be considered as one target or subdivided into individual targets as appropriate based on the attack scenario. For example, an entire Port Authority may be the target in one attack scenario, but individual parts of it may be targets in other attack scenarios.

Step 2: Threat Assessment and scenario selection

"A Threat Assessment is used to evaluate the likelihood of attack against a given asset or location. It is a decision support tool that helps to establish and prioritize security-program requirements, planning, and resource allocations. A Threat Assessment identifies and evaluates each threat on the basis of various factors, including capability and intention. By identifying and assessing threats, organizations do not have to rely on worst-case scenarios to guide planning and resource allocations. Worst-case scenarios tend to focus on extreme consequences and typically require inordinate resources to address.

"While Threat Assessments are a key decision support tool, it should be recognized that they are dependent on intelligence data. Even if updated often, Threat Assessments might not adequately capture emerging threats. No matter how much we know about potential threats, we will never know that we have identified every threat or that we have complete information even about the threats of which we are aware. Threat Assessments alone are insufficient to support key judgments and decisions that must be made.

"It is important that the developed scenario or scenarios are within the realm of possibility and, at a minimum, address known capabilities and intents as evidenced by past events and available intelligence. For example, a boat containing explosives (a specific class of scenario) ramming a tanker (target) that is outbound through a choke point (specific circumstance) is one credible scenario. It is much less credible that a U.S. Navy ship will be commandeered and used to ram a bridge unless specific intelligence reports indicate otherwise. That is why a criticality assessment should be performed initially to focus efforts on critical targets.

Step 3: Conducting a consequence and vulnerability assessment

"A vulnerability assessment is a process that identifies weaknesses in physical structures, personnel protection systems, processes, or other areas that may lead to a security breach, and may suggest options to eliminate or mitigate those weaknesses. For example, a vulnerability assessment might reveal weaknesses in an organization's security systems or unprotected key infrastructure, such as water supplies, bridges, perimeter security, under-passes below runways at certain airports.

"For example, at many passenger terminals, experts have identified security concerns including the distance from parking lots to important staging areas and buildings as being so close that a car bomb detonation would damage or destroy the buildings and kill people in them. To mitigate this threat, experts have advised to increase the distance between parking lots and buildings, even though modern airport design encourages exactly the opposite to facilitate passenger access to and exit from the terminal. Another security enhancement might be to reinforce the windows in buildings to prevent glass from flying into the building if an explosion occurs. Such assessments can identify vulnerabilities in port operations, personnel security, and physical and technical security.

"A consequence assessment evaluates the negative impact of a successful attack. It is a method to evaluate the likely outcomes of a scenario. The consequence analysis promotes the consideration of an attack's impacts including deaths and injuries, economic, public safety/national defense, environmental, and symbolic effect. In this step each target/attack scenario will be evaluated in terms of the potential consequences of the attack and the vulnerability (or invulnerability) of the target to the attack.

Step 4: Determining mitigation strategies and implementation methods

"Mitigate means strategies that should be developed to reduce risk for that target/ scenario combination. A security plan should contain the scenario evaluated, the results of the evaluation and the mitigation measures.

"The true value of these assessments is realized when mitigation strategies are implemented to reduce consequences and vulnerabilities. The desire is to reduce the overall risk associated with the identified target.

"As an example of a possible vulnerability mitigation measure, a company may contract for a stand-by tug to provide "sentry duty" to prevent ramming of a cruise ship. This measure would improve organic security and may reduce the overall vulnerability score from a "high" to a "medium." However this option is specific for that particular scenario and also carries a certain cost.

"Another option might be to dock the cruise ship in a more protected berth. This may reduce the accessibility score from "high" to "medium." This option may not require additional assets, but reduces the risk of this scenario, and may even provide mitigation for additional scenarios."[177]

---

[177] United States Coast Guard - Guidelines for Port Security Committees -"Navigation and Vessel Inspection Circular no. 902" - September 30, 2002 (Unclassified).

Threat Assessment implementation and reporting methodology

The most important element of a Threat Assessment is to provide early warning of events or developments that could have a major impact on national security. Occasionally, a single-source intelligence report will provide such warning, but more frequently the warning is derived from an assessment of all the information obtained through intelligence and other means in a given situation.

In most cases, Threat Assessments are produced and disseminated by departmental headquarters such as the Directorate of Transportation Security, and shared as a final product internally and externally. A modified approach is recommended though. Unless the threat is precise, specific, imminent in nature, and coming from a reliable source, the Directorate of Transportation Security must first ask its own regional security offices involved to quickly review the Threat Assessment and comment on it for operational on-site plausibility. This allows for evaluating its relevance to the transportation sector and to the context of the specific region involved before deciding on taking action and dissemination to partners and stakeholders.

The review must take place, and the recommendations of the regional security office assessed and taken into consideration by the Transportation Security Directorate before the Threat Assessment is finalized and communicated to security officers at airlines, airports and the port facilities, ships and shipping lines as well as other stakeholders as required. This is called for, because the adoption and implementation of protective/preventive security measures is an extremely disruptive and costly process for all concerned, and could result in serious loss of revenue, besides potentially harming the commercial reputation of the owners/operators.

When on the other hand intelligence about a specific or imminent threat originates at the regional operations level, the field security personnel normally share the information immediately with the Transportation Security Directorate headquarters to ensure that government at the political level is aware of the threat. Concurrently, and depending on whether this imminent threat is directed at aviation or maritime targets, the threat information must be shared with whoever is involved, namely the airport security officer, the airline security officer, the port security officer, the port facilities security officers, and the shipping line's security officer, keeping in mind of course that those individuals always possess the required security clearances[178].

---

[178] Security clearances for these individuals, the same way as for port and airport staff, are best obtained through the Transportation Security Directorate which acts as the coordinating middleman between the applicant and the security intelligence and law enforcement agencies which perform the background security checks.

A two-way threat and risk intelligence cycle

A forward-looking dynamic Threat Assessment process should not end when a threat materializes, irrespective of whether the occurrence of that threat is prevented or not. All stakeholders involved must be required to report to the Transportation Security Directorate regional office in whose sector they operate, which measures they undertook following reception of a Threat Assessment, as well as communicate any threats that may have come directly to their attention other than those received from the Directorate.

In this respect, the industry stakeholders must also provide the Transportation Security Directorate's regional office in whose sector they operate with a complete report on any threat that materializes anywhere in the system, nationally or internationally, whether its occurrence is prevented or not.

Such reports, received in total confidence (i.e. treated as classified when received), shall include details about the effect of the threat on the stakeholder's operations and Security Plan, and the Risk Assessment it has performed, including any additional preventive measures introduced as a result, and subsequently any significant changes to the Security Plan.

Following review of the stakeholder's report, and the comments and recommendations made by the regional transportation security office, the latter must forward a copy of the stakeholder's report and the Regional Office's views to the Transportation Security Directorate headquarters. This two-way communication provides the Directorate of Transportation Security with a means of documenting and trending specific threats to national security.

The Directorate of Transportation Security, through its regional security offices, is required to monitor the implementation of Threat Assessments by the industry stakeholders and audit the resulting Risk Assessment performed by them. This should be mandatory to ensure that the Threat Assessments are taken seriously, and that the stakeholders use them to make improvements to their security measures and/or to their Security Plans whenever required.

Therefore, to build on previous experience and allow for a lessons-learned analysis, it is recommended in the context of this book that the Transportation Security Directorate maintain a database of specific threats to the national transportation sector during a given year and the manner they were handled.

The process of evaluating threats/intelligence, calls on the Directorate to sensitize the industry stakeholders whenever required, possibly through ongoing working sessions with them about the types of prevailing threats, the driving factors and intent of terrorist groups, but also about the limitations of intelligence and the need for the industry to be more proactive in sharing its own threat-related information with the Directorate.

Intelligence analysts who prepare strategic or tactical intelligence reports create a product that is client-solicited. One adverse situation that faces analysts who produce both unsolicited and client-driven intelligence is, not knowing what happens to the intelligence they provided. For the most part, they have no mechanism to track intelligence they may have shared, nor a way to determine if it has been used at all.

In most cases intelligence received from various intelligence and law enforcement sources ends with the client department. In this case the Transportation Security Directorate. Intelligence-producing agencies are so busy that they do not have the time, or sometimes even the requirement to receive unsolicited operational feedback from the client organization. So the intelligence cycle is broken and the product ends up traveling one-way. In fact the analyst-client feedback loop must come full circle, and if the intelligence agency does not mandate a feedback, it is not doing its job properly and starving itself from vital information that gives intelligence the required actionability.

This two-way communication between the intelligence providers, i.e. the intelligence agency, and the intelligence consumers, in this case the Department of Transport, provides the Department of Transport with a means of sharing information with the source of intelligence, while offering the department itself with a mechanism to document and trend out specific verifiable threats to national security. Where would the department obtain that information? Certainly from airlines, airports, ports, shipping companies, etc.

The post-threat or post-incident report prepared and disseminated by the Transportation Security Directorate must be communicated to the intelligence or law enforcement agency that has provided the initial intelligence. This will allow the originators of the intelligence to acquire a full picture at to how the intelligence was used to prevent the threat from happening, or how it failed to do so. It will also complete the threat picture for them on the national level, but it will also help them ascertain the quality and reliability of the raw source of that intelligence for future tasking.

A Step-By-Step Guide on making it Work

1. Transportation Security Directorate (TSD) receives intelligence about a threat from internal or external sources.

2. In case of specific or imminent threat, TSD disseminates the information immediately for action on a need to know basis to the pre-identified

contact points within the Department of Transport National Headquarters and in the geographic regional offices for communication to the stakeholders.

3. If the information is neither specific nor imminent, TSD prepares a Threat Assessment based on the intelligence received and includes value-added as required, then forwards a draft for review to the various Regional Security Offices (RSO).

4. As soon as they have been notified, RSO review the Threat Assessment for plausibility and relevance to the region and transportation sector involved.

5. If decision is made by RSO, in consultation with TSD to notify the stakeholders, e.g. ports, airports, airlines, etc., the RSO will proceed to notify them accordingly and maintain contact with them until the event has been resolved.

6. Stakeholders perform or update their facility's Risk Assessment based on the Threat Assessment received from TSD, and communicate the results of their findings and measures they may have taken as soon as possible back to RSO following the same channels.

7. If a threat materializes, whether its occurrence is prevented or not, the stakeholder concerned shall provide the RSO with a complete report on the matter. Such report will include details on the effect of the threat on the client's operations including any additional preventive measures introduced as a result, and any significant changes to their Security Plan. The information shall also be entered in the stakeholder's operational logbook.

8. The concerned RSO reviews the report, adds comments and recommendations, then shares it with the TSD and maintains a copy in the stakeholder's file. The TSD will include the information and lessons learned in its threats database related to the industry sector involved, i.e. aviation, maritime or surface, in order to monitor threat trends. Finally, TSD shares the information with the source of the threat information, e.g. the intelligence service.

MANAGEMENT OF THREAT ASSESSMENTS
IMPLEMENTATION CHART

Transportation Security Directorate
1. Receives intelligence about threat
2. If imminent threat, disseminates information immediately
3. If not imminent, prepares Threat Assessment and consults
   with RSO at HQ and Regional levels
4. Disseminates Threat Assessment on a need to know basis

Regional Security Office
1. Reviews Threat Assessment for plausibility and relevance
2. Discusses releasability of the Threat Assessment to
   stakeholders with TSD
3. Communicates Threat Assessment to stakeholders
4. Maintains contact with stakeholders until event is resolved
5. Monitors implementation of Risk Assessment.

Stakeholders
1. Perform/update Risk Assessment
2. Report back to RSO on whether threat occurred or was
   prevented and on measures taken
3. Make changes to Security Plan
4. Enter occurrence in the operational logbook

Regional Security Office
1. Adds comments and recommendations to stakeholder report
2. Forwards copy of report to TSD
3. Maintains a copy in the stakeholder's file

Transportation Security Directorate
1. Includes information in threats database
2. Shares information with the source of threat intelligence

TSD = Transportation Security Directorate
RSO = Regional Security Office

Communicating imminent or actual threats to public safety/security

Receiving intelligence or information about imminent threats and handling it properly is half the problem as far as the Transportation Security Directorate is concerned. The other equally important half is how to communicate it internally and externally, particularly when the intelligence is highly classified.

1. Internally within the Department of Transport, the Transportation Security Directorate, which includes the department's multimodal intelligence branch as discussed, will disseminate imminent verifiable threat information directly to the following branches depending on the circumstances and nature of such threats:
   - Senior management at the headquarters and regional level
   - The Security Operations Branch
   - The Security Policy / Regulatory Affairs Branch
   - The Department of Transport Crisis Centre
   - Dangerous Goods Response Branch
   - Civil Aviation, Maritime, Rail, Mass Transit, Highway, Canals and Waterways Safety and Security Branches
   - Technology and Information Management Services Branch

2. The threat information may also need to be shared with the office of the Head of State and/or that of the Prime Minister, and the Ministers and other senior officials having emergency response functions, as well as with other government departments and agencies, etc, to allow them to take the necessary actions for prevention, enforcement, mitigation and disaster assistance within their sphere of influence.

   Imminent threats are normally communicated to these departments directly by the Intelligence Service. To obtain more technical and site details if the transportation sector is the target of the threat, the point of contact for the Intelligence Service will be the Transportation Security Directorate. The reason behind assigning the major role to the Transportation Security Directorate, and not say to the Intelligence Service, or to some political intermediary department, is that it constitutes a one-stop point of reference, and any additional or future information required by everybody that involves the overall transportation sector is within its grasp.

   In extreme cases, certain threats could lead to closure of and restrictions of airports and airspace, cessation of air traffic, grounding of aircraft, diversions/forced landings/boardings of aircraft, or ships, temporary closure of rail lines, bridges, shipping lanes, ports, harbours, locks and canals, etc.

Threat information will in most cases lead to increased security measures and levels of inspections of security at ports, airports, aircraft, and dangerous goods shipments. In such instances the Transportation Security Directorate will raise the security level at which ports and airports operate, and also communicate with the transportation industry stakeholders, major railways, airlines, ports, airports, shipping companies and other industry associations, or groups on an as required basis.

3. Certain threats will also be communicated to foreign government departments and international agencies, such as: ICAO, IMO, INTERPOL, the FAA to name but a few.

4. Communications with the general public takes place when Threat or Risk assessments prompt changes in security levels and requirements which affect the public or require the cooperation of the public. Typically, these communications take place through the media and press releases posted on the Department of Transport web site.

5. Threat information, including Intelligence Assessments, and certain Threat and Risk Assessments are usually distributed at various levels of classification, i.e. either Unclassified, Unauthorized Disclosure, Prohibited, Protected "A, B & C", Confidential and Secret. Messaging at higher classifications is typically handled by the Transportation Security Directorate Intelligence unit through person to person briefings.

6. Channels used to distribute information
    ➤ Urgent notifications of incidents requiring immediate action are typically distributed by telephone (1-800 numbers, hot lines, auto-dial lines, cellular phone, secure cellular or land-line telephone, in the office and at home of certain duty officers and all Intelligence staff), fax (incl. high capacity fax server system, secure fax); encrypted e-mail, etc.
    ➤ Highly classified Intelligence Assessments are usually distributed by hand in person, or through secure telephone lines.
    ➤ Messaging is disseminated to the public through the Minister of Transport, other Department of Transport officials, or through Public Affairs communications channels using the media, various modal advisories, press releases, conferences, interviews etc. Occasionally, these communications are coordinated through a lead department in charge of national security.

Managing threat information communications

Withholding information through media blackouts during a crisis sometimes hurts more than it helps. Therefore, it is essential that the Transportation Security Directorate establish a communications strategy, and that it participates in all incident or accident simulation exercises that the training department organizes periodically. An important aspect of the simulation exercise is to practice how to communicate the information about the developing situation to the public and the media, practice producing press releases, a final communiqué, and the results of the post mortem that will eventually be produced after termination of the emergency situation; all without divulging intelligence sources and information.

Many crises are handled professionally by the security management and staff, but the dissemination of public information about it to the media and through them to the public, while the events are still ongoing is occasionally handled unprofessionally.

There is a tendency sometimes to try and sidestep the issue at hand, and instead of sharing information in a reasonable but convincing way, "official spokespersons" either indulge in a defensive or an obfuscation exercise. Sometimes an unprofessional performance on their part is such that the public cannot but interpret it that way. If they lose their credibility, they harm their own department and its officials, cause alarm among the population that could have dire political, security and economic consequences.

Sometimes several individuals from the same organization go around giving their personal reading of the situation on national television and to the printed press. Occasionally they end up disseminating conflicting details, without prior coordination. Only one qualified senior media person, who is "camera material", and experienced in talking to the media, should be the official spokesperson, with a trained backup for him/her. This should prevent what could otherwise turn into chaos and public hysteria, which may lead to social unrest based on a misunderstanding of what is going on. The "official spokesperson" must be a consummate professional and not a dispenser of half-truths or outright lies. To ensure that this remains the case, public and media communications simulation exercises must also include the Communications Officers of the stakeholders involved, whether they are from the aviation or maritime sectors who deal with the media.

CHAPTER 9

KEEPING A HANDLE ON INTELLIGENCE ON AN ONGOING BASIS

Introduction

When people think of security, they generally think in terms of a central agency, perhaps with several branches across the country which is responsible for that vital aspect of governance. This of course is only partially accurate. The whole picture is certainly different.

In an article entitled "Meeting the Homeland Security Challenge: A Principled Strategy for a Balanced and Practical Response", published in the Journal of Homeland Security, Admiral James Loy and writer Robert G. Ross state that "… with many (security) responsibilities being fulfilled by state and/or local authorities, and with many potential targets being owned by the private sector, *a truly national program will necessarily extend well beyond the federal government*"[179]… including private sector, state and local government, and non-DOD (Department of Defense) federal agencies.

"The organizational relationships can be made more complex by physical and political factors. The Port of New York and New Jersey, for example is subject to the jurisdiction of two states.[180] Maritime activities in San Francisco Bay are affected by two major cities, three port authorities, a few large airports and nine county governments. Hecker, points out that "appropriate roles and responsibilities within and between the levels of government and with the private sector are evolving and need to be clarified. New threats are prompting a reassessment and shifting of longstanding roles and responsibilities, but these shifts are being considered on a piecemeal and ad hoc basis without benefit of an overarching framework and criteria to guide the process."[181]

Building law enforcement and security partnerships

In Chapter 3 we discussed Bruce D. Berkowitz and Allen E. Goodman's estimate that "one of the signs that something was wrong with the traditional model (for handling intelligence) was that intelligence officials would not rely on their standing organizations when a really important issue came along.

---

[179] J.M. Loy, and R.G. Ross, "Meeting the Homeland Security Challenge: A Principled Strategy for a Balanced and Practical Response, Journal of Homeland Security, September 2001, p.13.

[180] JayEtta Z. Hecker, "Port Security: Nation Faces Formidable Challenges in Making New Initiatives Successful", U. S. General Accounting Office, August 5, 2002, p.2, Washington, D.C.

[181] JayEtta Z.Hecker, "Homeland Security: Intergovernmental Coordination and Partnership will be Critical to Success", U.S. General Accounting Office, July 1, 2002.

Instead, they would establish ad hoc "task forces" and "intelligence centres." During the past decade, for example, the intelligence community has created new intelligence centres to cover critical issues such as proliferation, counterterrorism, narcotrafficking, and other special topics. The intelligence centres bring together the specific analysts and collectors needed to address a specific issue. The centres are also intended to connect intelligence consumers directly to intelligence producers. Indeed, establishing new organizations for high-priority assignments has become a reflex action."[182] The centres that Berkowitz and Goodman refer to are what is now known in the trade as "Intelligence Fusion Centres."

Within each state and major urban area, fusion centres have an important responsibility to build strong partnerships with other field-based law enforcement and homeland security entities at all levels of government, such as Joint Terrorism Task Forces, High Intensity Drug Trafficking Areas, Emergency Operations Centres, Intelligence Officers and Protective Security personnel.

State and major urban area fusion centres are owned and operated by state, provincial and local entities. The federal, or central, government recognizes these designations and has a shared responsibility with state and local governments to support the national network of fusion centres.

Fusion Centres overview

Fusion centres serve as focal points within the state, provincial and local levels for the receipt, analysis, gathering, and sharing of threat-related information among federal, state, local, and territorial partners. They

produce actionable intelligence for dissemination, which can aid other law enforcement organizations in their investigative operations.

Fusion centres focus on feeding critical information back to Federal intelligence and law enforcement officials. Each fusion centre has capabilities unique to the needs and requirements of the jurisdiction where it is located. This represents a major contribution to national security in terms of collecting specific intelligence.

The intelligence service's branch that is responsible for intelligence analysis serves the fusion centres by providing infrastructure and analytical context to information. This ensures that there is a true two-way flow of information between States and localities and the Federal government, and between law enforcement and the national intelligence community. The Intelligence Analysis Branch makes sure fusion centres have the infrastructure tools, access to all necessary information, right federal partners and training.

---

[182] Bruce D. Berkowitz and Allen E. Goodman, "Best Truth", p.63. In Thomas H. Hammond, "Intelligence Organizations and the Organization of Intelligence."

Operational Capabilities of Fusion Centres

1. Receive classified and unclassified information from federal partners;
2. Assess local implications of threat information through the use of a formal risk assessment process;
3. Disseminate threat information to other levels of local government and private sector entities within their jurisdiction; and
4. Gather locally-generated information, aggregate it, analyze it, and share it with federal partners.

Fusion centres contribute to the information sharing environment through their role in receiving threat information from the federal government; analyzing that information in the context of their local environment; disseminating that information to local agencies; and gathering tips, leads, and suspicious activity reporting from local agencies and the public. Fusion centres receive information from a variety of sources, including from stakeholders within their jurisdictions, as well as federal information and intelligence. They analyze the information and develop relevant products to disseminate to their customers.

These products assist homeland security partners at all levels of government to identify and address immediate and emerging threats. Beyond serving as a focal point for information sharing, fusion centres add significant value to their customers by providing a state and local context to help enhance the national threat picture.

Fusion centres provide the federal government with critical state and local information and subject matter expertise that it did not receive in the past – enabling the effective communication of locally generated threat-related information to the federal/central government. Threats not only emanate from outside a country's borders, but also from within the country. Integrating and connecting these state and local resources creates a national capacity to gather, process, analyse, and share information in support of efforts to protect the country.

Fusion centres empower front-line law enforcement, public safety, fire and emergency response services, public health, and private sector security personnel to lawfully gather and share threat-related information.

Fusion centre personnel are also given access to classified terrorism-related information residing in the Department of Defence classified network. Under this initiative, select fusion centre personnel with the appropriate federal security clearance can access specific terrorism related information resident on the department's secure intranet network

Fusion centres provide interdisciplinary expertise and situational awareness to inform decision-making at all levels of government. In the United States for example, some fusion centres have adopted an "all-crimes" approach, incorporating information on terrorism and other high-risk threats into their jurisdiction's existing law enforcement framework to ensure that possible precursor crimes, such as counterfeiting or narcotics smuggling, are screened and analyzed for linkages to terrorist planning or other criminal activity. (In our view criminal gangs avoid terrorists like the plague. Criminal activities are meant to make money as quietly as possible, while terrorist activity is only interested in scoring political points that make a lot of noise and create a lot of attention at the same time.)

Other fusion centres have adopted an "all-hazards" approach. In addition to collecting, analyzing, and disseminating information on potential terrorist planning and other crimes, these fusion centres identify and prioritize types of major disasters and emergencies, such as hurricanes or earthquakes, which could occur within their jurisdiction. In doing so, they gather, analyze, and disseminate information to assist relevant responsible agencies - law enforcement, fire, public health, emergency management, critical infrastructure - with the prevention, protection, response, or recovery efforts of those incidents.

Consistent with the statutory definition of a fusion centre, these centres typically bring together in one location representatives from several different state or local agencies, such as state and local law enforcement agencies - state police, county sheriffs, and city police departments - homeland security agencies, emergency management agencies, and the National Guard. Many fusion centres have federal personnel working on-site, such as DHS Intelligence operations specialists and Customs and Border Protection agents, along with others such as FBI intelligence analysts and Drug Enforcement Administration agents.[183]

Intelligence Fusion Centres work well as force multipliers because they enable states and localities to make effective, risk-based decisions about public safety matters and mitigate threats to national security. Local or state level fusion centres normally include a representative from the transportation sector, if they do not, they must very quickly fill this gap in view of the criticality of that sector.

Addressing the security needs of the transportation sector

Each of the sectors who are represented in the Fusion Centres has its own specific operating environment and requirements. Besides, because of their different modus operandi, partially by necessity and partially by choice, each sector also has its own specific operational partners with whom it must deal with at all times, they each have their own mini intelligence fusion centre so to speak.

---

[183] For further information regarding Fusion Centres, please refer to:
www.dhs.gov/files/programs/gc_1156877184684.shtml

Aviation, maritime and surface transportation equally have, or should have, their own security intelligence committees as opposed to the larger and more diverse fusion centres in light of their specific and highly critical role.

We must keep in mind, though, that not all countries have a system of Fusion Centres, and some may not find it particularly useful for their purposes.

THE ROLE AND OBJECTIVES OF PERMANENT JOINT REGIONAL TRANSPORTATION SECURITY COMMITTEES

To have an idea about the complexity of managing security at major airports for instance, let us see who is involved in security at a typical major North American airport. All-in-all, there are between thirty and forty organizations or more with some responsibility for security at such an airport, including stakeholders, such as private companies, who have their own security arrangements at the airport. The situation is much the same in so many major airports around the world.

1. Federal police agency
2. Federal police Drug Section
3. Federal police VIP Security
4. Federal Immigration and Passports
5. Federal Customs and Excise detachment
6. Federal police Head of State Protection Detail
7. Federal police Federal Enforcement Section
8. Federal police Proceeds of Crime detachment
9. City, county, municipal, or regional Police
10. National Intelligence Service
11. Metropolitan Airport Authority
12. Federal Passport Office
13. Department of Transport
14. Air Navigation Services
15. State troopers
16. Federal Post Office
17. Courier companies
18. Private security companies
19. County Fire Department
20. Metropolitan Fire Department
21. Airport Fire Department
22. Health Department
23. Metropolitan Transit Authority
24. Food Inspection Agency
25. Department of Agriculture
26. Department of the Environment
27. In-flight catering companies
28. Military Police
29. Military Commandos
30. Federal Aviation Administration
31. Secret Service
32. Department of Foreign Affairs
33. National carriers' security personnel
34. Foreign carriers' security personnel
35. Other aviation operators' Security

In the area of maritime security, the situation inside and outside a seaport's perimeter could be even more complicated by the fact that hundreds of bulk and container trucks and dozens of merchandise trains, and cruise ship passenger buses enter and exit ports every day and night, which adds another complication to handling security on an ongoing basis. That is without forgetting multimodal seaports which include railways, passenger traffic, cruise terminals, ferry terminals and naval facilities for the country's navy and coast guard.

The narrow, fragmented, and diffuse character of government agency jurisdiction constitutes a fundamental impediment to improved physical protection of ports and airports. "The fragmentation of federal, state, and local authorities in ports is not a new issue. No one agency has authority to coordinate planning and response against clandestine forms of attack on maritime facilities, either nationally or at the local level…a single act of terrorism directed against a port can easily cut across the jurisdiction of a variety of federal, state, and local law enforcement bodies. For this reason the fragmented structure of agency responsibility, i.e. jurisdiction, is a major source of vulnerability in protecting ports against terrorism."[184] The same could apply to airports.

Stephens described the two organizational divides: "the artificial barrier created by organizations focused almost exclusively either on the land or maritime environment, and the barrier between the public and private sectors. He identified the critical missing link as "an effort to rationalize the structure of governmental authority bearing upon port security, including its relationship to private sector firms."[185]

Outreach to the industry: Is it working?

There is a compelling argument regarding the importance of the outreach to the industry. Take the shipping and freight-forwarding industries as an example. These industries are well positioned through experience to identify indicators that there is something just not right with a particular shipment for example. That is why it is essential to engage the industry across the country, and review all those indicators and what the consequent actions should be if they are not comfortable with the transaction.

"The Transportation Security Administration (TSA) developed a series of products to share security-related information with transportation stakeholders such as annual modal threat assessments that provide an overview of threats to each transportation mode - including aviation, rail, and highway - and related infrastructure. Even though the survey targeted only U.S. stakeholders, it does give an example that other countries may benefit from, or may even want to try implementing in their own environment. The result of the survey it launched showed that fifty-seven percent of the stakeholders (155 of 275 who answered this question) indicated that they were satisfied with the products they receive. However, stakeholders who receive these products were least satisfied with the actionability of the information - the degree to which the products enabled stakeholders to adjust their security measures. They noted that they prefer products with more analysis, such as trend analysis of incidents or suggestions for improving security arrangements.

---

[184]Hugh W. Stephens, "A Framework for Sustainable Port Security", Journal of Homeland Security and Emergency Management (2004) v.1 issue (2) p.14. Quoted by permission from the Journal.
[185] Ibid., p.14

"Further, not all stakeholders received the products. For example, 48 percent (128 of 264) of the stakeholders reported that they did not receive a security assessment in 2010, such as TSA's annual modal threat assessment. Improving the analysis and availability of security-related information products would help enhance stakeholders' ability to position themselves to protect against threats. Stakeholders who obtained security-related information through TSA's Web-based mechanisms were generally satisfied, but almost 60 percent (158 of 266) of stakeholders the Government Accountability Office (GAO) surveyed had never heard of the Homeland Security Information Sharing Network Critical Sectors portal (HSIN-CS). The Department of Homeland Security (DHS) views HSIN as the primary mechanism for sharing security-related information with critical sectors, including transportation stakeholders. Forty-three percent of rail stakeholders, 28 percent of highway stakeholders, and 72 percent of aviation stakeholders - who consider TSA's aviation Web Boards as their primary information-sharing mechanism - had not heard of HSIN-CS.

"Among the 55 stakeholders that had logged on to HSIN-CS, concerns were raised with the ability to locate information using the mechanism. Increasing awareness and functionality of HSIN-CS could help ensure that stakeholders receive security information, including TSA products. Defining and documenting the roles and responsibilities for information sharing among TSA offices could help strengthen information-sharing efforts.

"Officials from TSA's Office of Intelligence consider the Administration's Transportation Sector Network Management offices to be key conduits for providing security-related information directly to stakeholders. However, officials from these offices differed in their understanding of their roles. For instance, officials told GAO that their role was to communicate policy and regulatory information, rather than threat-related information. While TSA officials look to the current Transportation Security Information Sharing Plan for guidance, it does not include key elements of the approach that TSA uses to communicate security-related information to stakeholders. For instance, it does not describe the roles of TSA's Field Intelligence Officers, who facilitate the exchange of relevant threat information with local and private entities responsible for transportation security.

"Of the 53 air cargo stakeholders that completed the survey, 6 provided open-ended comments indicating that TSA provides very little security-related information to their industry concerning unscheduled air carriers such as on-demand cargo operations. These stakeholders stated that the information they receive is usually related to either large cargo companies like FedEx and UPS or passenger air carriers.

"Furthermore, providing additional context about actionability would be more beneficial if they provided actionable information or additional guidance that would allow the stakeholders to adjust security measures or take other necessary actions to improve their security postures, and also identify ongoing trends to various sectors.

"U.S. rail operator Amtrak indicated that they have monitored open and sensitive data sources for rail-related security material. The analysts produce a weekly report called Railwatch that, according to these officials, helps them develop tactics to defend against terrorist activity. Amtrak officials further indicated that these analysts also work closely with government agencies, including fusion centres, to develop and share information that they described as much more rail-centric than the daily security information that DHS makes available to them.

"According to the Transportation Systems Sector Specific Plan (TSSSP), two-way information sharing between government and industry is one of the goals of maintaining the security of the nation's transportation system.

"As it is not practical for TSA to reach every stakeholder, it relies on communications with representatives from these industries rather than individual stakeholders. TSA works with industry associations to distribute security-related information because leveraging these partnerships allows TSA to broaden its ability to reach stakeholders. Keeping in mind that stakeholders who are not affiliated with industry associations may not receive these communications. For example, according to the United Motorcoach Association, as many as two-thirds of companies in their sector were not represented by an industry association. While in effect not all stakeholders can receive every product, stakeholders included in the survey were identified by TSA as those who should be receiving this information.

"The mechanisms used by TSA to share information with transportation stakeholders include the Aviation Web Boards, the Homeland Security Information Network (HSIN), and e-mail alerts. TSA's Aviation Web Boards serve as the principal information-sharing mechanism used to share information with the aviation mode, according to TSA officials. Both TSA officials and aviation stakeholders interviewed stated that the Web Boards might be viewed principally as a mechanism for disseminating regulatory information rather than threat-related information in some sectors.

"In addition, according to the 2009 National Infrastructure Protection Plan (NIPP), efficient information sharing enables both government and private sector partners to assess events accurately, formulate risk assessments, and determine appropriate courses of action. A network approach enables secure, multidirectional information sharing between and across government and industry. This approach provides mechanisms, using information-protection protocols as required, to support the development and sharing of strategic and specific threat assessments, threat warnings, incident reports, all-hazards consequence reports, risk assessments, and best practices. [This could also include sharing intelligence information within the parameters of proper security classification as usual].

It was also noticed that "awareness and usage of HSIN-CS varied by transportation mode. 72 percent of aviation stakeholders (124 of 173) responding to the survey had not heard of HSIN-CS and 9 percent (15 of 173) were unsure, and several commented that they would be interested in accessing the system. Among aviation stakeholders, the Web Boards were the more commonly utilized information-sharing mechanism.

"DHS officials noted that there is a HSIN-CS portal for the aviation mode, but without input from the industry committees, DHS cannot develop it to meet the needs of aviation stakeholders. By contrast, facilitated communications with highway and motor carrier and rail stakeholders have resulted in the development of mode-specific HSIN-CS portals and improved outreach, according to DHS officials. These committees include the Sector Coordinating Councils (SCCs) and the Government Coordinating Councils (GCCs). These councils create a structure through which representative groups from all levels of government and the private sector can collaborate or share existing approaches to critical infrastructure protection and work together to advance capabilities.

"The Field Intelligence Officer (FIO) program is an integral part of TSA's information-sharing environment. According to TSA, the FIOs serve as the principal advisor to Federal Security Directors and their staffs on all intelligence matters. Other responsibilities include developing and maintaining a working relationship with local, federal, state, and private entities responsible for transportation security, regardless of mode. While officers are based at the airports, they interact with the security officials from local rail, mass transit, highway, and port and pipeline (where applicable) modes to facilitate the sharing and exchange of relevant threat information."[186]

Under such conditions, the private sector, who has much to lose when there is a breach of security, could be left out in the cold, and at the mercy of these competing jurisdictions as well as competing public service empire builders.

As was mentioned earlier, intelligence is a two-way street. Intelligence agencies' headquarters share intelligence information with their own regional offices, and with their partners in government such as the Department of Transport among others. But what happens to the soft-intelligence regarding threat indices in their own backyard, i.e. at ports and airports. Ignoring that aspect denies the intelligence agency and the intelligence analysts an important component of the

---

[186] GAO Report #12-44 - November 2011on Transportation Information Sharing

overall picture they are tasked to look at. To illustrate this point the case of the young Nigerian Umar Farouk Abdulmuttalab (the underwear bomber) may shed light on how intelligence information does not reach all the stakeholders involved.

Attempt by Abdulmuttalab to destroy Northwest Airlines Flight 153

The post-mortem undertaken by the US administration following the December 25, 2009 attempt by Umar Farouk Abdulmuttalab to destroy Northwest Airlines Flight 153 was rightly considered by the administration as a failure of counter-terrorism, especially that there were pretty obvious suspicious indications about this passenger. In a message sent by the Director of National Intelligence Dennis C. Blair to employees of the United States Intelligence Community, aimed at improving procedures and systems to detect and prevent a similar attempt from succeeding, Blair said:

The fact "That Mr. Abdulmuttalab boarded Northwest Flight 153 for Detroit was a failure of the counterterrorism system. We had strategic intelligence that Al-Qaeda in the Arab Peninsula had the intention of taking action against the United States. We did not direct more resources against them, nor insist that the watch-listing criteria be adjusted. The Intelligence Community analysts who were working hard on immediate threats to Americans in Yemen did not understand the fragments of intelligence on what turned out later to be Mr. Abdulmuttalab, so they did not push him onto the "no fly" list."

"To prevent such situations from arising again, Blair underlined in his message that the Intelligence community "will take a fresh and penetrating look at strengthening both human and technical performance and do what we have to do in all areas." He added that he has "specifically been tasked to oversee and manage work in four areas":

1. Assigning clear lines of responsibility for investigating all leads on high-priority threats, so they are pursued more aggressively.
2. Distributing intelligence reports more quickly and widely, especially those suggesting specific threats against the United States.
3. Applying more rigorous standards to analytical tradecraft to improve intelligence integration and action.
4. Enhancing the criteria for adding individuals to the terrorist watch list and the "no-fly" watch list."[187]

Unfortunately the message did not indicate that airport security personnel and airline check-in counter personnel must be sensitized about a potential threat, nor does it seem they were given any particular briefing about suspicious passengers, whether their names were on a no-fly list or not.

---

[187] "Message" by Dennis C. Blair, Director of National Intelligence, to Employees of the U.S. Intelligence Community, January 7, 2010. www.dni.gov/press_releases/20100107_release.pdf

The young Mr. Abdulmuttalab, who was traveling from Africa, then across the Atlantic, on a one-way ticket, and without any luggage should have at least raised some suspicion. The fact that his father Umaru Abdulmuttalab was once a Minister of the Economy in Nigeria probably qualified the son by extension as a subject "beyond suspicion". That is even though the media reported that the father had met with a Central Intelligence Agency (CIA) official about his son. But the report was not circulated within the US intelligence community, thus raising concerns that US intelligence agencies have not cooperated adequately despite ongoing pressure to do so since the 9/11 attacks.

Streamlining the security intelligence function within the Department of Transport

As elaborated previously, the overall management of transportation security should be the responsibility of the Department of Transport and everybody else working with that department. Why? Because the Department of Transport is the crucial link between all modes of transport and the security and intelligence community, not to forget of course the military establishment and the Coast Guard.

The other pillar is that the Department of Transport is better suited for this task because of its regulatory mandate and operational prerogatives of ensuring ongoing communications between all the stakeholders involved at all times in all facets of the transportation industry, and not just during a crisis. It must also be underlined that stakeholders are partners in intelligence and not just a consulting body. Therefore keeping a handle on intelligence in the transportation sector on an ongoing basis can best be performed through "Permanent Joint Regional Transportation Security Committees."

It is essential to keep in perspective that ports and airports are each a system of systems: They are critical nodes in the specialized complex of economic inter-modal subsystems that move passengers, goods and cargo around the world. At both ports and airports, cargo and passengers are transferred to/from the maritime or aviation mode, then from/to other transportation modes (e.g. maritime, rail, road). Typically, ports and airports are spread throughout the country except of course in the case of very small countries with only one airport, and possibly no access whatsoever to the sea.

Depending on the size of the country, the Transportation Security Directorate, while operating from the headquarters of the Department of Transport, maintains regional security offices in various parts of the country. Each of these regional offices carries out its duties within the region it is responsible for in coordination with their headquarters, which bear ultimate responsibility in terms of security, especially in situations requiring the closure of a port or an airport, seizure of a ship or an aircraft, or denying them docking, anchoring or landing authorization.

In terms of security, the regions can, and should play a more active and important ongoing role than what they traditionally do. In some cases they are pretty active and contribute immensely to security, but there are situations in some countries where they are relegated to the role of gofer and paperwork chaser between the stakeholders and the Directorate's headquarters. Through their ongoing interaction with local law enforcement and intelligence agencies, and with stakeholders, they could be capable of exchanging threat-related information (soft intelligence) in the field. Keeping in mind that in most cases, it is rare that that type of soft-intelligence, both criminal or related to terrorism, makes its way to the attention of the security and intelligence agencies at headquarters level, and if it does, chances are that it will not be given the attention it deserves. This type of security information, it must be noted, is of significant importance when it comes to monitoring threat trends. Although Fusion Centres could provide that link, the speed at which aviation security crises travel calls for a more direct and instant interaction with federal decision makers.

Because of the inherent specificity of the aviation, maritime, and surface transportation industries; it evolves that each regional Transportation security office will have corresponding modal units, or simply a couple of individuals jointly managing the three modes, or maybe just one interacting with all three modes of transportation. The overall regional security units may be managed by one manager or director, who is the de facto transportation security specialist in the region. His/her position will provide him/her with an overall view of the security of the whole transportation system in the region. This person, who has acquired hands-on expertise in security, but also a deep understanding of the transportation industries involved, is indeed in a position of significant responsibility.

Workings of the Permanent Joint Regional Transportation Security Committees

How do we get those who have the intelligence, and those who need it to de-compartmentalise and work together - not just cooperate - on an ongoing basis?

What is recommended here is for the Department of Transport to create formal permanent Joint Regional Transportation Security Committees in each of the Transportation Security Directorate's geographic regions. As there will be a Regional Maritime Security sub-Committee, there will also be one for Aviation Security, and a third one for surface transportation security.

Their success rests of course on proper organization and management, provided they handle the various facets of security like a well rehearsed orchestra through the baton of one conductor, the Department of Transport.

Much of the day-to-day interaction between the Regional Transportation Security Officers on the one hand, the aviation, maritime and surface transportation industry security officers, as well as the local intelligence and law enforcement agencies on the other hand, will be conducted on a person-to-person, colleague-to-colleague basis. This semi-official, semi-unofficial interaction, which is not a bad thing of course, is still rather incomplete, as it does not formalize the relationship between the various stakeholders, and leaves no assurance that the same level of symbiotic relationship will continue when people move, retire, or are transferred.

The informal relationship does not allow the Regional Transportation Security Officer from sharing the wider view of the Transportation Security Directorate in terms of aviation, maritime and surface transportation security with his/her counterparts. Besides, it does not give him/her the formal and official platform to ask them for information pertaining to security matters, nor share information available to him. That is without forgetting that, due to the nature of their work and their environment, intelligence officers in general would not discuss intelligence outside the parameters of a formally sanctioned relationship. As will be described later on, without a formally sanctioned agreement with the headquarters of the intelligence service, the Regional Transportation Security office will not be recipient of pertinent ongoing soft intelligence to complete the puzzle picture of its various threat investigations.

One way to achieve the ongoing symbiosis between the various players mentioned above is to create an official forum for them to interact professionally under the leadership of the Directorate of Transportation Security. Hands-on experience in aviation, maritime and security intelligence permits us to confidently state that Permanent Joint Regional Transportation Security Committees in each of the Transportation Security Directorate's geographic regions constitute the best forum through which the objective of keeping a handle on intelligence and awareness in the maritime and aviation domains on an ongoing basis is best met.

A relatively similar approach is followed in the U.S., but essentially in the area of maritime security. In a 2005 report addressing the maritime sector, the U.S. Government Accountability Office (GAO) pointed out that "area (i.e. regional) maritime security committees provide a structure that improves information sharing among port security stakeholders. At port locations visited by the GAO in April 2005, federal and non-federal stakeholders said that the newly formed committees were an improvement over previous information sharing efforts.[188] The types of information shared included assessments of vulnerabilities at port locations and strategies the Coast Guard intends to use in protecting key

---

[188] "Maritime Security New Structures have improved information sharing, but Security clearance processing requires further attention", GAO Report www.gao.gov/assets/250/246013.pdf - April 2005

infrastructure."[189] In 2009 the Office of the Director of National Intelligence issued a report aiming at integrating maritime and air intelligence within his organization.[190]

Another similar approach was proposed in the 2007 British Cabinet document entitled "UK Border Security in a Global Hub."[191] "The British Border and Immigration Agency established a network of Airline Liaison Officers (ALOs) who operate in support of carriers overseas to help detect and deter inadequately documented passengers among several other functions."[192] "Knowledge of other agency priorities relies to a large extent on cross agency awareness training. This is largely welcomed by operational staff, and has generated positive results."[193]

"Truly effective interventions at the border rely on high-quality specific... intelligence... Some of the intelligence which results in successful interventions at the border is generated at the border itself. However, a large amount of useful intelligence is also generated by intelligence capabilities elsewhere in the same organisation, or in external organisations, that take a more holistic intelligence approach ... of which the border is only one dimension."[194]

"The Police National Maritime Security Strategy has also introduced strategic partnerships across the UK that enable the police, the other enforcement agencies and the industry to work together to protect maritime ports using all agency resources."[195]

"The Home Office and the Department of Transport (DfT) [communicated] with senior police and industry representatives to identify the most appropriate way to deliver this"[196] "... including requiring the operator at...a designated port or airport to chair a security committee to be attended by the relevant agencies. The purpose of such a committee would be to produce a security plan which is based on relevant threat and risk information and collective analysis; identifies and prioritises mitigating actions and facilitates the production of an agreement on the services the police will provide at a facility, in the context of the security activities of other parties."[197]

---

[189] Also consult Department of Homeland Security, "Coast Guard Members sought for Area Maritime Security Committees (AMSCS)"; Federal Register Notices, (USCG-2008-1217) v.73, number248, December 24, 2008.

[190] Office of the Director of National Intelligence - "Global Maritime and Air Intelligence Integration", January 2009.

[191] "Security in a Global Hub: Establishing the UK's new border arrangements, Border Review, Domestic Policy & Strategy", Cabinet Office, London: www.cabinetoffice.gov.uk/border_review.aspx
Crown copyright: November 2007.

[192] Ibid., paragraph 3.3

[193] Ibid., paragraph 4.19

[194] Ibid., paragraph 4.16

[195] Ibid., paragraph 4.68

[196] Ibid., paragraph 5.90

[197] Ibid., paragraph 5.91

The main difference between the American and the British examples and the approach proposed in this book is that the American maritime committees are managed by the U.S. Coast Guard, and the British aviation committees are managed by the port or airport authority. We, however, are of the opinion that committees organized and managed by the Department of Transport for the reasons given earlier in this chapter will be comprehensive of all modes of transport, more effective, and have a better reach. Besides they will be managed by one point of responsibility, namely the Department of Transport. The department is ideally suited for this task because of its regulatory mandate, its operational prerogatives which it can action post-haste, and its role within the transportation industry. All of the above helps ensure ongoing communications between all the stakeholders involved in all facets of the transportation industry at all times, and not just during emergency situations.

Committee organization, membership and benefits

From the perspective of the Transportation Security Directorate (TSD) in a given region, there would be three Regional Transportation Security sub-Committees: one for aviation, one for maritime and one for surface, each meeting independently, but are all chaired by the same person, namely the Regional Security Director.

As for the composition of the Aviation and Maritime Security sub-Committees, the following is suggested as an indication. There could be more or less participants such as representatives from the air force, the navy, the coast guard and others, depending on the country's specific requirements. As mentioned earlier, the committees should not be too large to become difficult to manage. One way to control the size of the Committee, especially in major metropolitan areas, is to have certain key working sessions with everybody in attendance, and other sessions with only those directly involved in a given situation.

Proposed composition of the Regional Aviation Security Sub-Committee

- TSD Regional Security Director (Chairman)
- TSD Regional Aviation Security Inspector(s)
- Airport Authority chief of security
- Airline companies security managers
- A representative from each of the federal, regional and local law-enforcement agencies involved in aviation security
- Customs representative
- Passports and Immigration representative
- The regional Intelligence Service representative in charge of transportation/ aviation security
- Transborder counterparts whenever applicable

Proposed composition of the Regional Maritime Security Sub-Committee

- TSD Regional Security Director (Chairman)
- TSD Regional Maritime Security Inspector(s)
- Port Authority chief of security
- Shipping lines and rail operators security managers
- Port facilities security managers
- Coast Guard representative
- A representative from each of the federal, regional and local law-enforcement agencies involved in maritime security
- Customs representative
- Passports and Immigration representative
- The regional Intelligence Service representative in charge of transportation/ maritime security
- Transborder counterparts whenever applicable

The Surface Transportation Security sub-Committee will be organized along the same lines, and may include rail, urban transit, ferries, highways and inland waterways.

Regional and local committees located in outlying areas, as opposed to major urban centres, especially those with infrequent aviation or maritime operations may only have a Security Inspector for all three modes of transport. Unless traffic volume and frequency increases appreciably, it will not be necessary to have more than one transportation security officer to cover all three modes of transport for the region due to the paucity of traffic.

Importance of the Regional Security Director

It is very important to underline the fact that the Regional Security Director, i.e. the man or woman in charge of overall Transportation Security, will be the anchor person for transportation security in the whole region. In turn, he/she will report directly to the Transportation Security Directorate at the headquarters of the Department of Transport in the national capital.

Security and intelligence call for special measures, and one crucial component of it is the special quality of the people recruited to be in charge, their career path, and proper remuneration.

The important role played by the Regional Security Director makes him/her the de facto highest regional authority in transportation security. By his/her knowledge of the security situation in all modes of transport, that person will hold a key position within the overall regional security and intelligence establishment.

This position calls for long on the job operational experience, and consequently, all the incentives required to maintain such a person in his/her position as long as deemed necessary. One more thing to keep in mind is that this person must be an integral partner in the country's intelligence apparatus. The same must be said of the Director General of the Transportation Security Directorate at the department's headquarters, who fills the same functions but on the national level. This means he possesses an overall view of the security situation in the area of transportation security across the country.

If you were to ask yourself today if a crisis takes place "Who is in charge?" Chances are that in most cases due to the proliferation of those who will respond "I do", there is an uncertainty as to who is really in charge. Many people will say "Call 911." This makes eminent sense of course, provided the 911 emergency operators have been told that when they receive an emergency call that is related to transportation security they must immediately advise the Transportation Security Directorate.

Role of the committees in keeping a handle on security on an ongoing basis

From a holistic government and industry perspective, the Committees will formalize the regional relationship among the various stakeholders involved; establish a secure mechanism for the exchange of intelligence-quality security information, particularly those related to threats to the transportation sector. The interaction among the committee members will also help identify the areas of cooperation and coordination among their respective organizations, and establish their role as a problem-solving and initiatives-generating group.

By integrating all the major players, the regional Security Inspectors in the various transportation sectors will become active partners with an integral role to play in the security and intelligence information exchange process. And, as mentioned earlier, the Regional Transportation Security Director will be the pivot of the overall transportation security network in the region.

Why are the Regional Security Committees conducive to better security?

Members of the committee are expected to exchange security intelligence related information among themselves at all times, and find solutions to specifically local security matters without having to wait for a formal meeting. This exchange will allow for an ongoing operational interaction between the stakeholders and the government security and intelligence representatives on the committee. All such exchanges will be handled at the proper security clearance level, and through secure channels, to ensure protection of classified information, third party intelligence, as well as the aviation and maritime stakeholders' own proprietary information.

The ongoing symbiosis created among the committee members during non-crisis times will render the inter and intra-departmental management of actual crisis situations, when tension is at its highest, to be more swift, more closely coordinated and performed in a non-competitive manner. This is because members of the committee would have already established, not just a close professional rapport among themselves in times of peace, but equally important, a personal comfort zone, and would thus feel much more bonded like a team working with each other in a coordinated fashion in emergency situations. Once more, this is akin to an orchestra, where on-going rehearsals and concerts build better harmony, not just in musical terms, but also in terms of how the musicians interact and play together.

The Transportation Security Committees' network will serve as a rapid conduit for the dissemination of security notifications. The Committees' work will also contribute to the ongoing Threat and Risk Assessments from a field perspective; as well as enhance the mechanism of communicating changes to threat levels. The committees will address special situations as they arise in consultation with the participants' respective headquarters. The Committees will be called upon to provide the vehicle to jointly manage the security aspect of other major transportation related events such as air shows, tall ships visits, state visits, summit meetings, major sports events such as the Olympic Games, and other special visits involving the transportation system, and finally they will also serve as a pool for conducting joint security simulation exercises for training purposes.

It is strongly recommended that joint training exercises triggered by simulated Threat and Risk Assessments be carried out periodically. The exercises, organized by the Transportation Security Directorate must include staff at the headquarters and regional levels along with aviation, maritime and surface transportation partners and stakeholders from the industry. This is where Transportation Security Intelligence should be added to the training program. The exercises will allow the participants to test handle various simulated threats and evaluate the risks and vulnerabilities to which the target could be exposed.

The importance of simulated exercises comes to light when assessing individuals' reactions, self control, leadership qualities, and ability to work efficiently under stress as a team. These qualifications appear very quickly when handling emergencies. Hence, it is certainly much better to detect any behavioural anomalies, not to say catastrophic behaviour, during an exercise rather than when a real crisis is unfolding, and when negative behavioural traits do exacerbate the situation and lead to possible loss of command and control.

CHAPTER 10

CLOSING REMARKS

In the key area of transportation security, the Department of Transport is the best agent to bring all security, intelligence and the stakeholders together.

PREPAREDNESS AND INTELLIGENCE SHARING

According to Professor William V. Pelfrey; "the "Cycle of Preparedness" within organizations tasked with preventing, responding to, and recovering from attacks provides a framework to better accomplish an "auto adaptive" capacity. This framework begins with prevention, (which may be) accomplished through collaboration and information sharing as primary elements, and threat recognition, Risk Management, and intervention as additional elements; followed by awareness that an event is occurring; and response in the form of emergency response activities; and finally consequence management and recovery to revitalize the jurisdictions." [198]

Security by its own nature is obstructive, expensive and non-revenue generating, but it is of course necessary. The whole perspective of many security and intelligence agencies regarding security is often skewed, as they consider themselves sometimes to be the centre of the universe, and everything revolves around them. Former Secretary for Homeland Security Tom Ridge expressed it beautifully when he said in one of his speeches that "we should move on from need to know to need to share."

The role of intelligence is to think in terms of the future, not what has already happened. i.e. stay at least one step ahead of spies and terrorists. Intelligence narrows the scope of sources of threat, filters wheat from chaff, and ensures that prevention is targeted and focused instead of being shotgun like, and very expensive.

Since it is impossible to prepare, protect, deter, preempt and mitigate for every possible threat, swift intelligence analysis and sharing for the common purpose of foreseeing or recognizing terrorist threats, actions, and behaviours is the quintessential element in the cycle of preparedness.

---

[198] William V. Pelfrey, "The Cycle of Preparedness: Establishing a Framework to Prepare for Terrorist Threats," Journal of Homeland Security and Emergency Management, v.2, Issue 1 2005, Article 5 p.1 - Virginia Commonwealth University. Quoted by permission from the Journal.

However, creating monstrous organizations by lumping together thousands of employees representing or hailing from so many departments each with its own tricentennial traditions, culture and modus operandi, may not be the most efficient way to do it, especially in areas such as security and intelligence that require a blend of long term trend analysis, yet rapid intervention almost at the same time.

"The responsibilities of the Department of Homeland Security (DHS) counting more than 200,000 employees are arguably the most diverse of any federal department. They include securing US seaports, airports, and land ports-of-entry; adjudicating applications for American citizenship; responding to hurricanes and other natural disasters; protecting the President and visiting heads of state; and protecting federal buildings."[199] In light of our own experience and the proposal that transportation security be managed by the Transportation Security Directorate, the U.S. Transportation Security Administration (TSA), which now reports to DHS, should have probably been part of the Department of Transport (DOT) to safeguard its operational specialization.

Understanding how "we" do intelligence is not enough to combat terrorists who come from different cultures altogether. We need to understand their culture, and their thinking and reasoning process, as well as why is it they really "hate us", not what some ignoramus, or worse still, criminally ill-intentioned neo-whatever attributes to them as the motive behind this hate. Sometimes they have a very good reason to hate us, which is why we should also look inwards at what we, or what our "allies" do or say that make people revolt in such violent fashion. Most of the time herein lies the best line of defence: know thy enemy!

Once we and the "bad guys" are set on a war path everybody goes into excesses and it becomes very difficult to go back to reason for both. Things get out of hand and we end up all losing in one way or another, even if we succeed in physically eliminating the bad guys. If one were to look around the wider Middle East, especially in light of the 2011 Arab peoples' insurrection in several countries at the same time, it does not call for too much intelligence to note that there are a lot of angry people out there, and for a cause. And please do not parrot what is being fed down our neck that "this is a tough neighbourhood." It is not tougher than any other once the people are left alone to live their lives in peace. Take for example the long despised, self-imposed and hated rulers like those of the Middle East to whom we accredit ambassadors and treat as if they were geniuses, while they are treating their nations worse than dogs and helping themselves and their children to the national wealth of the nation. When we blind ourselves and choose these self-imposed leaders as our allies we should not be surprised that those nations end up hating us. So we need to wake up too, at least for our sake and in our own interest.

---

[199] Harold M. Greenberg "Is the Department of Homeland Security an Intelligence Agency?"- Intelligence and National Security, (2009) v.24 number 2, pp.216-235.

No doubt the elimination of Osama Binladen is a serious blow to Al-Qaeda, both financially and in terms of leadership. Al-Qaeda has never appealed to the Arab and Muslim masses, and the death of its iconic spiritual leader may have sounded its disappearance. Whether another leader will emerge or not, he will not have the same aura - or the money - that Binladen initially brought with him. Al-Qaeda as we know it is essentially finished. Yet, the death of Binladen, and the possible return of Taliban rule in Afghanistan will decentralize Al-Qaeda even more and will render it inconsequential as an organization. But that is not necessarily good news, because there could be dozens of Al-Qaedas mushrooming all of a sudden somewhere in the world, then possibly disappearing to reappear elsewhere, which will render the fight against terrorism much more difficult. The root problems that led to Al-Qaeda, and that were never addressed at the proper time, did not start with 9/11, but way earlier. The Al-Qaeda phenomenon has been a catastrophe not just for world peace, but also for the overall Arab and Muslim nations.[200]

This is why intelligence has to be very close to and in step with foreign affairs and the executive branch. Ongoing intelligence would thus provide a very close insight into what's happening out there in general and not just among the bad people. It would not just be a means of prevention and protection, but also a source of deep understanding and better decision-making on our part. One of the first who need to understand these basic facts is our elected political leadership itself, which often embarks on foreign policies that reflect personal ideologies and corporate interests that may not necessarily be in the interest of the nation as a whole.

One should also note the separation wall similar to that between Israel and the West Bank, or the earlier one between the two Berlins, which separates between whatever is done at the intelligence level and the political masters' level. Intelligence can collect and analyse everything it wishes, but political decisions are often made with or without reference to intelligence analysis for reasons that are not related to national interest. This is a glaring example of "democracy not at work." When things go wrong, it is easy for the politicians and the media to blame intelligence as a whole, because they know that the latter cannot publically defend itself and its actions.

If we continue running intelligence detached from the realities of our world and in some kind of vacuum that does not take into consideration such things as the underlying triggers of terrorism and piracy as well as our own willful misguided policies, then we should not be surprised as to the result.

---

[200] A 2003 survey conducted in Saudi Arabia showed that Binladen had a 49% approval rating, but when asked if the respondent wanted to live under a Binladen style government, only 5% said yes. "Proceedings of a Workshop Convened to Consider Homeland Security in the Year 2015, footnote p.19 - Published by The Department of Homeland Security in cooperation with Georgetown University - January 2008.

WHO STANDS TO BENEFIT?

In the key area of transportation, the multiplicity of distinct security branches within government in general and the Department of Transport in particular, namely a branch for aviation security, a branch for maritime security, and a third one for surface transportation each separate from the other, is a recipe for losing control over security that could lead to a national disaster.

For intelligence pertaining to transportation security to be handled properly from all its aspects, it must all be integrated into one multi-modal intelligence unit in order for the right hand to know what the left hand is doing, and not divided among the various transportation sectors as is the case in several countries. While being multi-modal, it must be managed by one team of transportation security and intelligence professionals at the top. Threat information touching any module must be shared by all the modules among themselves in real time. Keeping in mind that Threat and Risk Assessments must be based on actionable intelligence and not produced simply because there is pressure to produce something.

The consolidation of the multi-modal intelligence and security function within the Transportation Security Directorate and the creation of the various Joint Regional Transportation Security Committees will result in the following benefits:

A - Internally within the Department of Transport

- Ensure that command and control and expertise regarding inter-modal transportation security, especially the intelligence functions involved, is concentrated in one centre of responsibility, namely the Transportation Security Directorate within the Department of Transport,
- Streamline the production, dissemination of actionable Threat Assessments and the ensuing follow-up,
- Provide the Department of Transport through the Transportation Security Directorate with the needed domestic intelligence information pertaining to security within ports, airports, airlines, shipping companies and other pertinent sectors of the aviation, maritime and surface transportation industries,
- At the regional level, it will structure and support the relationship between the Transportation Security Directorate regional offices, the security/ intelligence community, as well as the industry stakeholders by bringing them under the umbrella of an ongoing   operational   working   group, namely the Joint Regional Transportation Security Committees,
- At the national level, it will ensure that adequate ongoing transportation-related intelligence is being provided not only for the Department of Transport to fulfill its security mandate, but also for the security intelligence community to add an important   parameter to its intelligence-gathering and assessment role.

B - Airlines, airports and the maritime industry stakeholders

The stakeholders, whether they are airlines, airports, ports, port facilities, shipping companies, law enforcement and the intelligence service, will thus have a single point of contact in all matters related to transportation security. This will minimize the confusion that often happens during emergencies, and will ensure better inter-agency cooperation.

This should also help alleviate the financial burden on the stakeholders and the taxpayers as a result of the huge cost of supplying, installing and operating a never-ending protective physical infrastructure that keeps changing with every innovative threat.

C - The Intelligence and law enforcement community

Thanks to their ongoing interaction with the transportation industry, perhaps the biggest discovery that will be made by intelligence agencies in particular and law enforcement in general is that there is so much to learn from the transportation industry. And it is to the advantage of the industry as well as the overall national security that they do learn.

As mentioned repeatedly in this book, by understanding each other's world, and by creating this ongoing two-way working partnership on various levels, we will all be in a better position to determine: what intelligence to collect, where to collect it from, and how to analyze it to provide meaningful timely, precise and reliable actionable Threat and Risk Assessments, but also for pre-emptive targeting and interdiction before the bad guys go into action.

The bottom line for transportation security as well as intelligence professionals is to be able to identify the threat potential much, much earlier in the process, which is what we should always aim for. That is why intelligence has to be on the ball and ahead of everybody else.

All of which will substantially help protect our ports, airports, airlines, ships, waterways, roads and railways. It will reduce the cost of security for all concerned within reason, but, above all it will protect passengers, shippers, staff, and the population at large. This is how we can defeat the enemy.

APPENDICES

The following appendices expand on certain key historic conflicts that will continue to exacerbate the security situation not just in the region, but all over the world; unless of course reasonable and well thought-out solutions or settlements for them are found.

Understanding the underlying causes of trouble in various parts of the world adequately is part of the process of giving each issue its "proper label", to gauge its potential devastating dimensions, or better, to facilitate finding a possible realistic solution for it. The appendices have therefore been added in order to provide some depth regarding a select number of key international issues that have, or could have, future influence on the rise of threats to the transportation sector anywhere in the world. To render the overall exercise more useful, a heads-up is offered for some, and a proposed solution for others at least for discussion purposes.

APPENDIX 1: Why religion?

APPENDIX 2: Justifying suicide attacks: The world according to extremists

APPENDIX 3: A different approach to solving the Palestine-Israel Question

APPENDIX 4: The case of Iraq: An outlook to the future

APPENDIX 5: The Afghanistan super challenge

APPENDIX 6: The origins of piracy around the Somali coast

APPENDIX 1

WHY RELIGION?

"J'observe que toute les Églises ont eu la prudence de ne promettre le vrai bonheur qu'après la vie. Les Communistes sont perdus pour avoir promis le bonheur sur terre, alors qu'ils sont incapables de nous en montrer même un échantillon."201

You cannot run away from history, it will always catch up with you!

In most parts of the world one's identity is his or her religion. This applies to deeply religious people, but also for those who do not practice religion. To them it is inconceivable not to have a religion, as God cannot exist outside religion. Thus, not following a religion especially theirs is identical to being an atheist. To some of them killing an atheist is considered to be a good deed. Think of India, Ireland, Lebanon, Afghanistan or Saudi Arabia and you get the point. Being a Sunni Muslim, a Shiite Muslim; an Ashkenazi Jew, a Sephardic Jew; a Catholic, Protestant or Orthodox Christian is who they are, that is before being the citizen of this and that country. In some cases religious identity supersedes ethnic origin. That is why most of these countries' identification cards and passports include the bearer's religion and, in some cases the specific rite they adhere to.

A few weeks before going to print, and while walking down a street in Montreal this author came across a Hassidic Jew. So he asked him a question about a prayer, to which he wanted to refer to in one his lectures. The question referred to the well known prayer "Our Father who art in Heaven, etc.", and the fact that there was an identical prayer in the Quran, namely "Ayat Al-Kursi." So he wanted to know if there was one similar to both in Jewish liturgy. The Jewish man smiled and replied with a question in a pure New York accent as to which religion this author followed, but he never answered the question. The question was eventually put to the Rabbi of the local congregation in town and he directed the author to the famous prayer "Shema Yisrael". The story is told in order to give credence to the first sentence in this chapter, i.e. for some, you are defined by your religion. Period!

When Arabs for example ask a foreigner about where he is from, and he replies: "I am American." That is not enough for them. They will inevitably go to the next question, or find an indirect way to figure out if you are Christian or Jewish? Ultimately the reply will determine how they define this individual. In

---

201 Christine Ockrent, et Comte Alexandre de Marenches, "Dans le secret des princes", Éditions Stock, Paris 1986 (Comte Alexandre de Marenches was Director General of the French Intelligence Service known as " Service de Documentation extérieure et de Contre espionnage" (S.D.E.C.E) from 1970 to 1981, which preceded the current Direction générale de la Sécurité extérieure (D.G.S.E.), p.184. Tanslation: "I notice that all churches were prudent enough not to promise real happiness until in the after-life. The Communists are lost because they promised happiness on earth, but they are unable to produce even a sample."

today's world, when a suspect person happens to also be a Muslim, things get complicated. It is all unfortunate, but, warts and all, this is the world we live in, and not the one we would like to be in.

Everything in the Middle East and some other parts of the world are directly linked to what happened, or believed to have happened five thousand years ago or more. Centuries before the age of real science-based knowledge, and individual freedom of thinking, the self-appointed clergy of the three monotheistic religions assumed the responsibility of interpreting their concept of the creation, the creator, the end of times, the afterlife, how the amazingly complex universe was created, and even described how it will blow up one day (They never explained why it should blow up!), etc. Their conception was drawn without any proof and without being held accountable for what they propose. But it remains that in all religions the masses, educated or not, simply follow without questioning.

The authors of the relatively more recent three monotheistic religions have prescribed how humanity should interpret these phenomena over which nobody has or will ever have control or even complete understanding. Adherents of the Muslim faith swear that "Islam is the way", or that "the solution must be Islamic." Christians maintain that "Jesus is the way," and the Jews consider themselves to be "the chosen people." In a sense these three religions in particular are so different from each other in certain appearances, yet they are so similar in essence. After all, they all derive from the same source, namely very ancient Near Eastern cultures and religions, and later modified, changed and added to. Yet, despite the fact that the end product for all these religions is inherently the same, each group considers itself to be more special in the eyes of God than the other two.

The dangerous part in all of that is that throughout their history, believers and clergy in each of these religions have attributed a missionary political and militant message of one sort or another to their faith, which often includes the power of life and death over other people's lives. It so happens that most believers, not just the illiterates among them, strongly believe in these teachings, and are unwilling to use their common sense and think freely and independently outside the box. Some of these people are kings, presidents, prime ministers, politicians, military generals, university professors, scientists, or otherwise highly educated people who hold these beliefs and are willing to kill and die to achieve what they think God has ordained: A historically proven very dangerous state of affairs indeed.

In relatively recent times, Arab and Muslim peoples found themselves several times at a crossroad in their relationship with the Christian Europeans in general, but specifically with the British, the French and much later with the Americans. In modern times when relations between Muslims and both Britain and France were at their worst, the Muslims were very close to the Americans. Eventually the relations improved with the former and soured with the latter. If this is an indication, it is that religion is not the subject of agreements or disagreements between them, but politics and interests are.

Jewish fundamentalists subscribe to the notion that what they describe as "return to the Promised Land" is a God-given right and a promise that is not subject for debate. Christian fundamentalists believe it their duty to help the Jews reassemble in the same "Promised Land" so that when the Second Coming of Christ happens, it will be easier for them to convert all the Jews to Christianity, so that they are saved from eternal damnation. Other non-Christians are considered ineligible to have a place in the Holy Land unless they convert. Fundamentalist Muslims consider that at the end of times, only Muslims will go to Heaven. As to what happens to the others does not seem to fare any better than Muslims under extremist Christian or Jewish ideologies. Yet they all consider themselves to be the People of the Book and the sons of the mythical Abraham, and before him the equally mythical Adam and Eve.

People are free to create their own beliefs and live by them; i.e. live and let live. In the case of the three monotheistic religions as defined by the fundamentalists among them and the extremists and orthodox in particular, all three religions are on an ongoing collision course. Today, those who hold such deep beliefs carry guns, commission suicide bombers, lead armies, have access to weapons of mass destruction and have always found justifications for using any of them to assert their group's political and strategic interests. To all these, the clash of the end of times, i.e. the mythological Armageddon, is a fact, and so real that it will be a duty worth killing and dying for: A pretty grim picture of the future of the world.

When religion is hijacked by politics

Few outside academia and history buffs remember the various Catholic Crusades, which meant to liberate the Holy Land from the infidels, i.e. the Muslims. The Crusades were also a cover for an ongoing competition between kings and popes in Europe, each wanting to prove to the other who is in charge. That is when the Popes decided to make their point by organizing and leading armies under the sign of the cross to do the job.

When the Crusaders reached the lands of the 'infidels', they proceeded with the same ruthlessness they displayed on the way to massacre not only the infidels, but also any Arabs, Jews or Christians who followed the Eastern Orthodox church who did not toe the Catholic line. By the time the Crusaders reached the 'Holy Land', i.e. Palestine and the city of Jerusalem in particular, and established themselves, their opponents back at home, namely the European kings, had already noted that the Popes' led Crusades were successful. They also noted that the masses in Europe did indeed heed the call of successive Popes and marched to their beat. Not to be outdone, the Kings eventually joined the subsequent Crusades, and by the time the populations of the 'liberated' lands were pacified, the Kings set out to reap the economic and political benefits of what became now a military conquest followed by creating permanent settlements. At the end of the day, the whole Crusades initiative that lasted close to two centuries had turned into a pure colonial entreprise in the East, and the ultimate triumph of the kings over the Popes in the West.

The peoples of the regions occupied by the Crusaders, both Muslim and followers of the Eastern Christian church fought back against theweakening Crusaders until the whole Crusade movement collapsed under pressure partially by the resistance of the occupied populations, and as a result of home countries' internal problems, economic pressures and internal divisions.

Centuries later the process of using religion to seize the same Holy Land from its Christian and Muslim inhabitants, repeated itself with the creation of the State of Israel. While building Jewish settlements on land conquered or confiscated from them by force is considered to be a Mitzvah, i.e. a good deed ordained by no less than God, no wonder that in the minds of the Palestinians, both Muslims and Christians, who are losing their livelihood, the Jewish settlements are nothing but a repeat of the Crusader entreprise of the twelfth to the fourteenth century.

Religion did not seem to be a major source of conflict when the Arab rulers and populations of Christian and Muslim countries were allies and worked together, as happened many times in history, whether in the Levant or in Andalusia, Spain. But once they were on opposite sides politically, or for strategic or economic reasons, all of a sudden you would see crosses against crescents and vice versa.[202] This is what Samuel Huntington wrongly refers to as the "Clash of Civilizations."[203] This is also how Al-Qaeda and its adherents see it. There is no doubt for the group as to the existence of a clash of civilizations. In reality though, the real clash is the clash of mythologies not civilizations. The civilizational aspect of Arab and Western cultures rather included numerous examples of knowledge and scientific exchange that enriched both peoples over the centuries. The bottom line is that people stand up, react and fight to defend themselves and their countries when attacked irrespective of which religion they happen to believe in. Religion thus becomes simply one among many rallying cries.

A recent book by Amos N. Guiora, who spent a long career in the Judge Advocate General's Corps of the Israel Defense Forces, and was involved in "on the ground"

---

[202] While Christianity is rich with iconography and symbols, starting with the most visible symbol, the cross, Islam had never really had a distinct symbol. The crescent became considered as a symbol of Islam possibly at the behest of the European Christians as they fought back the Muslim Ottoman Turks. The crescent and the star are the visible symbols of the Turkish flag. The crescent on their flag was considered by their enemies to also represent Islam. Following that practice the Muslims have themselves adopted the crescent as representing them on flags, minarets, mosques, etc. Strictly speaking though, Islam as a religion does not have much place for iconography and material symbols other than the calligraphed verses of its holy book, the Quran.

[203] Samuel P. Huntington, "The Clash of Civilizations", Foreign Affairs, summer 1993 v.72 Number 3.

– as he terms it - implementation of the Oslo Accords in the Gaza Strip between 1994 and 1999, tackled the question of religion in a dispassionate way from a national security perspective in a book titled "Freedom from Religion"[204]

Here are some of the interesting observations made by the author that are worth retaining: "Religion is a powerful motivator for both positive social change and mass violence. It is an institution that is protected in civil society, whether by a nation's own constitution, domestic law, or international agreement…When religion is promoting the positive development of society, it is an institution that is tolerated or even celebrated. When religion is tearing down the fabric of society, however, it is rarely condemned in any meaningful way… Drawing the line between potentially questionable practices and those which truly endanger society is a difficult task…Religion is used as a motivator to commit wide-scale acts of terrorism, to justify individual acts of violence behind closed doors, and promote hatred of the "other." [205]

"Given that religious violence constitutes such a grave threat to democracies, governments must begin to examine this institution more critically than in the past."[206] I would qualify Guiora's last statement by saying that the threat is not just to democracies but to nations anywhere, since religions are also used by governments to justify their actions. "It is critical" says Guiora, "to understand that the motivation to act in the name of God is not endemic only to Islam, for Christians and Jews have similarly committed terrorist acts…predicated on "divine inspiration" on behalf of what they consider their God. The problem is not inherently religion; rather, it is the view of a religious extremist regarding his or her own belief system."[207]

---

[204]Amos N. Guiora, "Freedom from Religion: Rights and National Security", Oxford University Press, Terrorism and Global Justice Series, New York (2009). Quoted by permission of Oxford University Press, Inc.
[205] Ibid., p.9
[206] Ibid., p.9
[207] Ibid., pp.11, 12

APPENDIX 2

JUSTIFYING SUICIDE ATTACKS: THE WORLD ACCORDING TO EXTREMISTS

Terrorists seem to be more eloquent at describing the inequities of the system they are fighting against than the benefits of the new world they want to create. It is also not the case that Islam and terrorism are synonymous. The world had to combat Catholic terrorists, like the IRA or the Basque separatist group ETA in Spain. There were Jewish terrorists, like the Stern Gang. There were Hindu terrorists, Sikh terrorists, Japanese terrorists, etc. Then there were the non-religious terrorists, like the revolutionary movements in Europe and the Middle East in the 1970s, and the secular terrorists, like the PKK, and of course Islamic terrorists. To assume that there is some particular and unique connection between Islam and terrorism is simply not true.

People don't wake up one morning; look at themselves in the mirror and say: "When I grow up, I will become a terrorist." Something happens that pushes them to "lose it".

What is it that happened over the years that left Muslims and Arabs boiling? Neo-colonialism, military bases, economic and foreign political support given to repressive regimes in the Middle East and other Muslim countries. We should not forget the invasions of Iraq and Afghanistan, one to get its oil, the second to get a pipeline route to someone else's oil. Then there is the across-the-board support for the government of Israel, irrespective of its actions, who has been slowly, but industriously, dispossessing the Palestinians of their homeland on the basis of Biblical justifications, etc. These are all ongoing crises that give birth to extremists and to young people who have no second thoughts about killing in revenge, including themselves.

Religious fundamentalists or extremists, whether Muslim, Jewish, Christian, Buddhists, Hindus believe in the supreme authority of their scriptures - or, at least what they understand to be their scripture. For any religious extremists, compromise is unimaginable, and every other religion is doomed. "Religious belief has priority over all other considerations, including morality and secular law. Even if those considerations include acts of violence...extremists believe that the scriptures they believe in come directly from God or via God's prophets, and therefore words are to be taken literally. Since many scriptures contain passages that describe violence and revenge, these words offer both justifications and commandments to the extremist follower. [208]

---

[208] Amos N. Guiora, "Freedom from Religion: Rights and National Security", Oxford University Press, Terrorism and Global Justice Series, New York (2009), p.11.

"For the actor who believes in the infallibility of his or her religion, whether he or she possesses a profound understanding of religious scriptures is not important. The key is that the individual's acts are performed "in the name of God." What allows a suicide bomber to justify his or her actions on behalf of religion is framing the act in terms of "self-sacrifice" and martyrdom. Is this a correct interpretation of Islam? The vast majority view would say no. Yet arguing theology will not result in a safer society."[209]

From an ideological perspective

Understanding how extremists and fundamentalists in general view the world from an ideological, political and tactical perspective is the starting point to knowing how to combat them before they turn to blind terrorism. Ideological extremists are not just individuals in some remote desert, but could also be democratically elected members of parliament, congress, senate, etc.

It is revealing that religious extremist groups in general use a motto practically identical to that of their adversaries: **"IF YOU ARE NOT WITH US, YOU ARE AGAINST US!"** Both sides share similar messianic political roots, for instance one wearing a Muslim hat, such as Al-Qaeda and its franchisees; the other a Judeo-Christian hat. Both based on unsubstantiated, perceived ideologies quite remote from the established facts of history, but both extremely harmful to the long term interest of the people they self-assigned themselves to speak for, and by extension to the rest of the world.

The kingdom of religious fundamentalists is being built in the afterlife. So much for wisdom, since nobody knows for sure if there will be an afterlife, how will it look like, and whether death - or martyrdom, as self-appointed Muslim wise men describe it - will necessarily lead to the biblical garden-like paradise the three monotheistic religions believe in.

Despite their remarkable organizational and motivational skills, the core ideology of certain fundamentalist groups such as Al-Qaeda's is not that of a social reform movement. Al-Qaeda lacks a social vision or program beyond vague invocations of the caliphate (Islamic style government) based on Sharia (Islamic jurisprudence). Reform movements strive to take the world forward, while the fundamentalists' ideology is meant to take the world backward. Fighting poverty, combating disease, eradicating illiteracy, or redressing economic failure are not of concern to fundamentalists. They are simply not part of their platform, as these are part of the realm of the living. Religious fundamentalists and other groups with similar ideologies live to encourage death, and offer a concept of an afterlife that they certainly have no control over. They are so infatuated with the past that the future becomes blurred to them, hence they fantasize it.

---

[209] Ibid., Amos N. Guiora, Freedom from Religion p.12

Javier Jordá and Manuel R. Torres from the University of Granada, Spain, along with Nicola Horsburgh from the International Policy Institute at King's College in London, wrote a well thought and correctly analyzed piece under the title of: "The Intelligence Services Struggle Against al-Qaeda Propaganda", published by the International Journal of Intelligence and CounterIntelligence. In their piece, they accurately point out that "History demonstrates that terrorist violence is not, in itself, an efficient instrument. Generally, most terrorist groups have become extinct before realizing their ultimate aims. Moreover, although the effects of terrorism are often spectacular and disproportional in the short term—both in the resources employed and the damage caused—terrorism itself is not a decisive method of conflict. To maximize gains, terrorism should be complemented by a series of political and social actions. Above all, these complementary strategies must have the capacity to evolve with and adapt to complex forms of engagement. Terrorists have succeeded only when they have developed defined and limited goals, and when these are integrated into a wider strategy."[210]

"Al-Qaeda is not only a terrorist group; it is a project that nurtures its roots in radical Islam (with notable success in small circles) and antisystem vengeance (in a world in which thousands of people feel frustrated and victim of some injustice). Although the radical ideology that animates the group originates from an extremist and primitive form of intolerance, the organization and modus operandi reflect an advanced adaptation towards the new environment of globalization and the information revolution. Alarmingly, even if the original nucleus of al-Qaeda were to be destroyed, the network could still mutate and regenerate itself. Al-Qaeda's significant power derives in great measure from its success in terms of mobilization and propaganda. Funding is crucial, training as well, and the acquisition of explosives and weapons is of great importance, but the information and propaganda battle constitutes an essential pillar under which the organizational architecture resides and continuity is assured. Therefore, in the design of any global antiterrorist politic, special attention should be drawn to the measures taken by terrorists to ensure success."[211]

"Al-Qaeda is animated by an ideology that crosses borders, social classes, and ethnic groups. In this way, it manages to integrate dispersed groups of people who might have otherwise remained marginalized from the terrorist scene. In countries of Muslim majority, and in the capitals of the Western world, there exist subcultures that participate in the ideas of a global Jihad but would not have joined a terrorist campaign were it not for the success of several attacks and al-Qaeda propaganda. Once al-Qaeda's message, which permits universal understanding, is elaborated and distributed, the likelihood of forging transnational alliances and interaction between dispersed points is increased, all the while supported by the

[210] Javier Jordá, University of Granada, Spain, Manuel R. Torres, University of Granada, Nicola Horsburgh, International Policy Institute, King's College, London; "The Intelligence Services Struggle Against al-Qaeda Propaganda", International Journal of Intelligence and CounterIntelligence, 18: 31-49, 2005 p.31.
[211] Ibid., p.33

information revolution. The elevated number of states that have suffered attacks, or where members have been arrested, demonstrates the success of the Jihad discourse, in terms of both transmission and reception of the message, even if it refers only to a minority."[212]

"Although the majority of Muslims reject the practices of al-Qaeda and violence in the name of Islam, radical circles that share the principles of the network do exist. These groups seek continuity and expansion thanks to audiovisual and written propaganda, the interpretation this has on international reality, and the terrorist attacks that keep alight the flame of holy war. All this creates a transnational conscience and ties of virtual solidarity, which feed into the perpetuation of these marginal circles."[213]

"In general terms, a growing membership base is dangerous for terrorist groups because it threatens the clandestine nature of the network. This rule is not altogether applicable to al-Qaeda since it promotes a part-time (amateur) terrorism, practiced by nonprofessional terrorists, who often die on their first mission. This is possible largely because of the success of mobilization through propaganda, which facilitates recruitment and local coordination for the network. A terrorism of this kind is probably less effective in operational terms but much more difficult to combat on a great scale."[214] "Nevertheless, the differences between al-Qaeda and nonviolent Islamists are significant when deciding on the means to fight a netwar. For the ideological members of al-Qaeda, the armed Jihad is an indispensable instrument."[215]

The logic behind suicide attacks[216]

"Although the suicide bomber seems to have gained primacy of place within the mass media, this is not the only form of suicide attack. A suicide attack is appropriately viewed as one in which the attacker has no expectation of surviving the assault, who will die either by his or her own hand, or through the response of the survivors of his actions. Thus, an Israeli settler who enters a mosque in Hebron, killing 13 and wounding 60 before being overpowered by his intended victims and being himself killed, is as much an example of a suicide attack as any.[217]

---

[212] Ibid., p.33

[213] Ibid., p.34

[214] Ibid., p.34

[215] Ibid., p.35

[216] This section and the appertaining footnotes are adapted with permission from Tod Strickland's excellent article, "Toward Solutions: Understanding Suicide Attackers in the Contemporary Middle East", Canadian Military Journal, v.9, number 4, 2009, pp. 9-19.

[217] Baruch Goldstein, an Israeli settler from the United States entered the Cave of the Patriarchs in Hebron in 1994 during prayer time and machine-gunned Palestinian Muslim worshippers before being overpowered and killed by the crowd.

"Few suicide attackers are social misfits, criminally insane or professional losers. Most fit a nearly opposite profile, psychologically normal, better-than-average economic prospects, deeply integrated into social networks, and emotionally attached to their national communities. They see themselves as sacrificing their lives for the nation's good.[218]

"…In his book "Fighting Suicide Terrorism", I.W.Charney cites data collected by Marc Segeman, a Senior Fellow at the US Foreign Policy Institute and a specialist in terrorism and counter-terrorism who studied over 400 terrorists and showcased a profile of the attackers that many would not necessarily have expected. His data showed that 75 percent came from the upper or middle classes of their societies, with 90 percent coming from intact families, and 63 percent having been attendees at post-secondary institutions. Nearly three-quarters of them were married, as well as being employed in professional or semi-professional capacities."[219] It is not necessarily young, deprived men that are carrying out these assaults.

"As imagined or as inculcated into their minds, "the rewards (for their actions) supposedly carry on in the afterlife, where martyrs can expect "sweet honey and holy wine…seventy-two virgin brides…seventy five passes to this paradise for their friends and relatives. These rewards can easily be seen as powerful motivators to those seeking to induce others to join their cause", [220] especially in societies that frown upon male-female pre-marital relations; or among young individuals who are unsuccessful in courting females. It is still baffling to note that there are also professionally successful and happily married individuals with young children, who would go and commit suicide operations. The example of some of the 9/11 suicide hijackers is glaring.

"There is a significant body of Muslim clerics who supports suicide attacks, although they would not refer to it as such, opting instead to use a phrase akin to 'martyrdom operations,' and examples abound. In 1995, on the Al-Jazeera television network, [self-styled] Muslim evangelist Yusuf al-Qaradawi justified suicide attacks stating: "These operations…are the highest form of jihad and are most certainly permitted by Shari'a."[221]

[218] Robert A. Pape, "Dying to Win: The Strategic Logic of Suicide Terrorism", New York: Random House, 2005, p.23. Cited in Tod Strickland's article, "Toward Solutions: Understanding Suicide Attackers in the Contemporary Middle East", Canadian Military Journal, v.9 number 4, 2009, pp.9-19. It must be noted that Pape includes attackers from the entire globe, including the Tamil Tigers of Sri Lanka, whose profile may skew that of the typical attacker in the Middle East.

[219] Israel. W. Charney, "Fighting Suicide Bombing: A Worldwide Campaign for Life", Westport, CT: Praeger, 2007, p.149. Cited in Tod Strickland. Interestingly, no data seems to have been collected as to the whether the attacker was male or female.

[220] Michael P. Arena and Bruce A. Arrigo, "The Terrorist Identity: Explaining the Terrorist Threat", New York: New York University Press, 2006, p.141. Cited in Tod Strickland.

[21] Christoph Reuter, "My Life Is a Weapon: A Modern History of Suicide Bombing", Princeton: Princeton University Press, 2004, p.122. Sharia is Islamic law (jurisprudence). Cited in Tod Strickland.

"Importantly, these views are not held by all Muslims. Indeed, it is hard to determine an exact split of opinion, but for many, the views heretofore espoused are an anathema. In the bluntest possible terms, author Munwar Anees writes:

"...whatever the pretence, these acts are in dire violation of the teachings of Islam. There is no Quranic support for taking one's own life to kill and maim innocent children and women - even when in a state of war with the enemy. There is no evidence from the life of the Prophet that such acts were encouraged or permitted by him.[222] "Taking the firm view that such attacks are not the acts of martyrs", Anees explains [that] "the purpose of a Muslim's life is to live for the pleasure of God."[223] Further, he writes: "Islam teaches that life is a sacred trust given to human beings by the Creator. Like other Abrahamic faiths, it prohibits suicide as a grave sin. It is forbidden under all circumstances, including war."[224]

From a political and strategic perspective

The real problem in all Arab and practically all Muslim countries is actually the lack of a genuine working participatory democracy and the one-man rule, irrespective of how these rulers portray themselves. It is not a question of religious extremism. Religious extremism is just one of many means of acquiring power and exercising control: A concept not very different from that of the dictatorship of the proletariat at the base of Communist ideology.

Those autocratic rulers, who have usurped power in various ways, occasionally use religion to compete with the fundamentalist religious groups in order for them to strengthen their hold on power, while at the same time act like an institutional state mafia.

When the West goes and supports those types of rulers and the goons surrounding them in the name of promoting democracy by paying them huge sums of bribe money, euphemistically called 'foreign aid', Western governments weaken the qualitative and educated segments of society and play directly into the hands of the extremists. To the population at large, and in particular to those who are culturally or intellectually in tune with Western culture, such foreign policies damaged both the West, and in particular US standing, but also the whole concept of democracy. It is also amazing to note that the major two or three Western powers have the tendency to always ally themselves with the worst people in other countries. It is as if other countries allied themselves with organized crime in the US for example and called these groups their American allies. One could imagine what the reaction of the American public would be.

---

[222] Munwar A. Anees, "Salvation and Suicide: What Does Islamic Theology Say?" in *Dialog: A Journal of Theology*, v.45, number 3, fall 2006, p.279. Cited in Tod Strickland.

[223] Ibid., p.275

[224] Ibid., p.277

The critical path to extremism

Over the past forty to fifty years, most of the attempts to call for change by the educated elite and the intellectuals, either as individuals, or as members of political parties, were strongly opposed by the regimes in power in Arab countries. They were jailed, tortured savagely, killed, emigrated, chose self-exile, or simply shut up.

Enter the fundamentalists, who were crushed by some Arab regimes, such as Egypt and Syria in the sixties and seventies, but definitely encouraged later by others such as Saudi Arabia. They rose crusade-like in defiance of the mafia system prevalent in their respective countries. Their definite intention was to seize power. The resulting savage clashes between the regimes and the religious fundamentalists reached such high levels of ferocity, as happened in Algeria, Saudi Arabia, Egypt and other Muslim countries, that the fundamentalists lost control of their actions and lost sight of the original motive behind their uprising. The regimes too went overboard to protect their own narrow interests. The issue became who is going to damage the other more. Gone were the initial assumed pure ideals.

Politically-speaking, the Islamic extremists' principal goals are the removal of "apostate" Arab rulers, or what they refer to as pseudo-Islamic regimes. According to them this should be followed by setting up franchise-like Islamic governments or *"emirates"* across the whole of the Muslim world. Their declared ultimate goal is to convert as much of humanity as possible to the same vision they have. But aside from the idealists or the unaware, the underlying goal of the top leadership of these movements has effectively nothing to do with the initial teachings of Islam as a spiritual medium, a code for morality, and a way of life for individuals, society and nations that calls for moderation in everything. A lopsided version of the original teachings of Islam became the essence of their call, and was used as a stepping stone to taking over power to run yet another dictatorship.

When Osama Binladen started his political "crusade" against the Saudi Royal family, he had a case. When he could not achieve his goal, he turned his attention to their ally, the West, and the U.S. in particular. His crusade against them simply followed the famous adage "the friend of my enemy is my enemy." The same happened in the case of his ally, and successor, the Egyptian Dr. Ayman Al-Zawahri. Al-Zawahri was settling political scores with Presidents Sadat and Mubarak of Egypt. Now of course, he is left without his traditional enemies. The question today is what happens if the extremists in Egypt succeed in wrestling power not just from both the armed forces and the majority of the population, but eventually from the Muslim Brotherhood, who is now the other partner with the army in governing Egypt. Would they ally themselves with Dr. Al-Zawahri?

The perception about the USA overseas, gained mainly through American movies and TV programs produced as a "sound investment", portray America in a perverse way as a haven for violence, prostitution, drug smuggling, drunkenness, crime and rape; which do not reflect the traditional way of life of the vast majority of Americans. At the same time we continue to see Arabs and Muslims through the eyes of the fanciful coverage of that same media. It is the perception that turns people off. So when the US government tells them they must introduce 'our' democracy into their countries, the population says "No way! We do not want your style of democracy"- as they perceive it from the movies, and as they experience it thanks to the support the US provides not just to their hated leaders, but also to their regional enemies. Under such conditions, democracy in those countries took on a totally different definition from what the expression is supposed to mean.

Contrary to other peoples around the world, mass upheavals and choreographed revolutions are traditionally not something common in Arab society, though flaring riots and short-term violence are. Today all of that may have changed. Unfortunately, Arab educated intelligentsia seems to always excel at rhetorical debates and intellectual divergences, but always incapable of producing real constructive institution-building, problem-solving effective leadership. The 2011 "Arab Spring" uprisings may have changed the formula, but that will take some time before it is clear how the situation will evolve in the region. Without effective leadership, that "Spring" could risk becoming an Autumn of ongoing discontent.

Intellectual revolutions, or simply revolutions, call for a leader, who not only embodies the ideals he/she preaches, but also has the looks, plays the role convincingly and has both innate and visible leadership qualities. Middle Eastern societies do not function otherwise, partially because they have a problem working together. Unless they are led by such a leadership figure, things simply do not move. The history of the region continues to revolve around three figures who symbolize the often missing leadership, and who are considered by the believers to be prophets of God, i.e. Moses, Jesus and Mohamed. In a way, these prophets continue to lead even today. When everything else fails, populations turn to the Creator and put their faith in Him as the ultimate leader in order to get them out of their misery.

It is revealing that after six months of the 2011 Arab Uprising not one person we could describe as a genuine leader has appeared on the horizon in any of the countries involved. The fear is that some charismatic charlatan would rise and take over the insurgency, yet again for his and his cronies' sole benefit.

When most people everywhere thought erroneously that any revolt was going to come at the hands of the religious extremists, the recent insurrections in 2011 showed that the people who really wanted the change and were ready to pay the price with their own lives were the non-religiously committed Muslims and Christians, i.e. just across the board common people. Initially the religious extremists stayed home as this battle for the future is not theirs. But as time went by and they noted that the rather secular uprising was succeeding, they also took to the streets to take over the revolution. The attack on the Israeli embassy in Cairo in September 2011 is one indication. Should they continue their game, chances are that the Egyptian people may find themselves willy-nilly hoping for a military takeover; i.e. back to square one.

When the people rose in rebellion during the spring of 2011 against those tyrannical leaders and called for the institution of a democratic system in their countries, what was our response? Silence, followed by hesitation, then confusion among the allies, then procrastination, pussyfooting, and even support to one of the dictatorships (Saudi Arabia), who sent its army into Bahrain to help put down a perfectly peaceful and legitimate insurrection by the overwhelming Shiite majority.

An unusually candid view of the dangers accruing from U.S. policies in the region appeared five years ago in an unclassified study published by the Pentagon-appointed U.S. Defense Science Board on 24 September 2004. Contradicting President George W. Bush, the board stated: "Muslims do not 'hate our freedom,' but rather, they hate our policies. The overwhelming majority voice their objections to what they see as one-sided support in favour of Israel and against Palestinian rights, and the long-standing, even increasing, support for what Muslims collectively see as tyrannies, most notably Egypt, Saudi Arabia, Jordan, Pakistan, and the Gulf States. Thus, when American public diplomacy talks about bringing democracy to Islamic societies, this is seen as no more than self-serving hypocrisy."

- "American direct intervention in the Muslim World has paradoxically elevated the stature of and support for radical Islamists, while diminishing support for the United States to single digits in some Arab societies."

- "Furthermore, in the eyes of Muslims, American occupation of Afghanistan and Iraq has not led to democracy there, but only more chaos and suffering. U.S. actions appear (to some) in contrast to be motivated by ulterior motives, and (to others as) deliberately controlled in order to best serve American national interests at the expense (of these nations)."

- "Therefore, the dramatic narrative since 9/11 has essentially borne out the entire radical Islamist bill of particulars. American actions and the flow of events have elevated the authority of the Jihadi insurgents and tended to ratify their legitimacy among Muslims. Fighting groups portray themselves as the true defenders of an Ummah (the entire Muslim community) invaded and under attack - to broad public support."

- "What was a marginal network is now an Ummah-wide (nation-wide) movement of fighting groups. Not only has there been a proliferation of "terrorist" groups: the unifying context of a shared cause creates a sense of affiliation across the many cultural and sectarian boundaries that divide Islam."

- "Finally, Muslims see Americans as strangely narcissistic - namely, that the war is all about us. As the Muslims see it, everything about the war is - for Americans - really no more than an extension of American domestic politics and its great game. This perception is of course necessarily heightened by election-year atmospherics, but nonetheless sustains their impression that when Americans talk to Muslims they are really just talking to themselves."

"Thus the critical problem in American public diplomacy directed toward the Muslim World is not one of "dissemination of information," or even one of crafting and delivering the "right" message. Rather, it is a fundamental problem of credibility. Simply, there is none - the United States today is without a working channel of communication to the world of Muslims and of Islam. Inevitably therefore, whatever Americans do and say only serves the party that has both the message and the "loud and clear" channel: the enemy. Arguably the first step toward mitigating and eventually even reversing this situation is to better understand the values and worldview of the target audience itself." [225]

Unfortunately this darkness that fell on Arab/Muslim - Western relations had reached the nadir of blind suspicion and mutual desire on each side to harm the other. The vast majority of the Arab/Muslim populations stayed on the margin of it all, neither totally condemning the West, nor totally condemning the now called Islamic terrorists. They just buried their head in the demands of daily life and signaled their detachment from what is happening around them. Little did they reason that it is they who are the ultimate losers.

As the populations lost their means of expressing themselves through parliamentary representation and through the media, most of the population gave up the struggle and took on passive but visible resistance to the 'system': Visibly they did that either by living an eccentric and ostentatious lifestyle, or by doing the opposite, namely by donning conservative clothes or wearing beards, which they interpreted as Islamic attire. This was their visual, or iconographic, way of distancing themselves from these regimes, but also as a protective shield from the militant, but lethal, extremists.

---

[225] Report of the US Defense Science Board Task Force on Strategic Communication www.dtic.mil/docs/citations/ ADA428770 September 2004 pp.40-41.

Al-Qaeda's reach

The religious discourse maintained by Al-Qaeda and other extremist groups may find echo mainly, but not exclusively, among some unaware, devout as well as misguided orthodox Muslims alike, but its erstwhile domestic and international political discourse rang a bell in millions of ears. Al Qaeda's original extremist political message reflected what most of the population in that part of the world was suffering from in terms of harsh realities in their countries but was unable to express or do anything about it. Al-Qaeda's initiative provided them with a much needed psychological outlet for the stress they lived under.

Things have changed though with the further radicalization of Al-Qaeda and those who followed in its wake. The personal crusade pitting Binladen against the Saudi royal family and Ayman Zawahri's feud with the Egyptian government they both covered with a religious veneer became more and more apparent to the masses. The bloodiness and blindness of their methods, which did not distinguish between innocents, whether Arab, Muslim, Christian or foreign, and its wanton destruction of human life rendered these extremists highly suspect by Muslims and Arabs. Today most Muslims across the board consider that the extremists have hijacked their faith, twisted its tenets, politicized its message and thrust millions of people into harm's way at home as well as abroad for no long-term benefit to anybody starting with the extremists themselves.

Al-Qaeda, its affiliates, franchisees or subsidiaries, and those who use its name, attack Western countries and Christians in general, but increasingly with a large number of Muslim casualties. Al-Qaeda considers Muslim or Arab fatalities either as "collateral damage", or deserving Muslim apostates it considers at best as insufficient Muslims, and at worst as traitors, enemy agents and collaborators. Al Qaeda's original aim was to score points in a conflict they consider as inevitable as that of the Communist belief in the inevitability of the implosion of capitalism.

The more recent attacks by individuals such as the underwear bomber or home-grown youths of Indo-Pakistani and Arab origin in the UK and other European countries, or those committed in sub-Saharan African countries are more the actions of angry disoriented youth using Al-Qaeda as a cover for their actions. In some cases they are simply gangs operating for ransom money.

While Al-Qaeda occasionally includes Israel in its rhetoric, neither Al-Qaeda, nor any extremist Islamic group has ever attacked Israel or Israeli interests. Attacks by Palestinians including the Islamic Resistance Movement (HAMAS), whether as acts of aggression against Israeli targets; revenge or retaliation, or in self-defence against Israeli initiated attacks within the limited context of the Palestinian-Israeli conflict, has a totally different cause and effect as discussed in Appendix 3. Ironically, attacking Israel by outsiders on behalf of the Palestinians is against the interest of the Palestinians. The Israeli war establishment would love to see an organic association between Al-Qaeda and the Palestinians to bring the whole world against the Palestinians.

Why is it that Muslims, who do not agree with the extremist rhetoric, do not raise their voices in opposition to acts of terrorism perpetrated in their name?

Over the centuries, religion among Western societies, namely Judaism and Christianity, has been partially relegated to a relatively secondary role, but it remains part of people's culture and identity. In the case of Muslims and Jews, faith is not latent; it continues to be vehement among the majority of believers. But why don't Muslims, who do not agree with the extremist rhetoric both political and religious, why don't they raise their voices in opposition to acts of terrorism perpetrated in their name? There are several reasons for that:

1. The complex social fabric and the obsessive restrictions put by the rulers on democratic debate in most Muslim countries make opening ANYTHING for discussion or debate a hazardous entreprise.

2. Media sensationalism and generalisations about Muslims in general, and more dangerously those disseminated by media outlets controlled by questionable allegiances, perverse agendas, or financing, have succeed in conditioning a sizeable part of Western public opinion and the political establishment against Arabs and Muslims in general.

3. Muslims, like any community in distress, react like other communities in history when they are under real or perceived attack: They circle the wagons.

4. Muslims, at least originally, viewed that some of the terrorists' targets are not often above blame, and much of the time, they were the original initiators of the conflicts. This renders criticizing and blaming only the extremists and the fanatics by their coreligionists to be inacceptable.

5. Muslim communities find it equally impossible to reason with those fanatics, who have hijacked their religion as a cover for their terrorist designs, and are unable to stop their violence, which is detrimental to the community itself because they are not armed like them, and their whole approach to religion, politics and life or death in general is almost totally different.

6. Like members of the other religions, Muslims are a diverse people who happen to believe in the same religion. The community of believers is composed of widely different types of nationalities and ethnic groups, just

like Christians and Jews. Yet, the whole Muslim community is castigated and lumped together for anything wrong perpetuated by a fringe among them. Unfortunately, some Muslims do exactly the same thing and blame all the Jews or Christians as a block without distinction for the aggressive policies of their respective governments or some of their leaders.

7. The dynamics within the various Muslim communities are pretty diverse. Pakistani Muslims react differently from Arab Muslims, and Malaysian Muslims react differently from Algerian Muslims. Even within the same Arab community the reactions are different. The Egyptians, the Lebanese, the Saudis, each community has its own internal dynamics that are different from the other. But then, within Islam itself there are various sects such as Sunnis and Shiites and a few others. Interestingly enough, Al-Qaeda has succeeded in bringing all the extremists together irrespective of their ethnic belonging within at least one of these groups - the Sunnis - though, normally; they would barely know anything about each other. What ultimately united these extremist groups was more their blind hatred for the West than their understanding of Islam.

8. Finally, while some Muslims have adopted a militant path in countries of immigration, many more have either stayed clear of political Islamic activism, or simply turned their back altogether on religion.

In the Arab countries, the only way out left for the people to express themselves was to become radicalized politically or religiously, which eventually led them along a critical path towards violence and even terrorism, which was ultimately against the interest of all.

Having said that, one must still point out to the spontaneous insurrection that started in Tunisia in early 2011; henceforth known as the "Arab Spring". That type of insurrection took everybody by surprise as it was believed that, either the political left or the extremist religious right to be the future agent of radical change. As the success of the insurgents became apparent, both extremist religious groups and centers of power, at least those partially related to the old regime, have started vying for positions to take over the fruits of the popular uprising. As a matter of fact, as of mid-January 2012 more and more signs of a ruling condominium composed of Islamists and the military seems to be the new model that is being imposed. The process appears to be supported, or at least encouraged, by Western powers hoping to both please the people by letting 'moderate' Islamists (who have nothing to offer in terms of modern governance) come to power, while ensuring that the military (who are not disciples of democracy) maintain control.

The way out is first to put notions of pre-medieval religious teachings attributed to God, whether propagated at home and taught in schools where they belong, namely outside government, schools and politics. Then return the military to the barracks. Rational thinking aside, this is still a daunting task indeed that took Europe centuries of wars to achieve. The military cannot govern other than autocratically, because this is how the military establishment works. On the other hand, when people insist that it is God who has ordained this or that, or that if you are not of their religion, then you should be excommunicated and promised eternity in Hell, or when one people says that God promised them a land, and the other says that God promised paradise to them and only them, it is high time to cease and desist from attributing to the Almighty what He never communicated to anybody other than in man-made tales and mythologies.

APPENDIX 3

A DIFFERENT APPROACH TO SOLVING THE PALESTINE-ISRAEL QUESTION

PREAMBLE

All the traditional approaches have been tried and tested over so many decades in relation to finding a solution to the problem between the Israelis and the Palestinians. It is certainly time to think outside the box and not to reinvent the wheel, but to go back to old fashioned reason and common sense.

While this is not a problem that *a priori* has anything to do with either aviation or maritime security, it was indeed the trigger for the 1970s series of airplane hijackings that led to the institution of the current regimes of airline and airport security. The issue gained a maritime component with the various attempts to break the Israeli naval blockade around the Gaza strip in 2011. While the wave of aviation hijackings mainly involved leftist Palestinians with support from European, Japanese and Latin American supporters, the blockade busting attempts using chartered ships included some Palestinians but many more Turks, Europeans, North Americans several of them Jews.

Unless reasonably resolved, the Palestine Question will always be a trigger or an excuse for unrest, read violence, and not only in the Middle East. But this should not be the sole reason to solve the problem. To start with, the solution should not be for anything less than being just the right thing to do for the interest of both people and the rest of the world.

The following is a proposal that is different from what has been discussed so far as to how to break the current deadlock. The proposal, which calls first for a mutually acceptable accommodation between the Israelis and the Palestinians, leads towards a solution that could be envisaged, and hopefully tried. Without a direct hands-on role played by a major power such as the USA and its major allies, not just as facilitators, where they put all their weight and forces at play, then there will be no viable solution. The current state of affairs between Arabs and Jews both politically, and as a result of stubborn religious beliefs on all sides is not conducive to anything but perpetuating a permanent disaster zone.

CAN THERE BE A SOLUTION TO THE ISRAELI-PALESTINIAN STANDOFF?

The answer is: <u>Yes.</u> While it is psychologically impossible for anyone to bargain over his homeland, it follows that it is extremely painful for both the Palestinians as well as for the Israelis to do that. However, if we look at things as they are today, it does not hurt to try and salvage what can be salvaged for the sake of both peoples and the rest of the world.

Introduction

To discuss politics or religion realistically and effectively, each of the parties involved in the discussions has to know the issues and tenets on both sides of the table. i.e. the Palestinians must appreciate the Israeli position, and the Israelis must put themselves in the shoes of the Palestinians. Each side must be willing to question its own religion and political nevers. It must be willing to hear things it does not usually like or want to hear. Above all, each party has to be able to put itself in the shoes of its counterpart and understand where his/her position is coming from. It must come to the table with the intention of solving problems and not just to engage in polemics. It must be prepared to compromise. It must approach any realistic solution with creativity, but also differently from previous attempts. Finally both parties must be patient, patient, and again patient.

Before even mentioning the word "peace", there must first be a will on each side to genuinely take the other into consideration, until both people regain a certain sense of normalcy in their respective lives. This is not a problem of security as it is almost always described. Lack of security is the reflection of the problem, and not the problem itself. Therefore, establishing a cooling-off period in the region as a whole is a *sine qua non* condition to start with, during which the Palestinians will be able to breathe and live like human beings. It will also allow the Israelis to live in peace without having to wage war generation after generation.

Under the existing realities on the ground, the starting point should not begin by pondering again over a contentious non-starter, i.e. haggling over a division of cities and real estate between Israel and the Palestinians, not even talking about it. It is too early for that. We must think in terms of people rather than in terms of real estate. Furthermore, expecting that the two antagonists could talk or listen to each other rationally under the currently existing conditions would be an exercise in futility.

SEVEN STEPS TO PEACE

Each one of the contenders will need a "lawyer" to represent him. At time of writing, despite their major handicaps vis-à-vis Israel, the United States remains to some extent the only lawyer the Israelis may at least partially trust. Being the country that was at the origin of the problem, Britain could be in a better position than most to act as the lawyer for the Palestinians. The two powers have been involved the longest in this issue, and they command the respect and attention of both people. The representatives of the USA and the UK must absolutely not be the same individuals who played that role so far, and were almost intentionally bent on sabotaging all agreement between the two parties.

The most difficult part will be choosing representatives for the Israelis and for the Palestinians who will be partners in the process. Negotiations and agreements must be handled by people on both sides who are capable of being politically balanced. These empowered representatives must be chosen among the most highly respected, qualified and knowledgeable individuals within each nation, who are familiar with the roots of the problem on both sides, who believe in settling the conflict equitably, and who can reach an accommodating settlement between the two parties.

Negotiations towards a mutually satisfactory accommodation would be undertaken by, guaranteed and enforced by the British and the Americans acting on behalf and in consultation with the parties they represent, i.e. the Palestinians and the Israelis respectively. Arab governments, which are incapable of solving their own internal problems, which were created by them in the first place, may be consulted occasionally for their opinions, but they certainly should not be directly involved in the negotiations or implementation unless it is a bilateral border-related issue. Otherwise, implicating the Arab governments during the initial stages of negotiations will certainly lead to a dead-end.

The proposed mutually satisfactory accommodation between the Israelis and the Palestinians calls for seven steps, and requires an ability to escape the restricting inflexibility of the mental straightjacket. Some steps must be accomplished in sequence in the proposed order, while others can take place simultaneously depending on the prevailing conditions.

This gradual approach towards a mutually satisfactory accommodation would allow the Israelis not to be unduly edgy about security threats. It would also allow the Palestinians not to keep looking over their shoulders every minute of day and night fearing an Israeli attack of one kind or another. It should offer both parties a physical separation and a breathing space for as long as needed in light of the prevalent situation. As for peace, i.e. when the two parties will be ready to enter into direct bilateral negotiations to establish peace between them, the process may require several years, and possibly a generation or two, before the magic word is even mentioned. This gradual approach will allow both parties to be able to converse like civilized partners, not like prehistoric cave dwellers.

Step One: Cessation of hostilities

The first step on the path to a meaningful accommodation between the two sides must be a simultaneous positive, highly visible, concrete and meaningful gesture by both parties towards each other consisting of a mutual declaration of cessation of hostilities, which includes a freeze on confiscating more Palestinian lands and home demolitions, as well as stopping all attacks by the Palestinians against Israel.

Step Two: Border security

Step one will be accompanied by the stationing of a sizeable, well-armed bilateral military force, and not a UN peacekeeping contingent. These troops from third parties acceptable to both the Israelis and the Palestinians will be equipped with heavy armament and their operational mission will be to seal the borders between Israel, the Palestinian territories and the neighbouring Arab countries, i.e. enforce a total separation between these three entities.

It is proposed that both Moroccan and German forces be called upon to take on that role. The Moroccans will monitor the borders between the Palestinian territories and the neighbouring Arab countries (i.e. Jordan, Syria, Lebanon and Egypt), and will also ensure that no infiltration or launching of rockets across the borders from the Palestinian or Arab territories against Israel takes place.

While being a well-disciplined military force, the Moroccans have gained a protracted experience in preventing border infiltrations during their long war with the Polisario. The Moroccans are technically from outside the region, while still being Arabic speakers, hence close to the Palestinians. They would be more acceptable to the Palestinians and less objectionable to Israel, in view of the fact that Morocco has a Jewish community of its own, and Israel counts a sizeable Jewish community of Moroccan origin. This is in addition to the fact that the two countries have managed to maintain a reasonable relationship despite the Palestinian-Israeli conflict.

The task of the German forces will be to protect the Israeli-Palestinian borders from attacks by either side, including by or against the armed extremist Jewish settlers. The Germans are relatively new in this role and have never led or participated in any military operation against the Palestinians. On the other hand, the German government maintains a privileged relationship with Israel, especially from a military point of view. This is in addition to the fact that Israel has an important community of Jews of German origin, and Germany counts an expanding and influential Jewish community.

Step Three: Leadership change

The Palestinians must be brought to change their leadership in both the West Bank and Gaza in preparation for the reunification of the two territories. They must also invite experienced technocrats from among the Palestinians living overseas to join the administration as advisors for a number of years. Their task will be to harmonize governance between the two territories and set up the essential modern infrastructure needed to establish a viable economy, and to ensure a rather normal daily life for the population, in step with other advanced countries.

Step Four: The separation wall and movement of populations

The existing separation wall built by Israel will be maintained integrally during those early stages, then moved back gradually towards the Israeli territory wherever the wall separates agricultural land belonging to Palestinian villages along the green line to reinstate territorial contiguity in the West Bank. This will also return to the Palestinians badly needed economic resources for their survival.

As soon as this is completed, borders will open between Jordan and the West Bank to allow the Palestinians to travel and trade, subject to the existing bilateral agreements and regulations currently enforced among advanced countries. Similarly, borders between Gaza and Egypt will be opened along the same lines until the Gaza Strip is reconnected to the West Bank as described under Step 5. (The cautious step taken by Egyptian authorities of opening the Rafah Crossing border between Egypt and Gaza following the overthrow of President Mubarak's regime, could have served as a litmus test as far as opening the borders is concerned to allow the Palestinians, starting with the population of the Gaza Strip, to communicate rather normally with the rest of the world. This was a step in the right direction; but rather a bit too early. The Egyptians kept the crossing open for less than two days, but then went back and closed it, most probably under intense pressure or warnings from the USA and Israel. Relieved of as much tension as possible, the Palestinians in Gaza would have had less reason to fire rockets across the border with Israel.)

No Palestinians will be allowed to cross the border to work in Israel during this stage, but opportunities will be available for them to work in their own territory, i.e. in the fields reconnected to their original villages. Once the borders with Egypt and Jordan are open, Palestinians will also be able to work in any other country in the world needing manpower, as is the case for so many other migrant workers around the world. They could always return to a home in Palestine, i.e. Gaza and the West Bank, at any time.

Step Five: Reconnecting the West Bank and Gaza to the rest of the region

This step shall witness the beginning of initial work to build an underground rail and car tunnel like the Chunnel between continental Europe and the British Isles, or like the underground metro that is being built right now between the two shores of the Sea of Marmara in the city of Istanbul. The proposed tunnel will connect the West Bank and Gaza, and thus link the two parts of Palestine together without crossing through Israeli territory. The tunnel would also provide the West Bank with an outlet to the Mediterranean and to the Egyptian border, as well as link Gaza with the Arab hinterland east of the Jordan River. It will equally provide Jordan with an access to the Mediterranean. As a matter of fact, this connecting tunnel would connect Jordan, Syria, Lebanon and Iraq again to Egypt and North Africa for the first time since the land route via Palestine was cut following the creation of Israel in 1948. The positive economic repercussions of this project on the economy of Palestine and the adjacent countries including Israel would be enormous.

Step Six: The future of Palestinian refugees

All Palestinians wherever they are, including Palestinian refugees, would automatically become citizens of Palestine. They can reside on its territory at their pleasure. They could also opt for a permanent foreigner resident permit in their current countries of refuge, by agreement with and subject to the laws of such states. If such countries wish to naturalize any number of refugees, this can be done at the discretion of the governments involved. The question of compensations for the 1948 refugees would be addressed in future stages later in the process.

Step Seven: The future of Palestinian and Jewish populations on both sides of the dividing line

Start the gradual repatriation of Jewish settlers in the West Bank towards Israel, beginning with those living in the midst of Palestinian populations such as those in Hebron, for instance, followed by those living in isolated areas. Should some Jewish settlers elect to live among the Palestinians under Palestinian sovereignty, whether they opt to carry Palestinian citizenships or just a Permanent Residence status, that choice would be open to them. This means that they would be residing subject to the laws and regulations in force in Palestine, i.e. they would be equivalent to the Palestinians living in Israel and carrying its citizenship. If they opt to simply live like foreigners, then they will carry a renewable Residence Permit.

Palestinians who are citizens of Israel would maintain their citizenship in that state or move to the areas that will become Palestine. The same applies to

Palestinian residents in Jerusalem. Such Palestinians may choose to become Israeli citizens as well as obtain Palestinian citizenship, exactly like Israeli Jews who are dual nationals of Israel and other countries.

As for the future of Jerusalem, it will maintain its current status at least for the time being until an effective peace is reached between the Israelis and the Palestinians. Today, Israel has Jerusalem firmly in its hands. Anybody who thinks that Israel will relinquish it, even partially, through negotiations or even under threat is certainly naïve. They will keep it, and the Palestinians will keep the West Bank and Gaza. The Palestinians will be able to visit the Muslim and Christian Shrines in Jerusalem, and the Israeli as well as non-Israeli Jews will be able to visit the religious shrines in Hebron and elsewhere, the same way Muslim pilgrims do when they visit holy shrines in Saudi Arabia. They apply for a visa, visit, do some tourism while there, and certainly go shopping too if they wish, then return home to their respective countries.

WILL IT WORK?

There will certainly be those who will immediately express their doubts about this approach on either side. Doubters about everything and anything exist everywhere, and they should not be allowed to spoil the party. Both Israeli and Palestinian communities have the potential for sharing beautiful things in the future, yet due to the existing clash between them, they can only exchange the worst humans can exhibit.

The world is doing the impossible to save the environment and accommodate the habitat between wildlife and human beings. Sadly enough, humans have so far been incapable of simply accommodating fellow humans, who have become instead an environmental hazard to each other. Perhaps finding a solution to this intractable problem could set the example for future solutions to other problems facing humanity.

To conclude, suffice it to say that the Palestinians are more than just refugees, and the Jews are more than just Holocaust survivors. Should an illuminated soul wake up one morning and discover that "what's good for the Palestinians is good for the Jews", perhaps the whole perspective towards this problem could change. After all, given the proper atmosphere, the best neighbours the Israelis could have are Palestinians, and some of the best allies the Palestinians have today are Jews.

APPENDIX 4

THE CASE OF IRAQ: AN OUTLOOK TO THE FUTURE

The situation in Iraq has its own complications because religion, but also ethnic origin, does play a major role in this country. At least for the time being it is mainly internal to Iraq and among Sunni and Shiite Muslim communities, rather than between Muslims and non-Muslims. Attacks on Christian communities have generally been attributed to foreign elements such as Al-Qaeda and its affiliates. The worst may still come though as the Kurds and the Iraqis will have to reach an agreement, or in case of failure, prepare for what could be a very bloody civil war.

OIL, IRAQ, KURDS, TURKS, IRANIANS, AND EVERYBODY ELSE

The backdrop

As always in that part of the world, had it not been for oil, and to some extent the presence of Christian communities, the outside world wouldn't have lost sleep over what is happening in Iraq. That is the global perspective. Local and regional accounts to be settled will be left to the people involved, until the smell of booty beckons the adventurers to seize the opportunity. Finally, like everywhere else, there will be winners and losers.

"Iraq is disintegrating as a united state", writes Patrick Cockburn in a column entitled Iraq: the beginning of the end published on December 11, 2005. "The unitary state created by Britain after the First World War may be passing away. A Bosnian solution to the Iraq crisis is now on the agenda", says Ghassan Attiyah, a veteran Iraqi commentator. The Shia and Sunni Arabs and the Kurds - the three main Iraqi communities - show every sign of voting along ethnic and religious lines. Secular and nationalist groups looking for support beyond their own community have their backs to the wall. As far as the Christians are concerned, they will probably be in for a rough time and may want to draw their own conclusions before it is too late.

"Iraqis...talk about partition as a likely outcome of the crisis. This has already happened in Kurdistan. The Kurds, a fifth of Iraq's 26 million, already have quasi-independence. Iraqi Arab leaders largely accept what has happened in Kurdistan, if only because there is nothing they can do about it. Under the new constitution the Kurdish and Shia super-regions will own new oil reserves when they are discovered. This will give them economic independence."[226]

"As US troops are primed to leave Iraq and the situation in Iraq's disputed territories remains unresolved, the likelihood of escalating tensions along the so-called trigger line increases. While communication and cooperation between the Iraqi army and Kurdish regional guard forces has improved, they continue to face off across this unmarked line of control, which meanders through an elongated territory that is rich in ethnic diversity and, by twist of nature, oil, stretching from the Syrian to the Iranian border. Their tenuous relationship could come unglued when the US presence in their midst changes from military to civilian.

"In May 2011, the latest reminder of how explosive the situation remains, bombs killed scores in Kirkuk, the city and governorate at the core of the conflict. Kirkuk's ethnic communities each have contending claims to the area's status: the Kurds wish to attach it to the adjacent Kurdistan region; the Turkoman (population) would like for it to become a stand-alone region under neither Baghdad's nor Erbil's control. The Arabs mostly favor the status quo - a province directly under Baghdad's rule. In pressing their claims, demographics - who has the right to live and vote in Kirkuk - have become the principal battleground. Had oil been absent from the equation, the status question would have become a good deal less incendiary; the significance of the area's ethnic makeup and numbers would largely have faded; and there would have been no need for the deployment of rival security forces.

"The US military presence has succeeded in keeping the lid on tensions that never cease to boil just beneath the surface. It is for this reason that Kirkuki politicians of all stripes have called for an extension of the US troop presence in Iraq...Lacking mutual trust, suspecting each other's motives, and manipulated by more powerful forces outside Kirkuk, Iraqi and Kurdish politicians have been unable to come to a basic agreement even over how to govern the area, regardless of its status.

"Very little is likely to happen before US troops pull out, and all sides are now starting to prepare for that eventuality. The Kurds have been the first to move, citing security concerns. During the Eid al-Adha, the feast of sacrifice, in late 2010, they deployed Asaesh security personnel throughout Kirkuk city, angering Arabs and Turkomans. In February, they sent troops to the city's southern gateway, violating a security arrangement with their Iraqi and US partners in the so-called combined security mechanism, a system of joint checkpoints and patrols that has served to keep the peace.

[226] Patrick Cockburn - "Iraq: the beginning of the end", Counterpunch, December 11, 2005.
www.counterpunch.org/patrick12122005.html

"The Kurds' military assertiveness has been widely interpreted as an attempt to probe their adversaries' resolve. Perhaps they feel heartened by the result, but they would be wrong to interpret Iraqi Prime Minister Maliki's passiveness as a potential willingness to acquiesce in a Kurdish takeover of Kirkuk once US troops are no longer there to ease the Kurds back out. No Arab leader in Iraq could hope to survive politically if he is seen to surrender Kirkuk to the Kurds, and inversely Kurdish leaders would lose all their credibility if they failed to stand up to an Iraqi army bid to drive the Kurds out of Kirkuk. This means that if the current standoff persists, unilateral moves, by either side, will without doubt trigger armed conflict once the US security blanket is removed.

"While this process gets underway, the shadow of the big questions - status, security, demographics, oil - can be reduced if leaders in Baghdad, Erbil, and Kirkuk were to focus on local pragmatic solutions. Rather than addressing the status question head-on, they should work to improve governance and development, and let results serve to build trust, which could then allow for progress on status. To remove the weight of demographics, the sides should agree that any solution to the status question should be the result of negotiations and not of an ethnically-based referendum. In the absence of a federal hydrocarbons law, Baghdad and Erbil should seek a deal to share both the management and the revenue of the area's oil wealth. And a local police force needs to be built up as a viable, and ethnically diverse, alternative to the presence of federal military and Kurdish regional guard troops."[227] Unfortunately "peaceful negotiations and consensus-based compromise", as Hilterman suggests in his article, are not considered qualities in that part of the world, but rather a sign of weakness.

NORTHERN IRAQ FORECAST

Iraqi oil fields in northern Iraq are located in an area surrounded by a majority of Kurds whose region is a *de facto* politically and even geographically independent entity with its own flag, government, parliament, customs and border posts, etc. Besides, it has escaped the inter-confessional mayhem that has smitten Iraq. Ethnic Turkmen and Iraqi Arabs are in the minority there. In relative terms, but keeping in mind their historic internecine clashes, the Kurds are pretty well organized, strongly led, and the population stands steadfast behind its traditional leaders.

The Kurds in Iraq are followers of Jalal Talbani the current President of Iraq (who used to be Iran's man in the formula, but now seems to play the Iraqi hand and the American hand by extension. In northern Iraq, the Kurds are led by Masud Barzani, (who used to be the Iraqis' and the Americans' man in the formula or vice versa, but now plays neutral). He is the son of the prominent Kurdish national leader Mustafa Barzani, a former honorary general in the Russian Soviet

[7] Joost Hiltermann, "Of blood, oil and Kurdistan", The National Interest, June 2nd, 2011.

Army during the Stalin regime. Masud is currently the President of the Kurdistan Regional Government in northern Iraq. These alliances, we must keep in mind, can change from one sunrise to the next.

In a region where religion and spiritualism are paramount, we should keep in mind also that each of the two Kurdish groups follows a different mystic Sufi order. They have always competed with each other, and will continue doing that, with short periods of cooperation until each gets what they want. Then they go against each other again. These two groups are physically sitting on and around rich oil fields, which rank close to third in terms of reserves in the world.

The Kurds gained more and more power since the demise of Saddam Hussein's regime, and as a result of the fratricidal war going on between the Iraqi Sunnis and Shiites. With early support from the US (think oil), and with occasional logistical military support from the Israelis (think disrupting Arab countries); the Kurds found that that was the best opportunity for them to obtain their long sought independence. An independent or even semi-independent Kurdish government in northern Iraq is viewed as a future hornet's nest in the region and a source of more trouble in the years to come.

To make things even more complicated, the Kurds in the region are not just the Talbani and Barzani followers. There are the large Turkish-Kurdish communities who populate south-eastern Turkey, but some of whom actually live in the Kurdish region of northern Iraq. A large number of those Kurds, but not all at this point, are active supporters of the PKK. These Turkish Kurds, or Mountain Turks, as the Turks insist they are, are certainly not too happy to see a Kurdish state being built without them who have been fighting for one for years; especially that the state in today's configuration is no more a confederation of nomads and shepherds, but rather a rich oil producing and exporting state-in-the-making. There is tons of money involved now, plus immeasurable power to be gained because of that.

The Turks are loath to imagine an independent Kurdish oil sheikhdom with plenty of petro-dollars in its coffers at their borders, unless they weave an agreement with the Kurdish administration on condition that the new state is PKK-free. The relationship between Turkey and a Kurdish state in which a PKK that maintains its current claims to south-eastern Turkey as a full member will be bloody. If the Turks have been incapable of defeating a relatively poor, but doggedly determined PKK guerrilla movement before, a potential coalition of PKK and the rest of the Kurds with lots of oil money in their pockets, is something Turkey will never allow to happen.

Aside from constituting an immense source of instability in the region thanks to a large pro-PKK Kurdish population inside Turkey itself, if the Kurds were to be in control of the oil, they will oblige the Turks to drive a very hard bargain. But the

Kurds, true to themselves, could still quarrel among themselves and destabilize the region. This is where the Americans and the Turks may cooperate to literally fight the Kurds. Turkey will not wait to be begged.

Along with American support Turkey could actually take the side of Iraq under such circumstances and help it regain control of its northern territories. This means pitting the Kurds and the Iraqis against each other. That could usher yet another long and destructive war. Not a pretty sight either. The Turks will continue to watch the situation very closely, but no matter which scenario may prevail, the long term destabilization of the region is something the world may have to live with for a very long time indeed.

But then you also have the Iranians watching the Kurds closely, because they have their own axe to grind with them too. Iran, anxious to reduce the Kurds to size, will be happy that everybody is rushing to do its own dirty work for her. The Iranians are also quite involved in supporting certain elements among the Shias in Iraq, whom they would like to see in control of the whole country. While all Iraqi Shias, who are Arabs, are not necessarily supporters of Iranian policies, and certainly would not want to see Iraq under its hegemony, they find themselves unable to stand against their fellow Shias who are. The reason being the ongoing rift between them and the Iraqi Sunnis; or at least those among the latter who toe the extremist Wahhabi line. The Iraqis, or should I say the poor Iraqis, by their own stubbornness and insistence on fighting each other in a religious war based on myths and ancient tales will be destroying what is left of their own country.

THE BOTTOM LINE

The central government in Baghdad is not going to accept that the country be divided, particularly when the main resource the country relies on, namely oil, is now partially in the Kurdish controlled area, and partially in the Shiite controlled area. The Kurds will not relinquish their control of the oil, and trying to take it away from them by force is not going to work. Besides, neither the Iraqi government, nor the neighbouring states look with approval at the close cooperation between the Kurds and the Israelis, who also have a population of Jewish Kurds in Israel.

What about the Iraqis? The poor Iraqis will do to themselves what former President George Bush, using fabricated intelligence post 9/11, wanted to do to them: Return to the pre-industrial age. Not a pleasant picture. Perhaps the best thing that could happen to Iraq is the appearance of a latter day saviour: i.e. an improved but polished version of Saddam Hussein. But even that may be too late now.

Just a few months before going to print, a major academic journal published by one of the top US universities carried quite an astonishing article echoing something like the 1916 Sykes-Picot Agreement that led to the dismemberment of the Middle East and helped lead it to the sad state it is in today. The article calls for joining all Kurdish areas in Iran, Iraq and Syria together to resolve the Kurdish problem. If this is the kind of thinking going on in Washington that a major think-tank in the USA finds fit to publish, then the world better watch.

APPENDIX 5

THE AFGHANISTAN SUPER CHALLENGE

It will be a miracle indeed if anything changes in Afghanistan in the next one hundred years. This means of course change for the good of the country and its people. Neither armies, nor security, nor foreign aid, nor intelligence services are going to change anything in that country. Only when the people of Afghanistan decide on their own that enough is enough, straighten their priorities, and start putting order in their own house, that there may be hope. The best thing for Afghanistan now is to leave the country alone; but not quite. Indirect, discreet and on-demand assistance through non-Western, non-Christian parties without drums and whistles, to help rebuild the devastated regions of the country that may ask for and accept such assistance will go a long way towards improving the lot of the country and its people. That is step number one.

Afghanistan will still require a fundamental change in order to achieve long-term stability and live the way it wants to live and not what outsiders tell the Afghans how it should be. Despite what outsiders judge as incomprehensible socio-cultural behaviour, the people of that country have their own way of doing things just like everybody else on the planet have their own. And like everybody else, they have their own definition of dignity, which may or may not be shared by others.

Perhaps the starting point of possible change should first be in the Northern and Western provinces where the ethnically diverse population is traditionally relatively more receptive to dealing with outsiders. The attempt to do the same thing in the South and South-eastern regions of the country, particularly the Pashtu areas, where the Taliban originated and operate in their natural habitat, should be somewhat delayed until there is reasonable evidence of receptive fertile ground for any change. That change has to come from them, and not be imposed from outside. Try to impose something on the Turks or the Scots!

In all cases, "it is certainly clear that a majority of Afghans do not want the Taliban to return to power, since they know that the Taliban cannot provide development, jobs, education – anything that would develop an Afghan economy. They also know that the return of the Taliban would inevitably lead to a renewal of the civil war with the Northern Alliance."[228]

When the Taliban were in power, they "had no economic or social vision; t insisted (before, and continues to insist) that bringing in Sharia (i.e. Islamic urisprudence) would resolve all people's problems. It had no concept of what a

---

[8] Ahmed Rashid, "Prospects for Peace in Afghanistan", Asian Affairs, v.41 number 3, November 2010, p.357

functioning economy or education system required…Its principal appeal (at the time) lay in the fact that the Afghan population were fed up with Soviet occupation and the status quo. The details of the Taliban's policies mattered little under these circumstances; what mattered was ending the instability caused by the civil war"[229] that followed Soviet troops withdrawal.

Freedom in the Western political discourse is a relative freedom within the margins of the rule of law. In many other countries where the rule of law does not exist, or exists only partially, or is mixed with the rule of God, people think that freedom means a state of free for all without restraint; i.e. big fish eat small fish. So if you believe you have God on your side, then you fight to prove to all that you are the big fish.

One cannot but chuckle when the media broadcast news about the imminent organization of elections in a country like Afghanistan under any type of foreign-supported regime. First of all the Republic of Afghanistan is a country composed of many Afghanistans, and Hamid Karzai, the current president, is only the imposed president of one or two of them. He is a fish out of water, and the wrong man at the wrong time for the wrong purpose on the Afghan stage. The other Afghanistans have their own traditionally accepted tribal rulers, and that includes the Pashtuns and the others.

"In hindsight, the emphasis on making Afghanistan appear to be a democracy was set far too early; before there were enough solid building blocks inside the country that could have sustained this political process. For example, when presidential elections were held in 2004, half the population did not even know what an election was, given that they were not alive when the last election was held in the 1960s. But despite these obvious limitations there has been continued pressure to hold elections."[230]

In any future attempts to bring change to the whole of Afghanistan, the Pashtun areas, with their Taliban phalanges, are not to be left out completely. With time they may learn by example or by osmosis from their neighbours, who will probably become better off before them. They may also be irretrievably stubborn and not change at all. But as long as nobody bothers them, they, in turn, may not bother anybody either.

"It is important to recognise that Afghanistan is 70–80 percent rural and therefore the most effective way to undercut the power of the Taliban and the local warlords is to develop an agriculture sector that will encourage fighters (along with the 5 million refugees of the war) to return to the land."[231]

---

[229] Ibid., p.363

[230] Ibid., p.358

[231] Ibid., p.360

Putting order in the house of Afghanistan only is not sufficient by itself without taking stock of the whole neighbourhood. "A well thought out analysis published in 2009 to which several writers contributed under the title "The Future of Afghanistan" proposes that "a focused, coherent, and long-term approach to Afghan and regional stability is necessary to get Afghanistan out of its vicious cycle of insecurity, insurgency, impunity, and corruption. Any effort to establish stability through troop increases alone will ignore larger issues and lead to short-term improvements at best."[232]

The study underlines the fact that "insecurity, whether due to insurgency, terrorism, regional meddling, or warlordism undermines the potential for progress on all other fronts in Afghanistan, and that success is impossible without competent Afghan security institutions. However, within the international coalition, the goal of establishing internal Afghan-focused security was subordinate to the goal of destroying the international terrorist networks there that were orchestrating a campaign of spectacular attacks. Yet stable Afghan governance and security forces are required to create a viable long-term alternative to the Taliban.

"Of equal importance is the legitimacy of the Afghan government itself and its will and capacity to implement the rule of law. The report argues that U.S. expectations for Afghan democracy were dangerously overblown during the Bush administration, wrongly believing that "democracy would be the panacea to resolving the myriad challenges facing Afghanistan following such a protracted period of conflict."[233] In the long run, however, democratic governance may not be the ideal initial treatment that would stabilize the patient and stop the bleeding. Stabilization is what Afghanistan needs to start with, and administering democracy as we think of democracy may not be the right approach. Besides, creating police forces or an army with Western support will never bring security to Afghanistan. The contrary is more likely to happen.

"The future of Afghanistan also depends upon the ability of its national and local leaders to organize for a common, positive purpose", the analysis goes, but one must underline 'local leaders' because of the historical and socio-political make up of the country since it existed. While Afghanistan had a central government under the monarchy and the republican regimes, the real power was constantly in the hands of the local chiefs. The central government, when headed by leaders around whom there was consensus, was the arbitrator, the problem solver and the contact point with the outside world. Inside the country the local chiefs looked after their flock exactly like during Biblical times or earlier in other traditional societies.

Finally, we must also "work with Afghanistan's neighbors to create a regional environment conducive to Afghanistan's success. Regional competition

[32] J. Alexander Thier, editor, "The Future of Afghanistan" (2009) by the Endowment of the United States Institute of Peace www.usip.org/peaceops/afghanistan/book.html - Summary. By permission from USIP.
[33] Ibid., p.1

continues to undermine Afghanistan's long-term prospects, whereas renewed regional cooperation could provide a significant security and economic boost in Afghanistan, Pakistan and the region as a whole. What is needed now…is to realign joint priorities and expectations. The international community will be much better off with a right-sized, Afghan-appropriate vision that can actually be implemented than a grand international confection that continues to wilt under the glaring realities of the day", the authors say.[234]

But Afghanistan does not exist in a vacuum; for "all of the major countries that surround Afghanistan are preparing for the withdrawal of the United States and its allies in 2014. Russia, China, Pakistan, Iran, Tajikistan, Uzbekistan, Turkmenistan – all of them are maneuvering for the inevitable, and in the long-term, the future actions of these countries are much more important than the killing of Binladen."

"Deep inside, none of the countries mentioned above want the United States to leave Afghanistan. It should not be too difficult to understand why. If Afghanistan implodes and becomes a haven for radical Islamists, Central Asia, which the Russians consider their biggest security concern, will be destabilized. No one, not the Russians and not the Chinese, have anything to gain from such a scenario. Indeed, these two countries would prefer that the United States stay forever to do their dirty work for them, while they profit from the mineral wealth of Afghanistan – something the Chinese have already begun to do." (According to unconfirmed reports, there is a new factor at play in Afghanistan today, namely the reported discovery of huge untapped mineral deposits in Afghanistan, which include lithium, iron, copper, gold and cobalt. The discoveries were made close to the border with Pakistan and in the Pashtun areas in particular.)

"Afghanistan is thousands of miles away from Peoria, Illinois; it is next door to China, Russia, Iran, and India. If Afghanistan implodes, it is they, not the United States, which will feel the first and the biggest impact. "Weak though it may be, Pakistan has the power, more than any other country in the region, to wreak havoc in Afghanistan. It is not in their interests to do so, but who says the Pakistanis have always followed their interests?"[235]

ANOTHER APPROACH? - THE AFGHANISTAN-ARABIAN SEA HIGHWAY

Short of leaving the Afghans the way they have always been, one may propose for the sake of discussion, that Afghanistan be divided into two states: A Pashtu state in the south and everybody else, i.e. the Tajik, the Uzbek, the Hazara and the Balushi in a state of their own in the north. It is generally argued that the Pashtun populated areas in the south, where much of the Taliban originate, are

---

[234] Ibid., p.2
[235] Benjamin Ra, "Looking to the future in Afghanistan", The Washington Times, May 16, 2011.

the least amenable areas to change in the foreseeable future. The other tribal areas are considered to be relatively more amenable to accept some change over the years. Should the north set some type of example, perhaps the southern tribal areas would see something in it for them.

Yet, maybe there is another long term and less surgical approach to the Afghanistan question as a whole, but that would benefit the southern Pashtu regions in particular. Such approach could bring major changes to the whole of Afghanistan that it may have never seen in its history. It may sound a bit far-fetched and unrealistic to some under the prevalent conditions, but why not consider it a challenging case-study, even though it may be based on a huge assumption. The saying goes that "when the impossible has not worked, why not try the improbable"!

Afghanistan is a country that has historically been isolated from the rest of the world because of its landlocked geographic location. It has two major neighbours, to the west there is Iran, and to the east there is Pakistan, both of these countries share a common border along the shores of the Arabian Sea. The common border also juts about 500 kilometres inland where it meets with the borders of Afghanistan. Iran and Pakistan are blessed with a long sea front. Afghanistan has none.[236] If - and this is a really big "if" - the bond of Islamic "brotherhood" were really what Muslims claim it to be, could Iran and Pakistan do the unthinkable and cede to Afghanistan a tiny part of their respective territories, say a hundred kilometres wide strip for the sake of argumentation, to serve as a corridor linking Afghanistan to the Arabian Sea along the joint five hundred kilometres joint borders? This corridor will provide Afghanistan with an outlet to the open sea it never had in its history. Big question, and a challenge to all those who swear by Muslim brotherhood in this life and in the afterlife. But why not? Imagine the socio-cultural, economic and political change it could bring to that country.

Come to think of it, that stretch of rocky mountainous land, which does not bring value added of much consequence to either Iran or Pakistan, could make the big difference.[237] If Afghanistan, especially its southern Pashtu provinces, gains access to the open sea and establishes direct trade with the world, the socio-economic and cultural changes that this could bring over the years to those isolated areas of the country known to be the most backward and most extremist will be shaken to the core. History provides similar examples, even though most were rather by conquest rather than by common agreement. Think of the trade

---

[236] For further readings, please consult the following study by the US Department of State: "International Boundary Study" - number 167- March 28, 1979 Iran - Pakistan Boundary.
www.law.fsu.edu/library/collection/limitsinseas/IBS167.pdf

[237] A quick population and resources study of the Pakistan-Iran joint border area under discussion reveals that the population is pretty insignificant in terms of numbers; and both agricultural and water resources are quite limited due to the rugged terrain.

counters first established in China and Japan by the Europeans between the 15th and 17th centuries. That did contribute greatly to the opening of China and Japan to the world.

Proposed routing of the Afghanistan - Arabian Sea highway
(The black line across the borders of the three countries identifies the routing the proposed highway is to take.)

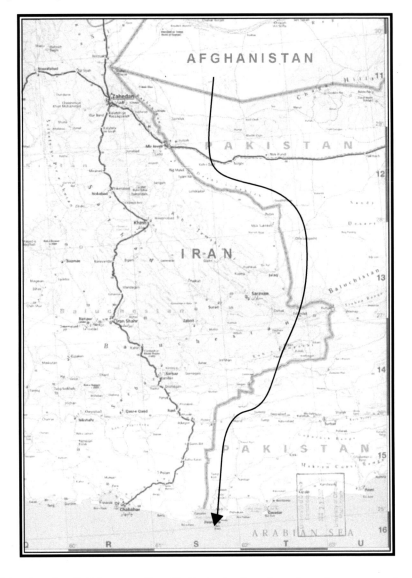

Will it take time? Of course it will. But what's a few decades, or may be two or three generations in the history of nations, especially in the history of such an old, noble nation as Afghanistan? Such a daring approach could possibly be the catalyst that may help bring long term peace in Afghanistan itself, but also to the region as a whole, and to the world. The real challenge is if' 'Muslim 'solidarity and brotherhood' could go beyond the words, or pure practical common sense can prevail, and whether the Afghans themselves are ready for the challenge. The Afghans may find interest in the proposal, but it will be more difficult to convince the Iranians and the Pakistanis.

In 2008 the government of China financed and completed the construction of the port of Gwadar on the Pakistani coast of the Arabian Sea, just a short few miles from the border of Iran. On May 24, 2011 China "accepted Pakistan's request to take over operations at the strategic Gwadar port." Pakistan also asked the Chinese government "if it could also build a naval base at the site of Gwadar... Pakistan further made a request for 4,400-tonne frigates to be supplied on credit and asked the Chinese to train its personnel for operating submarines.[238]

The China-Gwadar proposed pipeline and highway route
Source: www.truthwinds.com

⁸ "China takes over operations at Gwadar", Daily News and Analysis (DNA) India May 24, 2011.

In early 2011 it was announced that the port of Gwadar will be linked to central China by means of a super highway across Pakistan. If a several thousand kilometre highway can be built to give China a foothold on the Arabian Sea, a mere five hundred kilometre highway between Afghanistan and the Arabian Sea should be a piece of cake and a great contribution to world peace. Nothing hinders the linking of both proposed highways at a point where the Afghan and Pakistani borders meet and turn it into a joint venture for the combined benefit of all.

APPENDIX 6

THE ORIGINS OF PIRACY AROUND THE SOMALI COAST

"The origins of the piracy problem in Somalia are complex. The former Republic of Somalia has been without an effective central government since the overthrow of the military regime of President Siad Barre, in 1991. During the civil war that followed, some European and Asian countries took advantage of the chaos to send their commercial fleets to fish in Somali waters. European countries are also implicated in the dumping of thousands of drums of toxic materials, including nuclear waste, off the Somali coast.

"Without a coastguard to prevent these illegal activities, Somali fishermen began to organize and arm themselves to confront waste dumpers and demand compensation from foreign fishing vessels. The lucrative potential of this course of action was soon evident, and with an abundance of safe, deep-water anchorages along a 3,000-kilometre coastline, hijacking was the logical next step.

"The lack of a functioning central government, continued fighting, drought and economic collapse have contributed to a humanitarian crisis in Somalia, and exacerbated the piracy problem. While the first Somali pirates were former fishermen with what they considered to be justified demands for compensation, later others became involved, principally ex-militiamen and experts in operating the technology required to stalk and capture their targets. The illegal fishing and waste dumping that continues plays into the pirates' hands by allowing them to claim that they are defending Somali waters, a standpoint that gains support from coastal communities.

"The country's proximity to the Gulf of Aden ensures a rich source of potential targets, with more than 20,000 ships passing through the Gulf each year. A significant number of these are tankers transporting three million barrels per day of Persian Gulf oil destined mainly for Europe and the United States. The pirates, however, do not confine their attentions solely to crude carriers, nor do they limit their activities to the Gulf of Aden. They have also hijacked a wide range of vessels, from bulk carriers and container ships to fishing vessels and luxury yachts, over a 2-million square-mile area of ocean east and south of Somalia.

"With few exceptions, ship-owners and operators have readily paid for the safe return of a vessel and its crew. From the pirates' viewpoint, therefore, there is little risk involved in facing defenceless crews when the potential spoils are so enormous and offer the prospect of a lavish lifestyle in a region where 43% of people live in extreme poverty.

HOW THE GULF OF ADEN PIRATES OPERATE

"Many pirate attacks are opportunist, when the aim is often to take cash, crews' personal effects and equipment. At the other end of the scale, is the well-organized, well-armed attempt to take over a vessel when, typically, pirates operate in gangs of 10-15, either from shore using speedboats or skiffs, or from a mother ship. This vessel was initially a fairly slow-moving fishing boat which has been seized previously, but now they use modern freighters they capture on the high seas. When a potential target is identified, the attack is launched using three or four skiffs which can reach speeds of 20-25 knots. Pirates detect their targets by a number of means. These include visually, up to a range of approximately 10 km; with radar, up to a range of 20 km; and using Automatic Identification System (AIS), up to 40-55 km. AIS enables ships to exchange data, including identification, position, course and speed, all of which is useful information when planning an attack. AIS is mandatory for all ships voyaging internationally with a gross tonnage of 300 tons or more, and passenger ships of all sizes.

"With a reliable over-the-horizon navigation capability and handheld GPS and satellite phones pirates are capable of operating well beyond the visual range of the mother ship. With logistic support provided by this larger vessel, the pirates are free to operate far out to sea for long periods and able to press home an attack.

"Our analysis of data from the International Maritime Bureau (IMB) shows that in most cases the pirates fired upon the merchant ships in an attempt to intimidate the ship's master into heaving to. It also reveals that most hijackings occur during daylight hours. This makes sense, given the obvious difficulties associated with the pirates' modus operandi, which is to use makeshift hook-ladders to board a large, moving ship from a small craft in open sea.

"Clearly, slow-moving vessels with a low freeboard and readily available hook-points present little challenge to the pirates. Reduced crew numbers, and lack of vigilant watch keeping further increase a ship's vulnerability. In the case of tankers, the obvious danger presented by a flammable cargo may mean that crews are more likely to capitulate than to put up a fight.

"The ease with which the pirates are able to capture even the largest of ships was demonstrated by the hijacking of the Sirius Star in November 2008. On 15 November 2008, the MT Sirius Star, a Saudi-owned very large crude carrier, was hijacked by armed pirates approximately 450 nautical miles south east of the Kenyan coast. She was bound for the USA via the Cape of Good Hope and fully loaded with 2 million barrels of crude oil, the equivalent of a quarter of Saudi Arabia's daily oil output.

"The pirates took hostage the 25 crew members, two of whom were British, and sailed the tanker to the Somali coast where they anchored the vessel and demanded a ransom for the release of the crew and tanker. On 9 January 2009, both ship and crew were freed after US$3 million was paid. The hijacking was the most audacious at that time in terms of its location so far from land, the size of the vessel, an overall 332 metres; and the value of its cargo, which was worth at least US$ 100 million."

The MV Sirius Star. The largest hijacking in history
Source: US Navy Photo - By permission

"The pirates' operations have become increasingly sophisticated; they rely on satellite phones and GPS systems - and there are suggestions that they are also becoming more aggressive. Whereas in the past they relied on automatic weapons to intimidate ships' crews, now they are more likely to use rocket-propelled grenades (RPGs).

"Somalia is one of the most dangerous and violent places in the world, and cash generated from hijacking helps to finance the war. It is suggested, too, that some money reaches Al-Shabaab, which has been designated a terrorist organization by the US State Department and is fighting an insurgency war against Ethiopian and government troops. There is the potential for the pirates to become involved in international terrorism, for example by direct attacks on naval or commercial shipping, and using hijacked vessels as floating weapons.

"Sinking a large ship in the entrance to the Suez Canal would have a catastrophic effect on trade. Somali piracy could potentially fund the activities of terrorist networks around the world. In September 2008, the hijacking of a ship carrying weapons prompted an unprecedented level of cooperation to prevent the cargo falling into the hands of Somali insurgents believed to have links to al-Qaeda." [239]

---

[39] Excerpts from the Executive Summary of BAE Systems white paper, "Tanker Protection and Defence against Piracy". Adapted from Security Review (2009), p.12 and is reproduced with BAE's permission.

DIGGING DEEPER INTO THE SOMALI PIRACY CRISIS

Piracy along the coast of Somalia and elsewhere in the Indian Ocean and the Arabian Sea presents a much more complicated issue in terms of cause and effect than it is generally understood. In a comprehensive study by Roland Marchal, Research Fellow at the French Conseil National de la Recherche Scientifique (CNRS), Marchal dug pretty deep into the local, regional and international context that led to the current situation. Here is a brief summary of what he underlined in his detailed study, published by 'Humanity' in its spring 2011 edition.

"The fight against piracy near the Somali coast does not aim to tackle the very causes of the support that piracy enjoys among the Somali population at large, not least because the international community would then have to consider the violations of international law perpetrated by some of its major members. Hence, piracy is usually presented as a symptom of "state collapse" and a breeding ground for global jihad, while its moral economy is disqualified and the reconfiguration of a transnational Somali economy simply ignored.

"As so often, the international community claimed to be defending international law, even as it ignored or hushed up decades of illegal fishing and dumping of toxic waste off Somali shores by some of its members - including Japan, China, South Korea, Taiwan, France, and Spain. This helps explain why, although Somali fishing communities were the ones most often victimized by pirates, these same communities often also regarded the pirates as genuine nationalists, committed to taking revenge against numerous infringements on Somali sovereignty. A direct byproduct of the "economy of protection" that took shape during the civil war, pirates illustrate a form of social success that keeps at bay both Islamists and the secular government supported by the United States and its allies.

"Piracy in Somalia did not develop in a vacuum but in a context where Somalis were fighting internally for survival and for a better access to the spoils of the civil war, while facing increasing infringements upon their sovereignty by international actors. This generally misunderstood situation largely explains why and how a specific moral economy of piracy took shape.

"Piracy first started as an informal alliance between fishermen (or coastal communities) and militias. The former were able to handle sea navigation while the latter were instrumental in hijacking the ship and dealing with the hijacked crew onshore. The moral economy of piracy had consequences for the way in which ransoms were divided, since the respective shares were determined following the very rules applied in the fishery industry (beginning with distinctions between the owner and the fishermen, offshore operators and onshore personnel selling the catches, and so on).

"More crudely still, this was also an extension of the "economy of protection" that had taken shape onshore. If the hijacked ship could show an acceptable license, it was only required to pay a very minimal fee (duco). If this was not the case, the fine was heavy and those who stopped the ship were given a much higher reward. Those rules were adapted to commercial shipping. If the cargo belonged to a group of Puntland traders, it was released with a minimal payment.

"The fine/ransom depended on whether the owners of the cargo could find a shrewd representative in Puntland to mediate the case. The amount of the ransom essentially depended on the ability to get closer to the Puntlanders. Another aspect of this moral economy is still applicable today. Ships were (and still are) taken hostage only once. When they are released, they can move freely and no other group is supposed to target them. This is possible because part of the ransom is given to neighboring gangs, and this practice reflects the idea that pirates should not fight among themselves and have vested common interests. A few incidents that occurred in 2010 suggest that this "honor among thieves" has become more difficult than before.

"Indeed, things have started to change, in particular because businessmen have been increasingly involved and because the division of pirate labor has become more sophisticated. When crews are held hostage onshore, local businessmen may provide cash advances for their subsistence as well as payments to the militias guarding the crews: this is a way of not only defusing risks but also sharing the benefits of piracy by securing generous reimbursements once the ransom has been received. As in other cases of hijacking, one should also point out the role of the translator, who is often instrumental in guiding the militias and in maintaining the relation between pirate leaders and crews. But a much more important role is that of the *dilaal*, the intermediary who negotiates for the release of the ship and the well-being of the crew. In Somali culture, a *dilaal* can get a huge percentage of the transaction, and this may also be the case in piracy. In some cases, he can be the translator, but he can also be someone who has no direct connection with the military operation.

"Another dimension should be highlighted. Although initially pirates used little military hardware, their success allowed them to buy heavy weapons for use onshore to guard the crews and protect their operations; there is no evidence yet that the weapons they use offshore got more sophisticated. Long before 2008, pirates became significant military players in Puntland and aligned themselves with their respective clans in any confrontation opposing these clans to the Puntland administration or to other clans. This suggests that pirate gangs do not behave as sheer delinquents: they follow clan rules, they respect (up to a point) the authority of clan elders, and they do not behave as thugs when they are onshore. This also explains why they are not perceived by their fellow Somalis as the ruthless criminals described by the international and especially Western press.

"While piracy and jihadism developed in the same area, it is important to single out some differences that should caution against quick conclusions. Their coexistence can be explained by factors that do not necessarily involve collusion. For instance, pirate leaders move freely in territories controlled by al-Shabaab and are often seen either in Kismaayo or in the Bakaahara market in Mogadishu. First, pirates are much better armed than any other group and it would be very costly to confront them. Second, they have not yet been shown to have any political ambitions other than the need to operate without encountering obstacles, and as a result they are not really competing with Islamist groups. Finally, through either collusion or kinship, movements such as al-Shabaab may be able to get a (small) share of the money pirates distribute rather generously after ransoms have been paid.

"Last, but not the least, while most of the media focused on Somalia and developed a standardized narrative linking the pirates to the Islamists and the jihadists, one country was trying to use the crisis to advance its own interests: Yemen. Indeed, Yemen wanted the international community to pay for the creation of an anti-piracy base located on its coast. No chancellery dared to mention the role Yemen played in the Somali crisis. For more than a decade, experts have called attention to the weapons and ammunition trade going from Yemen into Somalia.

"To this day, the proliferation of small arms such as AK-47s or RPGs in Somalia is essentially made possible by Yemen, although other regional states such as Ethiopia and Eritrea or imports from Ukraine and Belarus also account for the arms trade. To the extent that the main traders [were] politically associated with the [former] Yemeni president, Ali Abdallah Saleh, who [was] fighting al-Qaeda in the Arabian Peninsula and allowed U.S. Special Forces to operate in Yemen, those criticisms have been sidelined or dismissed. In the same way, the continuing cooperation between some pirate gangs and Yemeni operators linked to human trafficking is not considered even though it took place from the early days of the Somali civil war.

"The most likely outcome of the international anti-piracy efforts will not be an exhaustion of piracy. It will be a form of piracy that is more violent toward the crews and more sophisticated militarily and that eventually attempts to sabotage the ships it fails to take over. While figures show that the success rate of attacks has been halved in two years, their numbers are still a major issue for maritime security in the area. Pirates are also operating in a much larger area today (the Seychelles are hardly included in Somali territorial waters), which makes the mission of the international force only more difficult.[240]

---

[240] Roland Marchal, "Somali Piracy: The Local Contexts of an International Obsession", Humanity: An International Journal of Human Rights, Humanitarianism, and Development, v.2 number1 pp.31-50, spring 2011.

Facing an increasingly sophisticated and technology-assisted piracy industry

Between 2004 and 2011 sixty two seafarers have died as a direct result of piracy in the Gulf of Aden and the Indian Ocean. Some died through deliberate murder by pirates, suicide during the period of captivity, death from malnutrition and disease, death by drowning or heart failure just after the hijacking.

"During this same period, over 3,500 seafarers have been kidnapped and held hostage by pirate gangs, who subject them to traumas such as being used as human shields, being forced to operate their ship as a pirate mother ship under pirate control, and to extreme mental as well as physical anguish," says Giles Heimann, Chairman of the SOS SaveOurSeafarers campaign. "Hundreds of these seafarers have been subjected to horrific torture including being hung by the ankles over the side of the ship, being shut in the ship's freezer room, having cable ties tightened round the genitals, being beaten, punched and kicked. Many of these seafarers remain traumatised and unable to return to their seafaring careers long after the hijack is over, if at all." [241]

The gangs, who pursue vessels in the sea use navigational technologies in their daily operation, satellite phones, Global Positioning System (GPS) and VHF radios are used as navigational aids to spot and identify potential preys. Fast fibreglass boats nicknamed Volvos because of their high powered engines. That is beside their ability to track their targets using the Automated Identification System (AIS) as mentioned above. It would not be unthinkable that the pirates' operations benefit from networks that include other than Somalis, such as European and American mercenaries who also stand to gain millions of dollars by cooperating with them. Neither intelligence agencies, nor law enforcement organizations have so far shown any effective success in monitoring, tracking and disrupting the pirates' operations whose networks extend way beyond Somalia, and all the way to some European capitals.

---

[1] "Seafarer death toll mounts as Somali pirates hijack, torture, intimidate, murder", PortNews Newsletter, June 26,)11.

SELECT BIBLIOGRAPHY

Alain Chouet, "Au cœur des services spéciaux - La menace islamiste: fausses pistes et vrais dangers". (Inside the Intelligence Service Special Branch - Islamic threat: wrong leads and real dangers), Éditions La Découverte, Paris (2011).

Amos N. Guiora, "Freedom from Religion: Rights and National Security", Oxford University Press Terrorism and Global Justice Series, New York (2009).

Arthur S. Hulnick, "Intelligence and law enforcement: The "spies are not cops" problem", International Journal of Intelligence and CounterIntelligence, v.10 number 3, pp.269-286 (1997).

Berko Anat, "The Path to Paradise, the Inner World of Suicide Bombers and their Dispatchers". Translated by Elizabeth Yuval. Westport, Connecticut: Praeger Publishing (2007).

Charles Enderlin, "Le grand aveuglement: Israël et l'irrésistible ascension de l'Islam radical", Albin Michel, Paris (2009)

Christine Ockrent et Comte Alexandre de Marenches, "Dans le secret des princes", Éditions Stock, Paris (1986).

Constable Kelly Ross and Constable Dale Duchesne; "The intelligence cycle: Why analyst-client feedback is crucial"; RCMP Gazette magazine, v.69, number 3, November 23, 2007.

Craig Unger, "Church and State: American Rapture" Vanity Fair, December 2005.

Department of Homeland Security (DHS) publications.

Dr Anja Shortland, Brunel University, "Treasure Mapped: Using Satellite Imagery to Track the Developmental Effects of Somali Piracy", Chatham House, Africa Programme Paper: AFP PP 2012/01, London, January 2012.

Emile Nakhleh "A Necessary Engagement: Reinventing America's Relations with the Muslim World", Princeton University Press. Also see his article in Review of Middle East Studies v. 43, number 2, winter 2009.

Hans Born, Ian Leigh and Aidan Willis, "International Intelligence Cooperation and Accountability", Routledge Studies in Intelligence, UK (2011)

ICAO Annex 17 to the Convention on International Civil Aviation - Safeguarding International Civil Aviation against Acts of Unlawful Interference - International Civil Aviation Organization, International Standards and Recommended Practices - Eighth Edition April (2006).

International Ship and Port Facility Security Code (ISPS Code) and SOLAS Amendments; 2003 Edition in various languages, International Maritime Organization (IMO), London.

Jack Davis, "Improving Intelligence Analysis at CIA: Dick Heuer's Contribution to Intelligence Analysis," in "Introduction" to Psychology of Intelligence Analysis, Richards J. Heuer, Jr. Washington, DC: Centre for the Study of Intelligence, p. xix. (1999)

Jim Harper, "Terrorism and Security Systems", Foreign Policy and National Security, December 30, 2009. www.cato-at-liberty.org/2009/12/30/terrorism-and-security-systems/

Mark M. Lowenthal, "Intelligence from Secrets to Policy", Second Edition, CQ Press, Washington, DC (2003).

Michael Scheuer, "Imperial Hubris: Why the west in losing the war on terror", Brassey's Inc., Washington, D.C. p.8 (2004) www.potomacbooksinc.com

Natalie Klein, Maritime Security and the Law of the Sea, Oxford University Press, April (2011)

Office of the Director of National Intelligence, "Global Maritime and Air Intelligence Integration" (2009).

Richard K. Betts, "Analysis, War and Decision: Why Intelligence Failures Are Inevitable", World Politics, v.31 number 1, (October 1978) pp.61-89.

Richard K. Betts, "Policy-Makers and Intelligence Analysts: Love, Hate or Indifference?" Intelligence and National Security v.3 number 1, (January 1988) pp.184-189.
Richards J. Heuer, Jr., "Psychology of Intelligence Analysis", Centre for the Study of Intelligence, CIA (1999).

Robert Bovey, "The Quality of Intelligence Analysis", American Intelligence Journal v.3 number 4, winter 1980-81, pp.6-11.

Robert R. Raffel, "Intelligence and Airport Security", CIA - Historical Document Posted: April 15, 2007. Last Updated: Jun 26, 2008

https://www.cia.gov/library/centre-for-the-study-of-intelligence/csi-publications/csi-studies/studies/vol50no3/airport_security_5.htm
(This document was discovered after the manuscript for this book was completed and readied for publication.)

Russell G. Swenson and Susana C. Lemozy, Editors, "Democratization of Intelligence: Melding Strategic Intelligence and National Discourse"; National Defense Intelligence College, Washington, D.C. July 2009.

Stephen Marrin - Improving Intelligence Analysis: Bridging the gap between Scholarship and practice, Routledge, Studies in Intelligence Series, UK (2011).

Stephen Marrin and Jonathan D. Clemente, "Modeling an Intelligence Analysis Profession on Medicine", International Journal of Intelligence and Counterintelligence, v.19 pp.642–665 (2006).

Stephen C. Mercado, "Re-examining the Distinction between open information and secrets", CIA studies in intelligence, v.49 number 2.

Yehoshafat Harkabi, "Israel's Fateful Hour", Harper and Row, Publishers (1988).

General Harkabi, whom the author met in the 1990s, was Chief of Military Intelligence in Israel in the late fifties. His book is based on a previous Hebrew work entitled "Hachraot Goraliot" published in Tel Aviv in 1986. General Harkabi, who was a super hawk among the hawks in Israel, saw the need to accommodate the Palestinians, perhaps not for the sake of the Palestinians per se, but for the sake of Israel itself. Without mentioning it, he and his contemporary Yeshayahu Leibowitz, though coming each from a different perspective, saw that "what's good for the Palestinians is good for Israel"

Yeshayahu Leibowitz, "Judaism, Human Values and the Jewish State". Harvard University Press; Cambridge, Massachusetts (1992) Chapters 22 to 25.

Israeli scientist and religious philosopher known for his outspoken and often controversial opinions on Judaism, ethics, religion and politics. From 1967 and until his death in 1994 Leibowitz was an outspoken defender of the complete separation between religion and state. In the last three chapters of his book, he called for an equitable solution to the Palestinian-Israeli Question by separating the two people from each other, "by a settlement imposed on both sides by the superpowers."

JOURNALS

Canadian Military Journal

Foreign Service Journal

Government Accountability Office (GAO) publications

Humanity: An International Journal of Human Rights, Humanitarianism, and Development

International Journal of Intelligence and Counterintelligence - Routledge Publishers.

International Journal of Law

International Journal of Middle East Studies

Journal of Air Transport Management

Journal of Homeland Security and Emergency Management

Journal of Strategic Studies

Routledge Studies in Intelligence

Studies in Conflict and Terrorism

The Brown Journal of World Affairs

The author

Hassan Eltaher was the former Chief of Civil Aviation Intelligence, then Chief of Maritime Security Strategic Planning with the Canadian Department of Transport. For several years prior to that, he held several lead positions in security with the Government of Canada, including as Senior Analyst, Threat and Risk Assessments.

His professional career has covered various operational and management functions related to both passengers and cargo with airlines and multi-modal freight forwarders in several countries in North America, the Middle East and North Africa. Mr. Eltaher designed and taught training programs in Airline and Airport Management and Operations at Embry-Riddle Aeronautical University in Florida, USA, then at Mount Royal University in Calgary, Canada. Following several years in various Marketing and Operations management positions with Pacific Western Airlines in Calgary, Alberta, he was seconded to the International Aviation Management Training Institute (IAMTI) in Montréal as Director of Airline Management Training Programs. At the end of his secondment, he joined the Canadian federal government.

He also maintained a part time activity as adjunct lecturer in Middle Eastern and North African Affairs with Carleton University, the University of Ottawa and the University of Calgary. After taking early retirement from the public service in 2006, he set up a consulting practice in the areas of Aviation and Maritime Security Intelligence Management. He follows both industries through frequent travel aboard ships and airlines.

Mr. Eltaher was educated in French schools in Cairo. He earned an M.B.A. in Aviation Management (With Distinction) from Embry-Riddle Aeronautical University in the USA, and a B.A. in Political Studies and International Relations from the American University of Beirut.